Print Like a Pro:
A Digital Photographer's Guide

Jon Canfield

Peachpit
Press

Print Like a Pro: A Digital Photographer's Guide
Jon Canfield

Peachpit Press
1249 Eighth Street
Berkeley, CA 94710
510/524-2178
800/283-9444
510/524-2221 (fax)

Find us on the Web at www.peachpit.com
To report errors, please send a note to errata@peachpit.com

Peachpit Press is a division of Pearson Education

Copyright © 2006 by Jon Canfield

Senior Acquisitions Editor: Pam Pfiffner
Development Editor: Linda Laflamme
Project Editors: Paula Baker and Karen Reichstein
Production Editor: Lisa Brazieal
Copyeditor: Liz Welch
Technical Editor: Jeff Greene
Compositor: Maureen Forys, Happenstance Type-O-Rama
Indexer: Karin Arrigoni
Cover Design: Aren Howell
Cover Photograph: Jon Canfield
Interior Design: Mimi Heft

ISBN 0-321-38554-3

9 8 7 6 5 4 3 2 1

Printed and bound in the United States of America

Dedication

To Kathy, my best friend and true love.

Acknowledgments

There may be only one name on the cover of this book, but trust me, most of the credit for the finished product belongs to everyone behind the scenes that pull all my scattered thoughts together into something cohesive and hopefully readable.

First and foremost, thank you to my amazing family. My beautiful wife Kathy is an inspiration and more supportive than I would have thought possible. She puts up with the crazy hours and schedules, always encouraging me to do what I enjoy. My children Ken and Erin are a source of pride and joy. They may be grown and out of the house, but they'll always be my kids.

I want to thank the incredible group of people at Peachpit Press that made this project happen. Development Editor Linda Laflamme gave me encouragement throughout the project and put up with my delays. I hope that I get the chance to work with her again, although she may run the other direction when she hears my name. Production Editor Lisa Brazieal did a great job of scheduling and book layout. She's the one that's responsible for how nice the finished product looks, and I thank her for that. Compositor Maureen Forys did a wonderful job with the layout of the book. Marketing Manager Zigi Lowenberg worked hard to get the word out on this book. I was lucky enough to have two project editors on this book, Karen Reichstein handled things at the start of the project before moving to other areas at Peachpit. Paula Baker stepped in and kept things going smoothly. Both did a wonderful job, making this one of the best projects I've ever worked on. Jeff Greene did an outstanding job as technical editor, and you can be sure that any mistakes that might be in this book were introduced after Jeff's review.

And, they may not have been involved in the book on a daily basis, but Managing Editor Becky Morgan, Acquisitions Editor Pamela Pfiffner, and Senior Acquisitions Editor Wendy Sharp all made the project possible to begin with. I hope this is the first of many books!

I wouldn't be where I am today without the support and help of some fantastic friends and writers. Ellen Anon was gracious enough to write Chapter 10 for this book, and her expertise and knowledge in the area of matting and framing can't be beat. Tim Grey, Peter Burian, and Charlotte Lowrie are always there when I have questions.

Finally, I want to thank all of the companies that helped with information, product loans, and questions. Teresa Weaver (Apple Computer), John Jatinen, Andrew Staples, Jane Fainer, and Dano Steinhardt (Epson), Jennifer Shanks, Scott Heath, and Geoff Coalter (Canon), Sebastian Macdougall (Matrox), Adrianne Bennett and Siobhan Flanigan, and Ann Johnson of Porter Novelli (HP), John Pannozzo of ColorByte Software (ImagePrint), Doug Little (Wacom), Sandra Sumski (Gretag Macbeth), Brian Levy and Matt Chilton (ColorVision), Norm Levy (Media Street), Ellen Pinto and Allison Rhodes (Pantone), and Thomas Frizelle (Kodak). To anyone I've forgotten, my thanks and apologies.

Contents at a Glance

Table of Contents

About the Author

Jon Canfield is the author of several popular photography books, including *RAW 101: Better Images with Photoshop and Photoshop Elements* (Sybex, 2005) and *Photo Finish: The Digital Photographer's Guide to Printing, Showing, and Selling Images* (Sybex, 2004). In addition, he currently writes the "Output Options" column for *PHOTOgraphic* and contributes to *Shutterbug, PC Photo, Outdoor Photographer,* and *Digital PhotoPro.* His images have been published in numerous books and magazines, including the *America 24/7* series. When he's not photographing and writing, he works for Microsoft, where he has helped develop such digital imaging products as Picture It! and Digital Image Pro.

About the Tech Editor

A member of both the National Press Photographers Association and the National Association of Photoshop Professionals, photographer **Jeff Greene** has been shooting professionally since 1982. He and his wife Christine own ImageWest Photography & Design in Paso Robles, California, where they have been producing award-winning digital images for a diverse selection of local, regional, and national clientele. Jeff's work has recently been featured in *American Photo, Outdoor Photographer,* and *Petersen's Photographic* magazines and in Tim Grey's bestselling *Color Confidence* (Sybex, 2004) and *Photoshop CS2 Workflow* (Sybex, 2005).

Introduction

My first attempts at printing images, almost 20 years ago now, were pitiful by today's standards. Of course, this was before digital cameras were available and a "high–quality" scanner was able to do 300 dpi in black and white. Color scanners? Dream on! My first color printer was an Apple ImageWriter II, a dot-matrix printer that was able to slowly print very basic color at noise levels that rivaled a jumbo jet. From there I moved up to a new technology: inkjet. The early HP DeskJet printers were light years ahead of that ImageWriter II in quality.

Still, the idea of printing a color image that resembled a photograph was just a fantasy. At the time, it was easy to be impressed by the simple fact that your page contained anything beside black text (of course, I still listened to music on a cassette or record player too). Comparing then and now is akin to comparing the original Pong to one of today's arcade extravaganzas. If you wanted prints of your favorite photographs, you still had to go down to the photo lab or your darkroom for reprints.

These days it seems as if everyone is into digital photography, capturing more images than ever. One of the promises of digital imaging is control. From capture to print, you expect to have control over how the image is captured and edited, and what the final print looks like. Unfortunately, it's the printing part that many people struggle with. It's unusual to find anyone who is able to just plug in a printer and get good results on the first try. It's almost as rare to find anyone who can identify a problem and fix it quickly and easily.

I've written dozens of articles on printing and print-related issues, most of them inspired by people like you who have written for help. Whether it's a problem with prints not matching the screen or the best way to optimize a photo for printing, the challenge of printing quality digital images can be a complicated and expensive process of trial and error. My goal with *Print Like a Pro* is to demystify the process, avoiding techno-speak wherever possible.

Getting professional quality prints doesn't need to be complicated, but it's hard to find all of the information you need in one place. As I was researching this book, I found that most of the information out there currently is either specific to one brand of printer or focuses on technical aspects rather than results. *Print Like a Pro* is different. What you hold in your hands now is a complete guidebook that will lead you through the printing process with clear examples, tips, and techniques that you can apply to your own photos.

Along the way, I found new techniques and tools that have made my life easier, and I hope that you find them useful as well.

Who Should Read This Book?

Anyone with digital photos to print should read this book—Mac or PC user, rank amateur or seasoned photographer, it doesn't matter. If you want better, more accurate prints, keep reading.

Perhaps you're struggling with prints that come out looking nothing like what you see on screen, or you're wondering why your enlargements look blurry or oversharpened. If so, you'll find the answers you've been searching for here. Don't know a printer profile from a printer driver? All will be revealed! From choosing the best type of printer for your needs to selecting the best paper and settings for different subjects, *Print Like a Pro* provides the information you need.

Whether you are looking for advice on how to resize and edit images for printing on your home printer or sending them out for publication in books, calendars, or posters, you'll find examples and simple steps to get the results you want.

What's Inside?

This book is all about results. I don't show you how to take photo-graphs, and I don't spend time on Photoshop features that don't apply to printing. There are plenty of other books out there that do a better job with those tasks than I could. What you will find is straightforward opinions, advice, and instructions on how to select a printer, optimize your photos for printing, work with photo labs, create special projects, and even present the finished product. Here's a sneak peek at what each chapter has to offer:

Chapter 1, "Understanding Digital Reproduction," introduces you to common terms and the differences between digital printing and conventional darkroom printing.

Chapter 2, "Setting Up a Print Studio," covers the types of printers that are available and how to select the one that's right for you.

Chapter 3, "Keeping an Eye on Color," is a short course on color management and why it's so critical to the digital process.

Chapter 4, "Using Printer Settings," explains what all those printer driver settings do. You'll find examples for Canon, Epson, and HP printers, and you'll learn what to select—and what to avoid.

Chapter 5, "Editing Your Photos," is all about using Adobe Photoshop, Photoshop Elements, and other tools to prepare your photos for printing. You'll find information on correcting color, converting to black and white as well as toned images, and adding creative borders to your photographs.

Chapter 6, "Resizing and Sharpening Your Images," shows you the proper way to handle these two critical tasks for different subjects and print types.

Chapter 7, "Printing Your Files," pulls all of the earlier information together and explains how to select the correct settings for high-quality prints.

Chapter 8, "Creating Special Print Projects," explains how to go beyond the basic print to create books and scrapbook pages, as well as how to print on fabric and other nontraditional surfaces.

Chapter 9, "Working with Service Providers," gives you the information you need when sending your photos out to be printed, including what to ask and how to keep your costs down.

Chapter 10, "Presenting Your Work," is all about mounting, matting, and framing your work. With information from Ellen Anon, a nationally known instructor and photographer, you'll see how to show your work in the best possible way.

Throughout the book, you'll see mentions to useful products, vendors, and service providers. So that you don't have to go hunting back through the chapters every time you need to reference one of these, I've compiled them all in an appendix of resources. There you'll find contact information for all of the products mentioned throughout the book as well as other sources that you might find useful as you explore the world of digital printing.

What's on the Web Site?

I've set up a companion Web site, www.printlikeapro.com, where you'll find updated information, sample files with which you can try the techniques presented in the book, and a gallery of images submitted by readers showing how they've used some of the techniques from the book. I encourage you to send me examples too. I'm happy to post them on the Web site for everyone to enjoy. You'll also find some surprise goodies on the site that I hope will be useful in your work flow.

Thank You!

To everyone still here, my thanks for picking up this book. I hope it takes your printing to the next level and that you enjoy the trip. I'd love to hear from you with comments and questions. I've met many interesting people doing things that I never would have imagined, and I'm sure that you'll take the information provided in this book to new levels of creativity.

—*September 2005*
Jon Canfield
jon@joncanfield.com

1 | Understanding Digital Reproduction

Before the advent of digital imaging, reproducing your photos meant giving up creative control to a print lab. Sure, you could specify glossy or matte finish and the size you wanted, but that was about it. Your only other alternative was to set up your own darkroom, which certainly gave you more control but at the cost of a steep learning curve, especially for color reproduction.

Now that photo quality digital output devices are available and affordable, there's no need to lose control and the learning curve is much more manageable. In this chapter, I'll introduce you to the digital advantage and some of the basic terms you'll need to know to understand the techniques in the rest of the book.

How Digital Differs from Analog

Analog media, such as traditional film and paintings, pretty much puts you in a take-what-you-get situation. Although you can change the way a photo looks by manipulating the negative, the amount of control is very limited and only available if you have your own darkroom. Paintings or drawings? Forget about it. Once the ink or paint dries, it's a little hard to change things.

Digital, on the other hand, doesn't care where you are in the creative process. Want to add or subtract elements? Erase or paint as you wish. Digital photos can be manipulated beyond recognition if that's your goal.

One of the reasons digital imaging has taken off so quickly is this level of control (**Figure 1.1**), along with the immediate feedback we crave (remember waiting for your film to be developed, hoping for a good shot?). Control has its drawbacks, though. You now have more to learn and more decisions to make from start to finish.

Figure 1.1 *Digital has earned its place in photography with the instant feedback and additional control offered. It's the perfect partner for today's "right now" lifestyle.*

More control

Control is good. The more control you have over your creations, the more personal they become and the more satisfaction you get when you finish a project.

This control is one of the reasons why digital camera sales soar past film in many parts of the world. If you want it, you have total control of how the image is captured, as well as the resulting file's format (RAW or JPEG). You can control the color balance of a photo for accuracy or mood, and even decide whether you want a color image or a black-and-white one, or perhaps something in-between.

The drawback to more control is that you as the photographer now have more work to do, both in the field when taking the photo and afterwards at the computer when editing the photo for output (**Figure 1.2**).

Figure 1.2 *Control has its price. Most digital photographers find themselves spending more time editing photos than they ever expected. It's easy to get carried away with the control that such programs as Adobe Photoshop give us over our images.*

And, with digital you don't have to worry about double prints or paying for prints you don't want. You print only what you want, and only when you want to. I don't know about you, but I don't miss the mini-lab and reprints at all (it's very likely they don't miss me either; I had no problem telling them to reprint my order when it wasn't right).

The Advantages of Digital

The advantages of using digital images are many:

- **Consistency.** Digital is great when you have multiple prints to create. Once you edit the file to your liking, you can click the print button once or one thousand times and get exactly the same print quality. With the proper techniques, which you'll learn throughout this book, you can use one digital file for any use you might have, without extensive re-editing (**Figure 1.3**).

Figure 1.3 *With proper editing techniques, such as using layers in Photoshop, you can reuse your images for many different outputs without having to start from scratch.*

- **Custom sizes.** Why stick to boring 8×10 or 5×7 prints when you can print to the exact size you want? If your photo looks better as a 6×8, print it that way. Perhaps you want a 24×30 poster of the same shot. Go for it! It's all up to you with digital (**Figure 1.4**). Digital printing has made panoramic prints very popular. The ability to stitch multiple images together to make a wide or tall print is included in many imaging programs, and if your printer supports roll paper, you can easily print panoramics of four or more feet long (**Figure 1.5**).

Figure 1.4 *The same image from the same file has printed well at very different sizes. Digital gives you the flexibility to choose what you want.*

Figure 1.5 *Digital photography has made the panoramic image very popular. It's easier than ever to combine multiple images into one for more detail and impact.*

Note

Not all printers can support long prints even if they use roll paper. If panoramic prints are important to you, be sure you check the maximum print size before buying a printer.

- **Unique media options.** The days of glossy or matte finishes being your only choice are long gone. These are still the most popular paper finishes for digital, primarily because people are familiar with them and they have the look of a "real" photo. Once you get past the need to have a real photo look and feel, you'll find there are a huge number of options available, including fine art paper that has a textured surface, true canvas that can be stretched and mounted just like a conventional painting, iron-on transfers, backlit film, and more (**Figure 1.6**). If it'll feed through your printer, it's very possible you can print on it for some interesting (if not always successful) results.

Figure 1.6 *You aren't limited to simple photo papers with digital. You can now print on fabric, puzzles, coffee mugs—almost anything. (Image courtesy of Kodak)*

More options

Obviously I'll be concentrating on printed output, but that's not all you are limited to with digital images. E-mail and Web display, as well as slideshows on the family television, are other choices.

With prints, you have a number of options available for paper types or even printing on fabric. Perhaps you'd like to make a calendar or puzzle from your photos—that's no problem with digital! The advantage here is flexibility. You can now use the same photo over and over again for different purposes—not something easily accomplished with a negative or slide.

A Digital Primer

Digital photographs are made up of *pixels*, which is shorthand for *picture elements*. The typical digital photograph today consists of millions of pixels, each representing one little dot. The size and quality of your digital prints are directly related to the number of pixels you have to work with. **Figures 1.7a** and **1.7b** show the difference in quality when printing the same image from a 3-megapixel camera at 4×5 and at 8×10.

Figures 1.7a and b *You can see the difference in image quality when printing a lower-resolution file, such as this one from a 3-MP camera at 8×10 (b). The 4×5 print from the same camera is fine (a), but the larger one is showing jagged edges and blurry detail from the enlargement. I'll show you how to keep this problem to a minimum in Chapter 6.*

The number of pixels available is only part of the equation, though, and throughout this book you'll see ways to maximize the quality of your prints regardless of the starting point. To be successful, however, you need to be able to understand the language of digital photography.

Resolution

The term *resolution* has several meanings depending on where you are. *Camera resolution* is typically measured in *megapixels* (MP), or millions of pixels, such as 6 MP. This is the number of photo sites on the camera's sensor. Larger numbers typically mean more detail and the ability to print larger photos. **Table 1.1** shows the resolution of common sensor sizes and the largest print size you can produce without resizing the image.

Of course, you aren't limited to printing only that size, just as you weren't limited to one size with traditional film. When selecting any size other than the native resolution, Photoshop interpolates your photo data to add or subtract information to fit into the new size. When you printed enlargements from a film negative, you began to see the grain as the print size increased. With digital, you begin to see the pixels that make up the digital image. Photoshop and other imaging applications can do a remarkably good job of interpolating data, and in Chapter 6, "Resizing and Sharpening Your Images," I'll go into detail on how to get the maximum quality possible when resizing up or down.

Table 1.1: Sensor Resolution and Image Size	
Resolution	**Native Image Size (approximate) in Inches**
3 MP	3×5
4 MP	4×6
5 MP	5×7
6 MP	8×10
8 MP	8×12
12 MP	9×14
16 MP	16×24
22 MP	20×32

The second context in which you'll hear resolution used is in relation to image dimensions. For example, if you want to use a photograph on the Web or in e-mail, a resolution of 800×600 might be specified. Although many people say *resolution*, they're really describing the *dimensions* of the photo. So, if you want to be one of the insiders and be cool during your next digital conversation, use *dimension* rather than *resolution* when talking about the size of your photos.

The third common use of resolution is to describe the *pixels per inch* (ppi) of a photograph. This specification has a huge impact on quality, especially for printed output. **Figures 1.8a** and **18.b** show the difference between an image printed at 72 ppi, which is the common resolution for on-screen use, and one printed at 300 ppi, which is the normal print resolution. In Table 1.1, I used the common resolution of 300 ppi to determine print sizes for each sensor. Because on-screen pixels become dots when printed, the term *dots per inch* (dpi) is sometimes used in place of ppi.

Figures 1.8a and b *A 72-ppi image (a) is typical for on-screen display, but when printed to the same size as a 300-ppi image (b) formatted for printing, the difference in quality is obvious.*

How Big Can You Go?

Digital files can be resized easily and with very good results (within reason). With the proper technique, you can get quality 8×10 prints from most digital cameras, and 11×14 prints from a 6-MP or larger sensor will look fine, with no obvious jaggies (see the accompanying note). Remember, like everything digital, the megapixel limitations and size guidelines presented in Table 1.1 are not hard-and-fast rules—just guidelines. What may be acceptable quality to me may not be acceptable to you, and vice versa. I'll go into image resizing in detail in Chapter 6. One of the main factors in determining how big of a print you can get is the initial quality of the image. Enlargements will start to show every imperfection in a photo. Keep in mind that digital can do some amazing things, but it isn't a miracle cure for low resolution or poor technique.

The other limiting factor will be the size of your printer. Most users have a standard-size printer capable of 8×10 prints, but 13×19 printers are gaining in popularity as their prices come down (**Figures 1.9a** and **b**). For serious photographers, the next step up is a large format printer (**Figure 1.10**). They're expensive and they take up more space than you realize, so unless you plan on doing lots of prints bigger than 13×19, you might consider sending this work out. For an in-depth discussion of choosing a printer, see Chapter 2, "Setting Up a Print Studio."

Figures 1.9a and b *The most common printer sizes for home-based photo reproduction are standard letter size (a) and wide format (b), which can handle media up to 13 inches wide. I'll cover specifics on these printers and others in Chapter 2.*

Figure 1.10 *Large-format printers are beyond the budgets or needs of most digital photographers. The three most common sizes are 17, 24, and 44 inches. If you do a large volume of printing, these printers can reduce your time and cost. Otherwise, you're better off sending the occasional large job out.*

RAW versus TIFF versus JPEG

Many of today's advanced digital cameras support RAW capture in addition to JPEG. Some also include TIFF capture. Which is best for printing?

RAW gives you the most control over your image after capture and has the most color information possible. When you take a photograph with a digital camera, it is captured in RAW format. If your settings are TIFF or JPEG, the image is then processed in the camera with the settings used at that time—white balance, sharpening, color, and so on. Saving as RAW allows you to make changes to any of these settings later, in the computer.

The other advantage RAW has is that more color information is retained. JPEG saves files in 8-bit format, with 256 possible values for each red, green, and blue color. RAW files are typically 12-bit or more. When opened in Photoshop, they are converted to 16-bit files (unless you specify otherwise during the conversion). You now have much more latitude when making color corrections to your images. This is especially important for shots with a broad range of tones in a particular area, such as the sky. The 8-bit file is likely to show banding, or abrupt changes in colors, while the 16-bit file will have smooth gradations between tones.

TIFF files saved in the camera have no real advantage over RAW. They're big and take up space on your memory card, and like JPEG, they've already had processing applied to them.

For detailed information on working with RAW files, I humbly suggest another of my books, *RAW 101: Better Images with Photoshop Elements & Photoshop* (Sybex, 2005).

Bit depth

Bit depth refers to the number of possible color choices in a pixel. A 1-bit image contains pixels that are either black or white (**Figure 1.11**). No shades of gray here; you either get a black dot, or you get nothing. It's the ultimate in take it or leave it. Move up to 8 bits, which is the typical black-and-white photo, and you now have 256 possible shades of gray for each pixel. Now we're getting somewhere! Even at 8 bits of black and white, however, you'll still feel very limited and photos will not have a lifelike look to them, but it's a heck of a lot better than the 1-bit choice. Moving up to color, those same 8 bits are now applied to each primary color—red, green, and blue. So, what do 256 shades of red, 256 of green, and 256 of blue combine to give you? A total of 16,777,216 possible colors for each and every one of the pixels in your photograph (**Figure 1.12**). Moving up the line to the highest possible image quality is the 16-bit image. If you shoot RAW (see the sidebar "RAW versus TIFF versus JPEG"), you have the full 16-bit color space available to you (**Figure 1.13**). This translates into 65,536 color values per primary color, for a theoretical 281,474,976,710,656 (yes, trillion) possible colors.

Figure 1.11 A 1-bit image is simply a printed dot or no printed dot. There aren't any color options. Does it remind you of early dot-matrix printer graphics?

Figure 1.12 *An 8-bit image contains a maximum of 256 different colors or shades of color such as gray. It's a huge improvement over the 1-bit file in Figure 1.11, but still very limited compared to what most printers are capable of.*

Figure 1.13 *A 16-bit image contains millions of color possibilities and will give you the maximum quality your printer is capable of producing.*

Halftone or continuous tone

Most printed images are *halftones*, meaning they are made up of small (okay, teeny) dots of ink with different densities and sizes. Larger dots placed closer together produce denser images, while smaller dots with more space between them appear lighter. When you view a halftone from a normal distance, your brain blends the individual dots and lets you see a solid image with smooth tonal variations (**Figure 1.14**). The inkjet printers that most people use for photo reproduction are based on halftone technology. Each printer has hundreds or thousands of nozzles to place dots of ink on the paper. For a real-life example of halftoning at work, take a close look at any newspaper photograph. You can readily see the individual dots with a magnifying glass, but when you hold the paper at normal viewing distance, the dots blend together, giving the image the illusion of a continuous tone.

Figure 1.14 Halftone prints are the type of image created by inkjet and laser printers. Without close examination, it's nearly impossible to tell the photo is made up of tiny dots of ink.

Continuous-tone images don't bother with varying densities and sizes of dots to make up a photograph. Instead, the colors overlap each other with no spaces between them to make a smooth transition from one color tone to the next (**Figure 1.15**). Continuous-tone printers for the desktop typically use the *dye sublimation* method, in which ribbons of color are overlaid on each other in several passes.

Figure 1.15 *Continuous-tone printers, such as the Kodak 1400, are the printer of choice for portrait and event photography. Continuous tone is created by using ribbons of ink that are fused to the paper, resulting in very smooth color gradations that are most noticeable in skintones. (Image courtesy of Kodak)*

Although they are not technically continuous tone, today's high-quality inkjet printers have, for the most part, caught up to dye sublimation in terms of quality and density of color. You'd be hard-pressed to spot individual dots from any of the current six- to nine-color inkjet photo printers in use today.

So, which should you choose: a printer that uses halftones or one that uses continuous tone to create prints? I'll go into specifics on printers in Chapter 2, but in general most people will want to use an inkjet printer, which means halftone, for most of your work.

Dithering

With the exception of continuous-tone printers, such as the dye sublimation models from Kodak and others, all printers use *dithering* to create tones within a print. Dithering is the process of reducing the number of colors in a photo to the number of colors a printer is capable of reproducing. It's also used with computer displays. For instance, when you edit a 16- or 24-bit TIFF file and save it as a JPEG file, the image must be dithered to fit into the 8-bit color space supported by JPEG. Modern photo printers have taken the art of dithering to amazing levels. It's hard to identify the dithering pattern used without high magnification on most of the current photo inkjets (**Figure 1.16**). Today's inkjets, particularly those designed for photo reproduction, can normally handle all the color your display is capable of reproducing so you most likely won't be worried about how your photos are dithered when printing at home. Dithering plays more of a role in prepress production where the resolution is lower and fewer inks are used. I'll get into prepress production techniques later in Chapter 9, "Working with Service Providers."

Figure 1.16 *Dithering is the method of reducing the number of colors in an image to fit within the output device's capabilities. The inset shows a close-up of how dithering affects the image.*

Moving On

This chapter served as an introduction to some of the digital terms you'll be seeing throughout the book as well as a background on the advantages of working with digital images. In the next chapter, you'll learn about the different types of printers, including more on the advantages of continuous-tone and halftone printers, and how to make a selection based on your needs.

2 | Setting Up a Print Studio

It's pretty obvious that one of the major decisions you'll make for your print studio is which type of printer to buy. Choosing a photo printer used to be easy, mainly because not that many choices were available. Now it seems that a new printer or technology is introduced almost weekly. Having lots of choices can be a good thing, but it becomes that much more important to sort out which features you really need, especially when what you need sometimes depends on what you *think* you might be doing with your prints a year from now.

Although the majority of users select either inkjet or dye-sublimation printers, other options are available that you may find more suited to your needs. I'll be up front and let you know that in my opinion, inkjet printers give the digital photographer the best set of features and performance of any printing process available.

But don't take my word for it. Read through the descriptions of popular printer technologies and inJks in this chapter to learn about their advantages and see what best matches your style of photography and printing. There's a little something for everyone, and there is no one perfect solution for every situation. At the end of the chapter, you'll find a handy checklist that you can use when shopping for a photo printer. Before you even set foot in a store, however, take some time to analyze your printing needs.

What Will You Be Printing?

What is your printing interest? If you're a portrait photographer interested in doing print packages for clients, your printing needs will be very different from those of the wildlife photographer. The second consideration is size (**Figure 2.1**). How big do you need to print on a regular basis? Sure, that 44-inch-wide printer looks great and can probably handle any job you might have, but if you normally only print up to 11×14, does it make sense to spend that kind of money for a printer?

Figure 2.1 *Size can be seductive—until you realize how big of a dent it puts in your wallet and in your office space. Most people will be happy with a printer that can produce 13×19 prints. And, when you see that 13×19 printer sitting on the 24-inch large-format printer, you quickly see how much difference 11 inches can make!*

For portrait photographers the question of producing either inkjet or dye-sublimation prints is a matter of taste. Remember from the previous chapter that *dye-sublimation printers* make multiple passes with different color ribbons to produce a continuous tone, and that *inkjet printers* use miniscule drops of ink to create an image. For portraits, the smoothness of dye sublimation is an advantage that many studios prefer. Today's inkjet photo printers are very nearly the equal of dye sublimation in print quality, but often lack the traditional photograph "feel" that many customers want in their images.

On the other hand, the wildlife or landscape photographer will likely be much happier with inkjet because of the options available for sizes and media, along with various ink options for special purposes. (For an in-depth look at each technology and its advantages, see the "Printer Types Overview" section later in this chapter.)

What Kind of Media Will You Use?

Your choice of printer will have a significant impact on the types of media to which you can print. Inkjet printers can handle just about every conceivable type of material that will fit through them—traditional photo papers, canvas, even fabric (**Figure 2.2**). Dye-sublimation printers, on the other hand, have very limited media options, typically offering only gloss or luster finishes of traditional-style photo papers.

Figure 2.2 *Inkjet printers offer the widest selection of media choices. You can print on anything from plain paper to fabric, although most of us prefer to stick to photo and fine art papers.*

Photographers are increasingly turning to fine art papers for some of their prints. These papers look and feel nothing at all like a traditional photo paper; they often have a textured and matte surface more similar to a watercolor paper.

If your printing needs vary as much as mine, plan on having more than one printer at some point. I use inkjet and dye-sublimation printers as needed for the project at hand. If I could keep only one, however, I'd stick with the inkjet because of the options available for both ink and paper types. The nice thing is that at current prices, it doesn't have to be a one-or-the-other decision.

Print Permanence

No matter what our specialties or media needs, we all wonder about the same thing: How long will that print last before starting to fade? The good news is that most of today's printers and inks have a much greater life span than ever. With the proper paper and ink combinations, you can plan on decades of display life for most prints, and in some cases prints are rated to last well over 100 years. The best way to improve your print's chances of survival is to understand the factors involved in determining the life span of your printed image.

Ink type

The type of ink your printer uses has a large impact on print permanence. I'll go into more detail about your choices later in this chapter; for now, just consider the basics.

Inkjet printers use two primary types of ink: dye or pigment (**Figure 2.3**). *Dye inks* tend to be brighter, and prints are more saturated than their pigment counterparts. The drawback is life span. Dye inks are often limited in display life, sometimes lasting only a few years before they begin to fade or shift color.

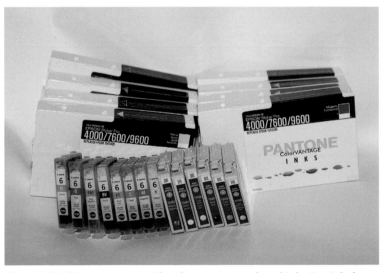

Figure 2.3 *Inkjet printers use either dye- or pigment-based inks. Dye inks have a slight edge in color gamut, or range, but pigment inks have a longer display life, which is important when selling prints.*

Pigment inks are not as vibrant as many dye inks but have the advantage of greatly increased display life. In many cases, pigment inks on archival matte finish paper will have a display life of over 100 years.

Dye-sublimation uses dyes as well, but they are transferred to the paper in a much different fashion. Dye-sub print life is similar to that of dye-based inkjet, especially when the protective coating layer used by some printers, such as the Kodak 8500, is used. Without this coating, dye-sub is more prone to damage from water and scratches.

Laser printing uses *toner*, similar to the way photocopy machines work. When pigmented toners are used, display life is long but does not approach the life span of inkjet primarily due to the lack of specific papers formulated for the pigmented toners.

Paper choices

As much as the ink used, paper type plays a critical role in how long your prints will last (**Figure 2.4**). Because of the way ink is absorbed into the paper, for example, matte finishes typically have a much longer display life than glossy prints, where the ink sits on top of the paper. If you plan to sell your prints, this is an important issue. After all, you don't want your customers coming back to you in 10 years wondering why their photo looks nothing like the one they bought.

Many printers, particularly inkjets, are optimized to work with specific paper and ink combinations for the longest display life. Even switching between different brands of paper with the same finish can have a tremendous effect on how long your prints will last. As an example, when using the Epson UltraChrome inks with Epson Premium Glossy Paper, you can expect a print life of about 70 years. Replace the Epson paper with a generic glossy photo paper and you might be looking at 7 to 10 years.

Figure 2.4 *Using papers designed for your printer and inks will give you the best results, especially when printing on traditional photo finishes such as gloss and luster. Generic brand papers can begin to fade in just a few years, while the right papers will last for decades.*

This doesn't mean you're limited to only the papers your manufacturer offers, however. Many popular fine art papers are available from third parties, and most of these are formulated for long print life.

When considering fine art papers, you'll want to check how they are made. For the best results, look for 100% cotton as found in such quality papers as Moab Entrada, Hahnemühle Photo Rag, and Somerset Velvet (**Figure 2.5**). Traditional photo papers, such as glossy and luster, typically use *RC*, or *resin-coated*, surfaces that swell up when the ink is placed on the page. RC papers don't have the display life of a cotton fine art paper, but in most cases they equal or exceed the display life of a traditional film-based print, and in many cases by decades.

Figure 2.5 *Fine art papers should be made from 100% cotton fibers. Available in a variety of finishes and weights, these papers are the choice of many pro photographers for their best prints.*

Table 2.1 compares the life span of some common print choices.

Table 2.1: Print Permanence by Paper Type	
Paper	**Estimated Display Life**
Premium Glossy	98 years
Premium Luster	165 years
Enhanced Matte	110 years
UltraSmooth Fine Art	175 years
Canvas	132 years
Somerset Velvet	128 years
Traditional Kodak Color Prints	22 years

Note

All of Table 2.1's estimates are for prints displayed in frames with ultraviolet (UV)-coated glass. You can expect less than half this time with the popular thumbtack display method.

Displaying your prints

Regardless of what type of ink or paper is used, the best way to extend the life span of a print is to display it properly. Using thumbtacks to stick your print up on the wall is a good way to ensure that the print lasts the shortest amount of time possible (I've seen prints fade to almost nothing in as little as three months).

For best results, you'll want to keep your prints either in an album or displayed behind UV-coated glass (**Figure 2.6**). Chapter 10, "Presenting Your Work," will show you how to properly mount and display your prints for their best presentation and protection.

Note

You'll often see two sets of numbers for print life. The lower number is what you can expect before noticeable fading or color shifting appears when the print is properly framed behind UV-coated glass and out of direct sunlight. The second, longer number is the expected life when stored in a dark location. Now, I don't know about you, but I can't see the print in a dark location so I tend to go with the shorter number.

Figure 2.6 *Storing your prints properly will greatly extend their life. Either keep them in an archival album or properly frame them behind UV-coated glass.*

Printer Types Overview

Inkjet, laser, dye-sublimation, electrophotography. So many choices and each technology does something better than the others. For 98% of you, the choice will likely be an inkjet or dye-sublimation printer. The next sections talk about what makes each type tick and why it's good at what it does.

Inkjet printers

Inkjet comes in two main flavors: *thermal*, which is used by most of the popular brands such as Canon and HP, and *piezoelectric*, which is used by Epson on the desktop and Roland, Mimaki, and others in large-format commercial printing.

Thermal

Canon invented the thermal process with its BubbleJet printers. As the name suggests, the technology uses heat to force drops of ink out of the printhead and onto the paper. A resistor heats up behind individual nozzles, forming a vapor bubble that forces ink out. As the resistor cools, the bubble collapses and draws more ink into the nozzle from the ink cartridge (**Figure 2.7**).

Depending on the printer, the printhead (**Figure 2.8**) may be part of the ink cartridge or a separate unit. The advantage to this method is that inks typically don't clog, and repairs are less expensive because the printhead is replaced more frequently.

Thermal Inkjet Process

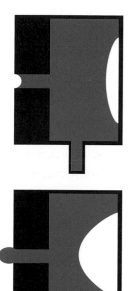

Element cool
No pressure on ink

Element heats
pushes drop of ink
through nozzle

Figure 2.7 *With thermal inkjets, a resistor heats and expands to force a drop of ink through the nozzle and onto the page. The resistor then cools and draws more ink into the printhead.*

Figure 2.8 *Thermal inkjets typically have user-replaceable printheads, which keeps clogging to a minimum and repair costs low.*

Until recently, thermal inkjets used dye-based inks exclusively, which gave them an advantage on vibrant, saturated prints but a shorter display life. Although pigment inks are now available on some models, reformulated inks have greatly improved the display life of dye inks. Canon's new ChromaLife 100 inks are rated for 100 years when stored in archival albums, and up to 30 years when displayed behind glass. The new HP Vivera inks, when used with HP Premium Photo paper, are rated to last 103 years.

The Canon Pixma and i9900, as well as the HP PhotoSmart and DesignJet series, are the most popular brands of photo-quality thermal inkjet printers.

In the Canon line, the Pixma 8500 letter size printer and the i9900 wide-format 13×19 printer both use eight colors with individual ink cartridges for the best possible photo prints (**Figure 2.9**). The Canon printers work well with both traditional-style photo papers and fine art papers, and are among the fastest inkjets available.

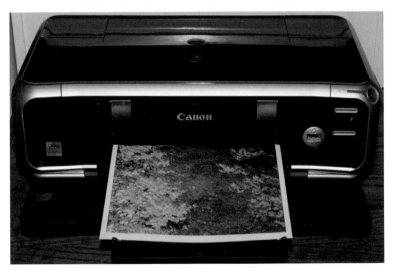

Figure 2.9 *The Canon BubbleJet printers, such as the Pixma 8500 shown here, are thermal inkjets that use separate ink cartridges for each color.*

The letter-size HP PhotoSmart 8450 is an eight-color printer, while the 13×19 PhotoSmart 8750 (**Figure 2.10**) is a nine-color 13×19 format printer. Both use three shades of black ink for excellent black-and-white prints and work well with a variety of paper styles.

Figure 2.10 *The HP PhotoSmart series uses the thermal process. The 8750 shown here is a nine-color printer but only uses three ink cartridges. With three shades of black the 8750 is able to produce very good black-and-white prints.*

Piezoelectric

The second major type of inkjet printer uses a piezoelectric process. Rather than a resistor heating up to force a bubble of ink onto the paper, the *piezoelectric* process uses a crystal that is subjected to an electric charge. This forces the crystal to flex and push a drop of ink through the nozzle (**Figure 2.11**). When the charge stops, the crystal returns to its original shape and pulls more ink into the head, ready for the next drop. The Epson Stylus printers use the piezoelectric process. These printers do not use replaceable printheads like their thermal inkjet cousins. The advantage is that the printheads are longer lasting. When you do have a problem, however, repairs are more expensive (it's probably cheaper to replace the printer than to repair the head). A final advantage of piezoelectric technology is that because the printheads don't change, profiles tend to be more accurate than those made for thermal inkjets.

Piezo-Electric Inkjet Process

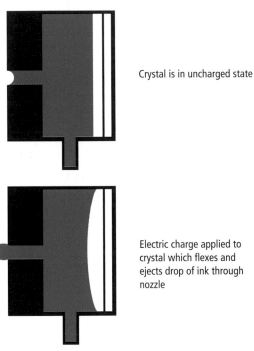

Crystal is in uncharged state

Electric charge applied to crystal which flexes and ejects drop of ink through nozzle

Figure 2.11 Piezoelectric inkjets use a crystal that flexes to force out a drop of ink when subjected to an electric charge.

Piezoelectric printers have traditionally used smaller droplets of ink than thermal inkjets, which translates into higher resolutions and finer details. Along with Epson, other examples of piezoelectric inkjet are IRIS, Roland, and Encad in the large-format size (**Figure 2.12**).

Figure 2.12 *The Roland large-format printer is a high-quality piezoelectric inkjet used by many print services.*

The Epson R800 letter-size and R1800 13×19 printers use an enhanced UltraChrome ink set with better color saturation and a special gloss optimizer for excellent results with glossy finish papers. The R2400 (**Figure 2.13**) is a 13x19 format printer that uses Epson's newest ink set, the UltraChrome K3, which includes three black inks. These are the same inks used in the 17-inch 4800, 24-inch 7800, and 44-inch 9800 professional printers and offer the longest print life of any inkjet prints. The quality of black-and-white prints using Epson's new Advanced B&W Photo mode is nothing short of amazing. If you're interested in black and white, these are the printers to check out.

Figure 2.13 *The Epson R2400 is a 13×19 printer that uses Epson's newest UltraChrome K3 pigment inks.*

Pigment versus dye

Pigment ink versus dye inks is something of a holy war among pro photographers and printer manufacturers. Each type of ink has its benefits and drawbacks, and with every new printer release the line between the two blurs a little more. Most of today's printers use dye inks; the Canon Pixma and HP PhotoSmart series are the most popular brands. Dye inks have the advantage of having more vibrant color and a wider color range, or *gamut*. Prints made with dye inks typically look more saturated than their pigment counterparts, which is all many people are interested in. The main drawback to dye inks is print life, which is shorter than pigment inks (see the "Print Permanence" section later in this chapter for more information).

Pigment inks, such as those used in the Epson UltraChrome series, have a much longer print life, particularly with matte finish papers. The biggest drawback to pigment inks is *metamerism*, which is seen as a shift in colors when prints are viewed in different lighting conditions. Earlier versions of the UltraChrome inks had a significant problem with *bronzing*, which is also known as *gloss differential*. This is seen when viewing a print at an angle: some areas of the print appear to be flat and dull when compared to other areas with the same color. The latest Epson printers such as the R800 and R1800 have added a Gloss Optimizer to reduce this problem. This optimizer is used automatically when printing on glossy paper.

Many of the current dye-based printers have begun using pigment-based black inks for truer blacks than previously possible with dyes, including Canon and HP. Canon has also introduced a new line of professional large-format inkjets that use all pigment inks.

Xerox solid ink

Xerox takes a very different approach to color printing. The Phaser 8400 (**Figure 2.14**) solid-ink printer uses what is known as *phase change* technology. Like the other piezoelectric inkjets, it uses an

Figure 2.14 *The Xerox Phaser 8400 is a solid-ink printer that takes a different approach. The ink is melted into a drum and then transferred to the page similar to traditional laser printers.*

electric charge to push the ink out. Where it differs, though, is the ink itself. The Phaser is also known as the "crayon printer" because it uses solid blocks of resin-based inks (**Figure 2.15**) that are heated to liquid as they are needed. Instead of going directly onto the page, the ink, in liquid form, goes into a drum that runs the width of the page. The ink is then transferred to the paper in a single pass, similar to traditional laser printing technologies.

The Phaser does produce beautiful color, but two issues prevent it from being a viable printer for photographers: The display life of its prints is so short that you'll notice fading in less than two years, and the images that it produces are less than photographic in appearance with a waxy, textured surface that sits above the paper. This is particularly noticeable when viewing the prints from an angle.

Figure 2.15 *Crayons or Gummi Bears? Nope, it's the solid inks used in the Phaser 8400.*

How many colors is enough?

Not long ago, most inkjets used four colors of ink and we were all impressed with the quality. Today's photo printers routinely come with six to nine colors, thus providing better color saturation and more accurate color tones. For photo printing, I consider six-color printers to be the minimum for high-quality output.

The new Epson UltraChrome K3 printers—the R2400, 4800, 7800, and 9800—use eight colors with three shades of black (one more than previous versions) for excellent black-and-white printing on a variety of papers. The Canon Pixma 8500 and i9900 printers are eight-color devices with red and green inks for better accuracy in those colors, while the HP PhotoSmart 8750 uses nine colors, including three blacks. The results from all of these printers are outstanding, and all produce color prints that rival or exceed anything you could get through traditional printing processes.

Dye-sublimation printers

Dye-sublimation, or dye-sub, printing typically uses a ribbon (**Figure 2.16**), which is heated by a printhead that runs the width of the paper. The elements in the printhead vaporize the dyes, which are then placed, or sublimated, onto the paper. Dye-sub printers make at least three passes for each print, with cyan, magenta, and yellow ribbons overlaying each other to create the continuous-tone final image. Some dye-sub printers include black dye, and some, such as the Kodak 8500 (**Figure 2.17**), include a protective coating for a total of four passes. The advantage dye-sub offers is continuous tone for rich details and smooth tonal shifts, making these printers excellent choices for portraits. The disadvantages are the limited paper choices—either glossy or semigloss (called luster)—and print sizes. Most dye-sub printers work with only one or two sizes of paper.

Figure 2.16 *Dye-sublimation printers typically use a ribbon that transfers colors by heat onto the page. Each print requires multiple passes, with one color of ribbon used on each pass.*

Figure 2.17 *The Kodak 8500 is a high-quality dye-sublimation printer that uses gloss or luster paper. Reasonably priced, the 8500 is a favorite among portrait and wedding photographers because of its excellent print quality and smooth skin tones.*

Color laser printers

Also referred to as *electrophotography* printers, color laser printers offer the advantages of low cost per print and speed but are limited in the available paper types and the maximum print size. Like a traditional laser printer, many units use a fine laser to etch an image onto rotating drums. In the case of color lasers, there are typically four drums: cyan, magenta, yellow, and black (**Figure 2.18**). The toner is electrically charged and is attracted to the drums, where it is then transferred to the paper.

Color laser printers are available from many manufacturers; Xerox, Canon, and Minolta are a few popular brands (**Figure 2.19**).

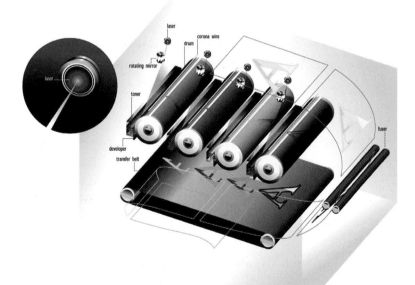

Figure 2.18 Color laser printers use four drums that are etched with a laser to attract toner, which is then transferred to the paper. LED printers work in a similar fashion.

Figure 2.19 Many color laser printers are part of a copy machine. The paper choices are limited, as are the sizes, and the print quality isn't as good as with other printer types.

The biggest limitations to color laser printing are the available media choices and the output sizes. Affordable printers seldom do larger than legal-size pages. For occasional use, color laser printers are a good compromise when text documents and speed are your highest priorities. For photographic prints, you're better served by other choices.

Digital photo processors

These are the big boys. Odds are that you won't be bringing a digital photo processor home for personal use; most of them start at over $100,000 and take up a fair amount of space. For that kind of money, you get continuous-tone prints on traditional photo papers and, depending on the model, in sizes that aren't possible with conventional printers such as inkjets. Examples of this type of printer are the Durst Lambda (**Figure 2.20**) and Océ LightJet. These printers use lasers or LEDs to expose regular photo paper, which is then processed in chemicals similar to the way traditional darkroom film prints are made.

Figure 2.20 The Durst Lambda is the granddaddy of digital photo processors. These devices use lasers or LEDs to expose regular photo paper, which is then processed in chemicals similar to the way prints are made in a traditional darkroom.

The other category of printers in this range is the minilab machines, such as the Fuji Pictography (**Figure 2.21**) and similar units from Agfa and Noritsu. You'll find these at most one-hour photo printers as well as most online print services. These devices also use chemicals to process traditional photo papers. And, like the Lambda and LightJet, they probably aren't going to fit into your home or budget.

Figure 2.21 *Many minilabs and online print services use the Fuji Pictography system. These units use normal photo paper and develop the prints in traditional chemicals.*

How much will it cost?

As you can imagine, there is a wide range of prices for printers. Much depends on the capacity of the printer—both number of prints and the maximum size. Leaving out the digital photo processors that are beyond the budget and size of almost everyone, you can expect to spend $100 to $300 for a quality inkjet printer capable of 8×10 prints such as the Epson R800, Canon Pixma iP8500, or HP PhotoSmart 8250. A 13×19 inkjet, such as the Epson R1800 or Canon i9900, will set you back $400 or so, while the pro-oriented Epson R2400 runs about $900. Expect to spend $2000 and up for a printer that can do 24 inches or larger.

Dye-sub printers, especially those capable of printing 8×10 or larger, will run a little more, with $900 to $1000 being typical for something like the Kodak 8500, while the Xerox Phaser and color laser printers mentioned earlier are in the $900 to $1500 range.

In the long run, the cost of the printer is trivial compared to the money you'll spend on consumables: paper and ink. Inkjet is the clear winner on a cost-per-page basis, but if you have specific needs that are filled by dye-sub or laser, then your choice is a bit easier.

Specialty Inks

Along with the inks sold by your printer's manufacturer, you can buy a number of specialty inks. For example, specialty inks can turn your printer into a custom black-and-white printer, and some color inks have a completely different look to them for printing on special media. If you print high volumes, you'll quickly find that inks are more expensive than the printer. At this point, the continuous-flow ink systems begin to look very attractive.

All of the options listed here are designed for inkjet printers. With other printer types, you're limited to what the manufacturer supports; this is another reason why inkjet technology is so popular among digital printers.

Black-and-white inks

Several products are available that will turn your printer into a black-and-white-only device capable of beautiful fine art prints that would be impossible to duplicate with color inks. These inksets work by replacing all of the color ink cartridges in your printer with various shades of black ink. Using special software, you can create prints with toning that simulates such custom darkroom processing techniques as platinum, selenium, and sepia.

Warning!

When you start to price new inks, the generic brands and refill kits available in the office supply stores or on eBay may look very attractive. I have one word of advice: *Don't do it!* Okay, that's three words, but regardless of my math skills, trust me on this one. You'll have far more headaches and grief than the savings is worth by using these inks.

Note

An RIP is a separate program that bypasses the standard printer driver to tell the printer exactly how much of each ink to place on the page for the utmost control. I'll cover choosing and using a RIP in detail in Chapter 7, "Printing Your Files."

Media Street QuadBlack

Media Street's (www.mediastreet.com) QuadBlack (**Figure 2.22**) currently works with a select set of Epson printers such as the R200. The kit uses six shades of black inks in total but only four at a time. Printing must be done through the QuadTone RIP (Raster Image Processor), where you select the tone you wish to use: cold, warm, or neutral. You can fine-tune your prints in the RIP to make further adjustments. The QuadBlack set is an excellent way to get into black-and-white printing and combined with the R200 gives you an inexpensive way to have a dedicated black-and-white printer without breaking the bank. QuadBlack costs about $210, but it will give you results you were unable to obtain for five times the price with other printers.

Figure 2.22 *The Media Street QuadBlack system turns a sub-$100 printer into a museum-quality black-and-white printer with a number of toning options.*

Lyson Daylight Darkroom

The Daylight Darkroom system (**Figure 2.23**) from Lyson (www.daylightdarkroom.com) is a complete black-and-white printing solution that currently works with Epson 2200, 4000, 7600, and 9600 printers. The Daylight Darkroom system uses seven shades of black ink to produce excellent quality black-and-white prints with some amazing specifications. The prints are rated to last over 100 years and can be used with glossy papers as well as other paper types. Like QuadBlack, Daylight Darkroom requires you to print through a special interface that bypasses the normal print driver. Lyson also provides a program to make custom profiles for the system. Daylight Darkroom starts at about $480.

Figure 2.23 *The Lyson Daylight Darkroom is a complete system for larger printers, with seven shades of black and excellent display properties.*

Pantone ColorVANTAGE

The same people who created the color standards used by almost everyone in the graphics industry also offer a set of inks available for Epson printers. The Pantone ColorVANTAGE (www.colorvantageinks.com) inks are pigment-based inks designed to have a wider gamut and more neutral blacks than the Epson UltraChrome inks. They'll even work with older Epson printers like the 1280 that used dye inks, with all of the advantages of pigment ink. The ColorVANTAGE inkset does a fantastic job and costs less than the Epson inks.

Note

I should disclose that I am a Pantone Innovator, which means that I use and endorse the ColorVANTAGE inks. I would use these inks regardless, though, and I receive no compensation for including them or recommending them.

Other specialty inks

Media Street, Lyson, and MIS Associates also make replacement inks for a variety of printers, either as refill kits, replacement cartridges, or bulk systems (covered next). While most of them mimic or improve upon the original inks used by the manufacturer, some add special features, such as the ultra-wide gamut in Lyson's Fotonic Ink, and Media Street's Generations Elite, which is designed for use in high UV lighting conditions such as direct sunlight.

Another popular option is the Small Gamut inks from Lyson, which are designed to give you outstanding results with toned black-and-white images. You'll find links to all of these and more in the Appendix A, "Resources."

Continuous-flow systems

It doesn't take long to figure out that printers are comparatively cheap when compared to how much it costs to feed them with ink. In fact, there are examples, such as the Epson R200, where it's actually cheaper to buy a new printer than it is to replace all of the ink cartridges. Doesn't say much for our environmental policies, does it? If you print in large volumes, you might be interested in checking out some of the continuous-flow systems available. Rather than use small ink cartridges with 10–15 ml (milliliter) of ink, these systems use external bottles of ink that are fed into replacement cartridges. These systems can greatly reduce the cost of printing, but their initial price isn't particularly attractive. Expect to spend $200 or more to get set up initially. After that, refill bottles of ink are very affordable.

These systems make the most sense for desktop printers that use the smaller ink cartridges. As an example, the Epson desktop models (up to the 13×19 size) use a cartridge that holds about 12 ml of ink and sells for about $12, or about $1 per ml. The larger printers use either 110 ml or 220 ml cartridges of the same ink and sell for $70 and $112, respectively, which comes out to about 63 cents and 51 cents per milliliter—quite a savings!

Media Street Niagara II

Media Street (www.mediastreet.com) makes its continuous-flow system available for a variety of printers, including most popular Epson and Canon photo printers. If you do a large volume of printing, using a continuous-flow system such as the Niagara II (**Figure 2.24**) can save you as much as 90% on the cost of ink. You also get the advantage of longer print life on your Canon prints because the Niagara system uses pigment inks. The gamut of these inks is very close to the original inks they replace, but you will most likely want to use new paper profiles to make the most of the change. Media Street is highly recommended if you're looking for a quality replacement ink with excellent results and strong customer support. Getting started with the Niagara system will run about $250, depending on printer model and the inks used.

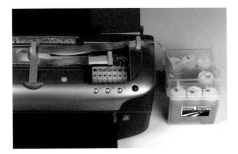

Figure 2.24 *The Media Street Niagara II Bulk Feed System can save you large amounts of money if you print in enough volume. The system works by replacing the printer's cartridges with special ones that are connected to bottles of ink that you can easily refill.*

MIS Systems

The MIS Continuous Flow System (CFS) from MIS Associates, Inc. (www.inksupply.com) is another quality system. Figure on spending about $150 and up for a complete setup, including ink. The MIS system (**Figure 2.25**) is available for most Epson printers and several Canon models. MIS offers several flavors of inks in the CFS, including dye, pigments, and black-and-white sets. As with the Media Street (and any other third-party ink), you'll have the best results by creating new printer profiles specifically made for your paper and ink combinations. Chapter 4, "Using Printer Settings," has complete information on creating and using printer profiles.

Figure 2.25 *The MIS Continuous Flow System is available for a number of Epson and Canon models and can be purchased with a variety of ink choices, including dye, pigment, and black-and-white.*

Lyson

For years, Lyson (www.lyson.com) has been providing high-quality inks and papers for a wide variety of printers and uses, including photo inkjets and industrial textile printers. The Lyson CIS system (**Figure 2.26**) is available in several different ink sets for Epson and Canon as well as large-format printers from Rolad, Encad, and Mimaki. The dye-based Lysonic Archival Ink set is designed for the Epson printers and when matched with their papers has a life of at least 65 years. The Fotonic Ink has a very wide gamut (as much as 20% larger than Epson dye inks), and the Quad Black kits are available in Cool, Neutral, and Warm tone sets. The CIS systems sell for about $300.

Figure 2.26 *The Lyson Continuous Ink System also uses several different ink sets including Lyson's Fotonic, which has the widest color gamut of any ink available.*

Printer Selection Worksheet

You've heard all your options; now how do you choose? To help you select the best printer for your needs, ask yourself these five questions when you're ready to shop:

1. **What is the largest size I want to print?**

   For 8×10 to 11×14, go with either dye-sub or inkjet. For smaller sizes, panoramics, or large prints, inkjet is the best option. For prints in the 16×20 and larger range, inkjet is the only realistic option for most users.

2. **What subjects will I be printing?**

   For portrait and wedding work, consider dye-sub for the highest quality when printing skin tones.

   For landscapes, wildlife, travel, or commercial photography, consider inkjet for more color options and media types, including black-and-white.

3. **What paper types do I want to use?**

   For glossy and luster only, choose either dye-sub or inkjet. For fine art, canvas, fabric, and specialty media, inkjet is your best option.

   For longest display life, pigment inks have an advantage over dye-based inks.

4. **How much printing will I be doing?**

   More than thirty 8×10 prints a month? Consider a larger printer or one that can use a continuous-flow system to save on ink costs.

   Fewer than thirty 8×10 or smaller prints a month? Any of the letter-size inkjet printers or dye-sub printers (see questions 2 and 3 for help on which type is better for your use).

5. **Will I be using the printer for more than photos?**

   If yes, consider inkjet or color laser. Inkjet will give you the best possible output for photos with very good text. Laser will give excellent text results and high speed with less-than-optimal photo prints.

Moving On

Now that you have a better idea of the types of printers that are available, and hopefully have decided on what will work best for your needs, you're ready to set up your system for color accuracy to help you get the most from your printing solution. In Chapter 3, "Keeping an Eye on Color," I'll explain display calibration and why it's a critical part of the digital workflow. Then Chapter 4 will show you how to use color management with your printer to get output that matches your display.

3 | Keeping an Eye on Color

Tip

When doing any image-editing work, your first step toward color management should be to change your desktop background to a medium gray. The gray may look boring, but that pretty background picture can make it very difficult to accurately judge color corrections.

If you've ever tried to get a good print from a computer that hasn't been properly set up for color management, you already know how frustrating, costly, and time consuming it can be. Your photo, so vibrant and glowing on screen, looks totally different, dark, or drab. You may even be thinking about giving up on printing at home completely. Don't. Instead, take a break from your computer to read this chapter and learn about color management, which will help you better match your printed results to what you see on screen. This chapter will take the mystery out of color problems and soon have you creating prints that actually look the way you want. You'll learn the essentials you need to get your monitor and printer playing together nicely and working for you.

And, you just might find that you have no desire to pull your hair out in frustration any longer!

Color Management Basics

Why do we even need color management? Here's a simple example. Get the biggest box of crayons you can find. Now, dump them all out of the box and onto the table with your eyes closed. Keeping your eyes closed, color in a blue sky, green grass, and a big yellow sun (remind you of grade school?). Okay, open your eyes and see what you've created.

It's possible that you have in front of you a nice picture with perfect colors. It's much more likely, though, that you'll be wondering what the heck you did. The odds of having a blue sky, green grass, or yellow sun are pretty slim. Even if you ended up with green grass, does it look right with a purple sky?

Tip

If you followed along with the exercise and now have crayon marks on your table, you can either clean them with WD-40, or if you have small children, blame them.

Now let's try something a little easier. Using only the yellow, blue, and green shades from your crayon box, try coloring another sun, sky, and lawn. I bet yours still doesn't look exactly like mine. Even if we both choose the same shade of yellow for our suns, do you think we'll both pick Kelly Green for the lawn, or Royal Blue for the sky? Probably not.

Getting your printer and display to produce the same colors is somewhat like the exercise above. Unless the printer knows what the display thinks green is supposed to be, it's unlikely that the two will match. Your display and printer each use *profiles* that describe how to create a color. When you print an image, the printer profile looks at the profile used by your monitor and translates the colors into the closest matches available (**Figure 3.1**).

Figure 3.1 *Trying to get accurate prints from an uncalibrated monitor is hit or miss, and usually miss.*

Creating profiles is like opening your printer's eyes: It will improve the match between your printer and display—improve, but not perfect. Resign yourself that your display and printer will never be an exact match for each other. There are two reasons for this mismatch. First, a display is *transmissive*, which means it creates light to display an image. A print is *reflective*; it doesn't create its own light but uses the existing light source to reflect colors. The second reason for differences between the two devices is the color space, or *gamut*, each is capable of using. I'll get into color space options and why they are important later in this chapter.

Printers use the CMYK color space, meaning they combine cyan, magenta, yellow, and black inks to produce each printed color. Monitors, however, use the RGB color space, combining red, green, and blue to tint each pixel. Why does this matter? Think back to your crayons. If your only way of making purple is to mix Sky Blue and Light Rose, the result will never look exactly like what I get from mixing Midnight Blue and Brick Red. (Chapter 5, "Editing Your Photos," will look more closely at color spaces and how to work with them.)

Profiling Your Display

Options for *profiling* or *calibrating* your display range from the very basic and not too reliable method of using your eyes and best judgment to make color adjustments, up to the *spectrophotometers* that cost well over $1,000 but generate extremely accurate results. Luckily there is a happy medium, and most people will be more than satisfied with the products available in the $300 range. I can hear some of you thinking: "I need to spend even *more?* Is it worth it?" The simple answer is absolutely yes. If you care anything at all about printing or displaying images, a calibration package is one of the best investments you'll ever make in digital imaging. If you're not quite ready to jump into another investment, you'll be happy to know that your monitor can be profiled for more accurate color using tools that may already be on your computer. Macs include Apple Display Calibrator Assistant, and Windows users who have Adobe Photoshop or Photoshop Elements installed can take advantage of Adobe Gamma. These options aren't as accurate as the hardware-based solutions, but they are certainly better than no profiling at all.

Why is profiling your display important? It all comes down to each of your devices speaking the same language. Like the crayons earlier, the monitor and printer each have their own idea of what Kelly Green may look like. Using a profile acts like a translation dictionary for your devices. The printer will now know how to "speak" Kelly Green.

Like the operating systems themselves, Macintosh and Windows systems take a very different approach to software calibration for your display. Macs include the Display Calibrator Assistant, while Windows users typically rely on Adobe Gamma, which is included with Adobe's Photoshop and Photoshop Elements.

Both Apple's Display Calibrator Assistant and Adobe Gamma do a serviceable job of calibrating your display, but because they rely on your eyes and the current room lighting, they aren't going to be anywhere near as accurate as the hardware calibration options discussed next, which use precise optical devices to measure the exact color being displayed. Still, if you don't have any other choice, visual calibration is better than nothing.

In the next few sections, I'll cover how each of these options—software and hardware calibration—work to give you more accurate color on screen, which will translate into more accurate results when printing your images.

Software calibration for Macs: Apple Display Calibrator Assistant

Macintosh computers use ColorSync to manage color between devices such as your display and printer. To create a profile for your monitor, you can use the included software calibration tool Display Calibrator Assistant, which is part of the Displays Preferences tool.

1. Open the System Preferences tool in the Taskbar (OS X). In Preferences, click Displays and then select the Color tab (**Figure 3.2**).

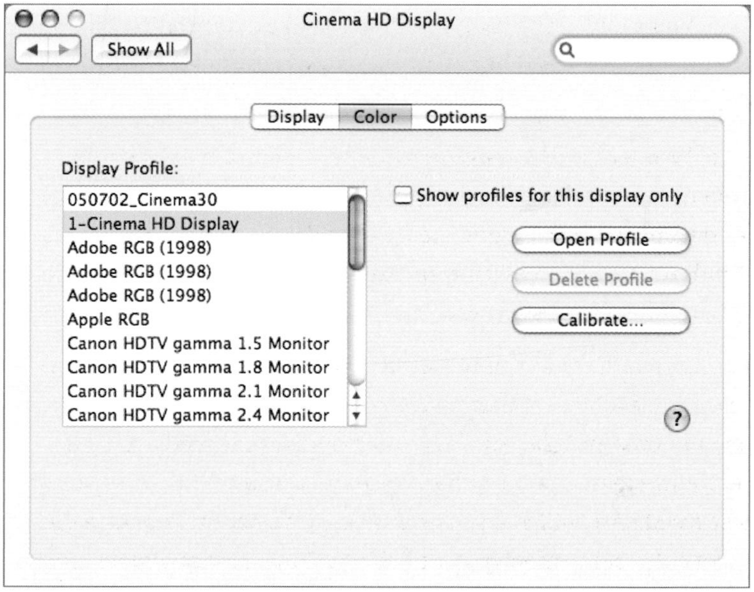

Figure 3.2 *The Calibrator Assistant is the Macintosh utility for calibrating displays. Access the Calibrator Assistant from the System Preferences Display control.*

Note

You can reduce the number of profiles displayed by checking the Show Profiles for This Display Only box. This is especially helpful if you want to modify an existing profile.

2. Click the Calibrate button to launch the Display Calibrator Assistant. The Assistant will step you through the process of calibrating your display and creating a profile. You'll see a check box for Expert Mode (**Figure 3.3**), which I think of as "worth the effort" mode. Turning off this mode leaves so few options that calibrating really isn't worth the time or effort. Use Expert Mode or don't bother.

Figure 3.3 *For best results, use Expert Mode for the Display Calibrator Assistant. You'll have more control, and it's still very easy to use.*

Note

The best choice for gamma is 2.2. The 2.2 setting, which is the default for Windows systems, is what most experts now recommend for imaging work on the Mac as well.

3. The first calibration is to adjust the native response, or *gamma*, for your display. You'll see a gray box with the Apple logo in the center and two boxes with adjustment controls. The left box adjusts the brightness of the Apple logo; move the blue control in the box until the logo blends into the surrounding gray as much as possible (**Figure 3.4**). The right box adjusts the tone of

the logo; move the blue control in that box until it is as neutral as possible compared to the background. The surrounding border of the box gives an indication of what tone will be added when moving the blue control in that direction. You can see that the border has hues of different color all the way around the box to indicate what color must be added to neutralize the background. Once you have optimized these settings, click Continue.

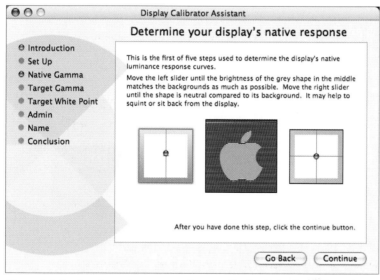

Figure 3.4 *Setting the native response for your display is the first of five adjustments for response.*

4. You should now see a similar set of controls, but a new shade of gray to match. Repeat step 3's adjustments, then click Continue four more times, matching a different gray value each time (**Figures 3.5a** through **3.5d**). Again, optimize to the best of your ability, aiming to get a seamless blend of logo and background at each step.

What Is Gamma?

After all this talk about gamma and native response, you might be curious as to what gamma actually is. For purposes of display calibration, gamma is the relationship between the voltage and the brightness of a monitor. Calibration of your monitor compensates for the native response, or what the monitor uses naturally, to a defined setting, such as 2.2 to get the desired on screen values for color. Not very exciting, but it is very important!

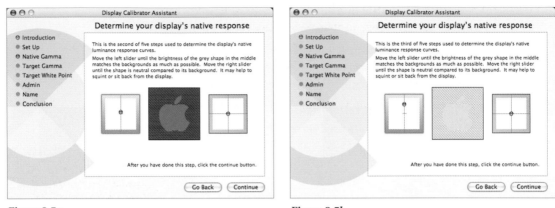

Figure 3.5a

Figure 3.5b

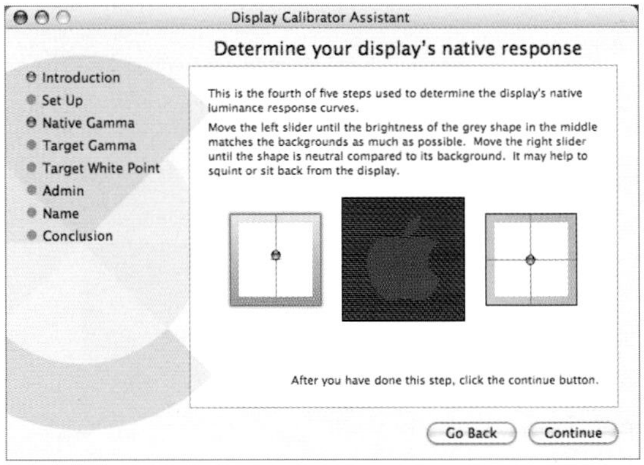

Figure 3.5c

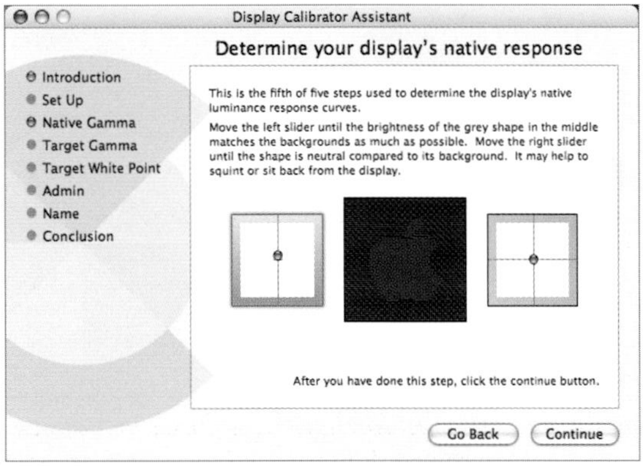

Figure 3.5d

Figures 3.5a through d *The remaining curve adjustments are all designed to get your display to the most accurate setting possible. You're trying for the best possible blending of logo and background in each of these steps.*

5. Next, select the target gamma for your display (**Figure 3.6**). Apple traditionally uses a gamma setting of 1.8, and the Assistant will recommend that for most instances. Windows, however, traditionally uses a gamma of 2.2. What's the difference? A gamma setting of 1.8 is brighter than a setting of 2.2.

When working in an environment with mixed computing platforms, this mismatch can cause problems with images appearing too dark or bright when moving from one system to the next. Because the majority of users are on Windows systems, many printing and web experts now recommend using the Windows setting of 2.2 for broadest compatibility. Make your choice, and click Continue.

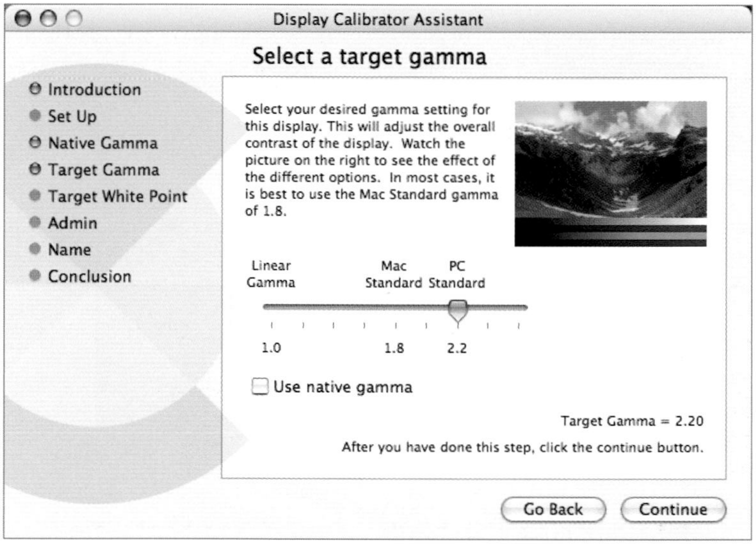

Figure 3.6 *The target gamma setting affects the overall contrast of the display. For maximum compatibility with other systems, I recommend using 2.2.*

Note

If you're using the Apple Cinema displays, clicking on the Use Native Gamma check box will show that even Apple displays use 2.2 natively.

6. The Assistant now asks you to set the white point for your display. For best results and the most neutral tones, I recommend using D65, which is a setting of 6500° Kelvin (**Figure 3.7**). Lower numbers will look warmer with a more yellow or reddish tint, while higher numbers will look cooler with more of a blue tint.

Most displays, especially LCD displays, will have a native white point of 6500° Kelvin. You can determine the native white point for your display by checking the Use Native White Point check box. It should be close to your desired white point setting. If not, I suggest manually setting the white point to D65 for best results.

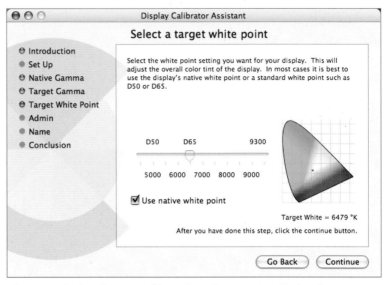

Figure 3.7 *Setting the target white point to D65, or 6500° K, gives the most neutral whites.*

7. The next step is setting administrator options. I can't think of any compelling reason to not use the profile for anyone using the computer, so check the box and click Continue.

8. Almost done! Give your profile a name that makes sense to you. I prefer to include the date and display name to let me quickly see how recently I profiled the display. Save the profile.

You should now see a summary screen showing the new settings (**Figure 3.8**). Whew! That wasn't too bad, was it?

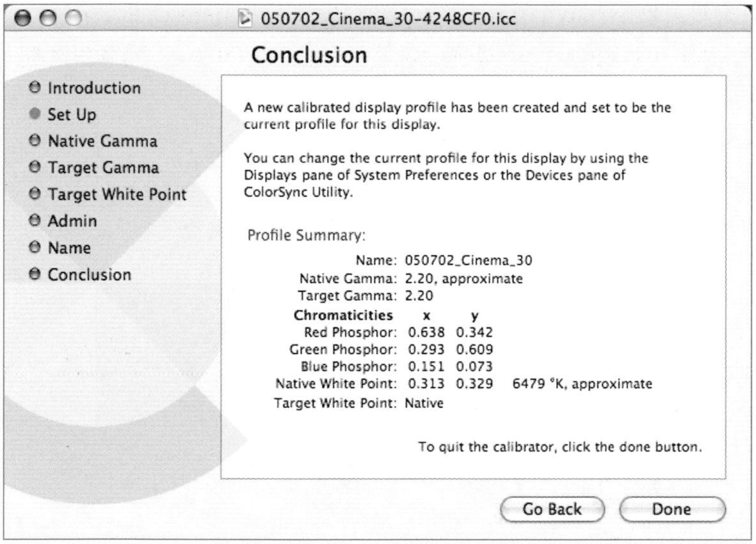

Figure 3.8 *The Assistant finishes up with a summary of the profile created.*

Go ahead and click Done if this is your only display. If you have other displays to calibrate, you can repeat these steps for each one. The profile you just created will be automatically selected as the default for that display.

Software calibration for Windows: Adobe Gamma

If you have Photoshop CS or Photoshop Elements 3 on your Windows computer, Adobe Gamma is there too. With Photoshop CS2, Adobe went a step further and made the program active with the assumption that most people don't use any form of calibration. If you're in this "most people" category, then lucky you—running Adobe Gamma just got a little easier. To get started you only need to go to your Start menu, select Startup, and then choose Adobe Gamma.

If you don't happen to have the latest and greatest version of Photoshop (CS2 as I write this) or Elements 3, then you need to do a bit of hunting to find Adobe Gamma. The first place to look is your Control Panel. Select the Start menu, and then choose Control Panel. If the Control Panel comes up in Category view (**Figure 3.9**),

Note

To run Adobe Gamma you'll need to be logged onto your computer as Administrator. If you're the only user on a non-networked computer, this probably doesn't mean anything to you. If you get an error message when you try to run Adobe Gamma, however, you need to change to Administrator.

you must switch to Classic view by selecting that in the left panel (circled in red in Figure 3.9). This should give you a view that looks like the one in **Figure 3.10**; I've circled the program you're looking for—Adobe Gamma.

Figure 3.9 *Windows users access Adobe Gamma from the Control Panel. If the Control Panel starts in Category view, switch to Classic view (circled in red) to access Adobe Gamma.*

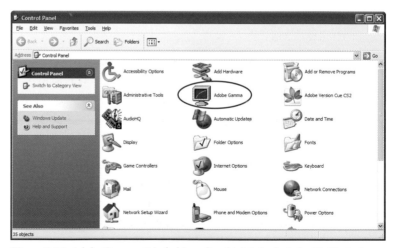

Figure 3.10 *Adobe Gamma (circled in red), which is included with Photoshop and Photoshop Elements, will enable you to profile your Windows display.*

Adobe Gamma has two different modes, a step-by-step wizard and a do-it-yourself Control Panel mode (**Figure 3.11**). Until you've gotten used to the program and have profiles to modify, I suggest using the wizard to make sure you get all of the needed information entered in the right order. So, get started by clicking on the Step by Step (Wizard) radio button and clicking Next.

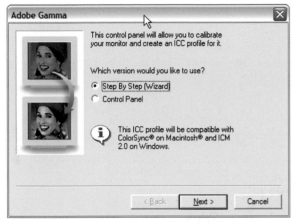

Figure 3.11 *Adobe Gamma offers a wizard mode (recommended) or manual Control Panel mode.*

1. The first step in creating your new profile is to give it a descriptive name. I prefer to use the monitor name and current date to make the profile easy to spot, and to remind me when I last profiled the display.

2. After clicking Next, adjust contrast and brightness for your display. Keep the surrounding white box as white as possible while blending the two black boxes together. Don't adjust until the center box goes completely black, and keep your eye on the white box. You want this to stay as bright as possible. Click Next.

    These settings are the first clues that you'll have changes that are subjective. Brightness and Contrast settings might seem different to you each time you use your monitor, so try to create the profile under your normal working conditions.

Note

Not all LCD displays let you change the Brightness and Contrast settings. This is particularly true with laptop displays. If you can't adjust these settings on your display, don't worry; just move on to the next step.

3. When asked to set the type of phosphors used by your display, simply click Next. Unless you know what your monitor is using, I recommend leaving this setting alone. The odds are that it's already correct for your display, and although choosing the wrong setting won't cause any physical damage, it will make getting an accurate profile more difficult.

4. Adjust the midtones by moving the Red, Green, and Blue sliders to blend the center box into the stripped outer box (**Figure 3.12**). Make sure that all three colors are showing by clearing the View Single Gamma Only check box. As you move the individual sliders, you'll see your entire display changing color balance. Don't worry about this. Once everything is set, the balance will be correct. It's likely to be different than what you had originally thought because you've just optimized the midtones for your display. The Gamma setting should be on Windows Default, which is 2.20. Click Next.

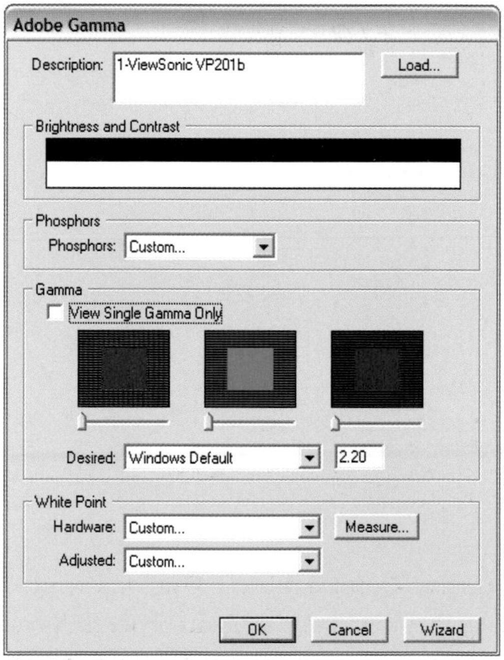

Figure 3.12 *Adjust the Red, Green, and Blue sliders to blend the solid center boxes with the surrounding lined boxes to optimize each color.*

5. The Hardware White Point should be set to 6500. This is the typical white point for computer displays and will give you the most accurate whites on screen. Higher numbers will give the display a cooler, bluer tone, while lower numbers will be warmer with more red. Click Next.

6. Leave the Adjusted White Point setting at its default of Same as Hardware, and click Next again to get to the final step.

7. Here's where you can see how much of a difference you've made to your display settings. The Before and After buttons toggle back and forth between the two settings (**Figure 3.13**). If there is very little change, don't worry—it just means your display was accurate to begin with! When you're satisfied with the profile, choose After, click the Finish button, and save the profile. I usually use the current date as part of the filename to remind me how long it's been since I last calibrated the display. So, on my system a typical profile name might be 050702_display.

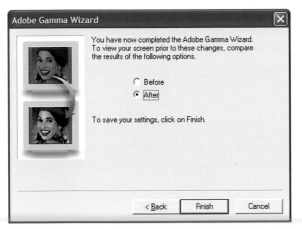

Figure 3.13 *Before and After buttons let you see what changes have been made before saving the new profile.*

Although Display Calibrator Assistant and Adobe Gamma are certainly better than nothing, they have the disadvantage of using your eyes and judgment to make subjective adjustments. A much better option, and one that anyone serious about digital imaging should consider required equipment, is a hardware calibration device.

Using calibration and profiling hardware

Hardware calibration is actually a joint operation using a special hardware device called a *colorimeter*, which uses precision optics to measure the exact color temperature of various shades of color on your display. The device's companion software then uses these measurements to create a profile for your monitor. Many of the programs included with these calibration units allow you to make adjustments to your profiles. By using a hardware device, you remove the human subjectivity from the process—which may seem impersonal, but it's one situation where machine has it all over human.

Your choices for hardware calibration run from under $100 for the ColorVision ColorPlus, to well over $1,000 for more sensitive hardware and advanced software. In the next sections, I'll show you how to use the two most popular choices: ColorVision's Spyder2 and Gretag Macbeth's Eye-One Photo. You can find more information on these and other calibration tools in Appendix A, "Resources."

ColorVision's Spyder2

ColorVision's Spyder2 (www.colorvision.com) includes both the company's Spyder colorimeter sensor and a software bundle (**Figure 3.14**). I'll be using the Spyder2PRO software for these examples; if you have ColorVision's ColorPlus package, your options and the basic workflow will be similar but your choices will be more limited. In both cases, the software is wizard based, making it easy to get an accurate calibration with minimal effort on your part. If you decide you're really interested in what is happening and want to learn more, you can make your own adjustments as you go along for total control.

1. To start, specify whether you'll be profiling an LCD or CRT display (**Figure 3.15**). Click Next.

Note

Some packages, notably the Gretag Macbeth Eye-One Photo (covered later), use a spectrophotometer rather than a *colorimeter*. These are more expensive devices and can also be used to create printer profiles as well (see Chapter 4, "Using Printer Settings"). The basics of how they work are the same, though. They sit on your display and measure color values.

Note

ColorVision has two different levels of sensor. The $100 ColorPlus package uses the older sensor while the $249 Spyder2 package uses the newer one. Either will work and do a good job, but the newer sensor is much more sensitive and gives more accurate results.

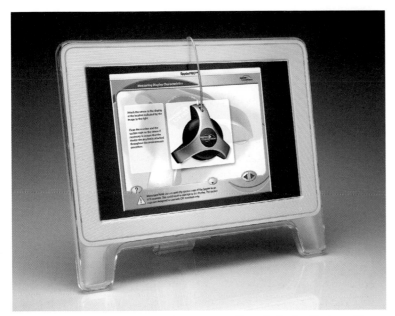

Figure 3.14 *The ColorVision Spyder2 is an excellent choice for display calibration. Easy to use, accurate, and affordable, it's one of the best tools available. (Image courtesy of ColorVision)*

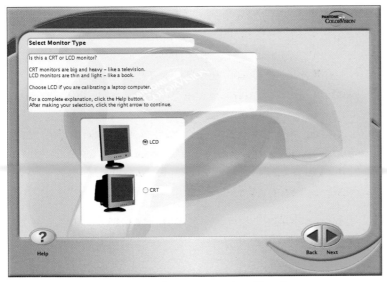

Figure 3.15 *The Spyder2PRO software uses a wizard interface to step you through calibration. The first step is to select your display type.*

Warning

For laptops and LCD displays, pay close attention to how the colorimeter is set up in step 6 to avoid damaging your display. Using a suction cup designed for CRT displays can seriously ruin your LCD and your day.

Note

If you have more than one display to calibrate, start with your primary display first.

2. Select the target gamma and white point from the Target pop-up menu (**Figure 3.16**). The best choice is 2.2-6500. The 2.2 indicates a gamma setting of 2.2, which is the default for Windows systems and what most experts now recommend for imaging work on the Macintosh as well. The 6500 refers to the white point temperature in degrees Kelvin. The most neutral white tone, 6500, should be used for digital imaging. Click Next to move to the Luminance Mode screen.

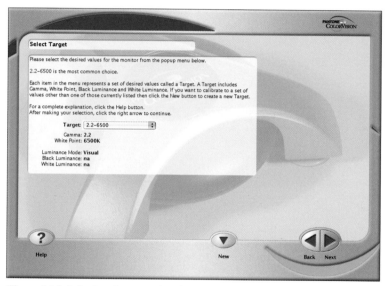

Figure 3.16 Selecting the target luminance and white point is next. I recommend using the 2.2-6500 setting for digital imaging work.

3. Luminance mode offers two choices, Measured and Visual. I suggest you choose Visual unless you're using multiple displays, and even then only if they're of very different types, such as an LCD and a CRT. Click Next, and you'll see a summary of the current settings along with information on the last time you calibrated your display and what the current profile name is. It's probably not that interesting, so click Next to move on.

4. This step differs depending on the display type you chose earlier. For LCD displays, you must tell Spyder2PRO whether you can set Brightness, Contrast, or Backlight (**Figure 3.17**). If you

selected a CRT to profile, set the White Luminance by adjusting the Contrast control to optimize the visual guide displayed in Spyder2PRO (**Figure 3.18**).

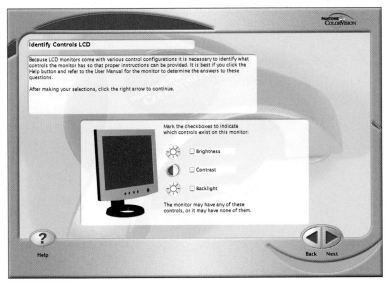

Figure 3.17 *If you selected LCD for the display type, you need to identify which controls your display has.*

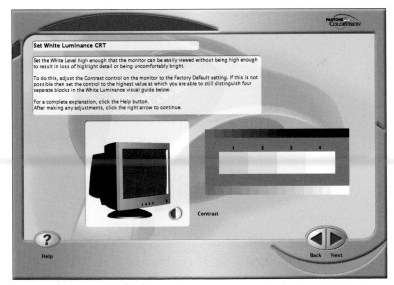

Figure 3.18 *If you're using a CRT, adjust the Contrast control for optimizing white values first.*

5. This step also depends on your display choice. For an LCD, check whether RGB, Kelvin settings, or Kelvin presets are available (**Figure 3.19**). For a CRT, set the Black Luminance as you set White Luminance in step 4 (**Figure 3.20**) before setting RGB and Kelvin as you did for the LCD calibration.

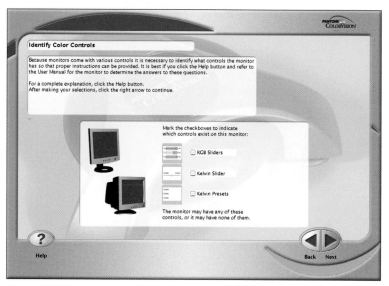

Figure 3.19 *If you're using an LCD, select whether RGB or Kelvin controls are present.*

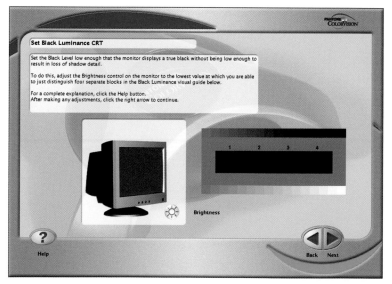

Figure 3.20 *Use the Brightness control to set black values for your CRT. The goal is to have each of the four blocks defined.*

6. Here's that important step I warned you about earlier. If you are calibrating a LCD, you *must* place the LCD baffle on the colorimeter (**Figure 3.21**). Using the suction cups on your LCD could very well damage the display, making you unhappy and leaving me feeling guilty. After selecting the correct option for your display type, place the colorimeter on the screen where shown and click Continue.

Figure 3.21 *Be sure that you use the LCD baffle when profiling a LCD or laptop display. Using suction cups will damage your LCD!*

Spyder2PRO now begins the actual calibration process, which consists of reading a number of color patches of red, green, blue, and gray, taking precise measurements of each to determine how to modify the final display (**Figure 3.22**).

Reading red samples.

Continue

Cancel

press esc to cancel

Figure 3.22 *Spyder2PRO takes readings of red, green, blue, and gray values to determine the accuracy of your display.*

7. When the program finishes reading the color patches (10 to 20 minutes depending on your system), save your profile. I usually use the current date as part of the filename to remind me how long it's been since I last calibrated the display. On my system a typical profile name might be 050702_display. Click Next until you see the before and after screens (**Figures 3.23a** and **3.23b**).

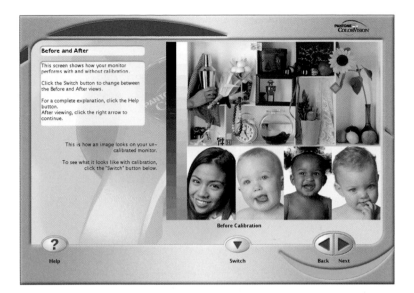

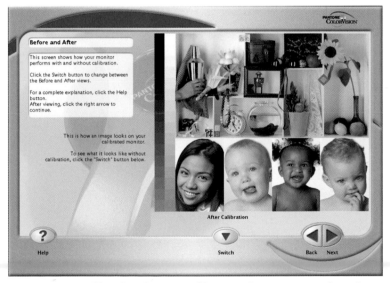

Figures 3.23a and b *When the new profile is complete, you can see the Before and After results. After (b) is noticeably different than Before (a), with more neutral gray tones and better skin tones.*

You can see how much the display has changed by clicking the Switch button to toggle between before and after displays. That's it! You should now have a very accurate display with a minimum amount of fuss on your part.

Note

Because I promised at the start of this chapter to not go into the gory details of color management, I won't explain how to use the advanced features of Spyder2PRO. But, if you want to adjust curves, or find out about the Candelas, DeltaE, or other techie details, they're all available under the Tools menu.

Note

If you're not happy with the calibration, you can choose Back to step through the wizard and start over, or you can leave the setting on Before to keep the original profile in use.

Gretag Macbeth Eye-One Photo

The Gretag Macbeth (www.i1color.com) Eye-One system is used by many pros, and with good reason. For photographers, I highly recommend the $1,495 Eye-One Photo package for a complete color management solution (**Figure 3.24**). Rather than using a colorimeter like Spyder2, Eye-One uses a spectrophotometer, which is slightly more accurate for monitor profiles and can also be used to create custom printer profiles. Another advantage of the Eye-One system is that it includes a measurement for ambient light. In other words, it measures the light in your work environment to ensure the most accurate monitor calibration possible.

Figure 3.24 *The Gretag Macbeth Eye-One Photo system is the choice of many professionals who need to profile monitors, printers, scanners, and cameras. (Image courtesy of Gretag Macbeth)*

Like the Spyder2, the Eye-One software has a wizard mode that walks you through the process of creating a monitor profile. Where the Eye-One departs from the other software is in the fine-tuning and analysis features included. The Eye-One package has several components, but I'll concentrate on Eye-One Match, which handles calibration.

1. Launch Eye-One Match and select the type of device you want to profile (**Figure 3.25**). Click on the monitor, then choose Easy mode. The Advanced mode offers a number of additional options, most of which are beyond the needs of all but the most critical applications. Click on the right arrow button in the lower-right corner of the Eye-One Match window.

Figure 3.25 *To use Eye-One Match for profiling devices, select the appropriate device from the starting screen.*

2. Choose the appropriate monitor type: LCD, CRT, or Laptop. Click the right arrow button again and calibrate Eye-One (**Figure 3.26**). This step checks your Eye-One hardware to make sure it's working properly before creating a monitor profile. Once the hardware is calibrated, click the right arrow button.

Place your Eye-One on the monitor.

Figure 3.26 Eye-One Match walks you through each step of the calibration process with clear directions and graphics.

3. Position the Eye-One on the monitor for the actual calibration by placing it in the correct holder as directed on screen, then click the right arrow. Eye-One Match reads several gray, red, green, and blue patches to determine the accuracy of your display. The process takes about 10 minutes, so sit back and relax while all the work is done for you.

4. When Eye-One has finished reading all the color patches, save the resulting profile. I usually use the current date as part of the filename to remind me how long it's been since I last calibrated the display. So, on my system a typical profile name might be 050702_display. You'll also be asked how frequently you want to be reminded to create a new profile, and you'll see some interesting information on the results from your monitor (**Figure 3.27**).

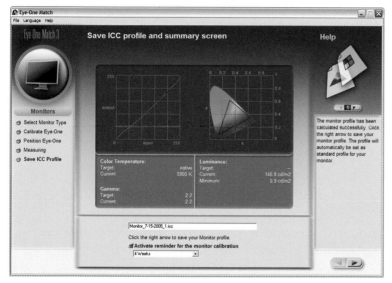

Figure 3.27 *When the calibration process is complete, Eye-One Match prompts you to save your profile and set a reminder period for updating the profile. The charts are useful to see how your monitor performed during calibration.*

If you wish to use Advanced mode, you'll also need to define a white point, a gamma setting, and luminance settings. One advantage of Advanced mode is the inclusion of an ambient light check. If you often work under different lighting situations, this can be very useful, because it lets you create a profile for each lighting setup and switch to them as needed. As you can see in **Figure 3.28**, a number of extra steps are involved with Advanced mode. Compare these to the Easy mode options in Figure 3.25.

Note

You should recalibrate your display on a regular basis. How often is regular? If you're using a CRT I suggest every two to four weeks, and more frequently with older displays. For LCD displays every two months is sufficient.

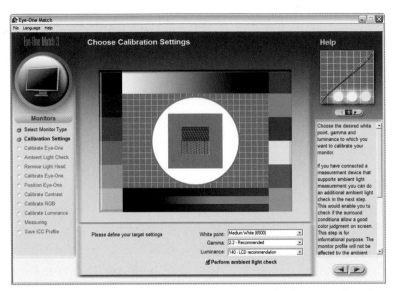

Figure 3.28 *Eye-One Match's Advanced calibration mode offers a number of additional measurements and can be very useful when working under differing lighting conditions.*

Moving On

I've covered quite a bit in this chapter, but it all leads to a more productive work environment. An accurate display is the only way to ensure accurate prints, so don't skip this important step. You'll find that many of the concepts covered here will be similar to those addressed when printer profiling is discussed in the next chapter. Because your monitor and printer are closely related, it's important to understand how these profiles work together. And, as promised, I've avoided the esoteric information that many of you might find less than interesting.

If you are interested in delving deeper into color management, check out *Real World Color Management, Second Edition* by Bruce Fraser (Peachpit Press, 2004) an outstanding book dedicated to color management from the photographer's perspective.

Now that you have display calibration under control, you're ready to move on to the other side: printer color management and optimizing your images for printing.

4 | Using Printer Settings

Like any working partnership, the one between your display and your printer will be more successful if both partners work from an agreed-upon set of assumptions. The previous chapter showed you how to specify the proper settings your monitor; now it's the printer's turn.

Most printers include a number of profiles for the papers made by the manufacturer. These profiles range from acceptable to excellent, but don't help your prints much unless you properly select and use them.

Photo printers have a number of options available to assist with getting top-notch photo prints, but they don't always make the choices clear. This chapter covers how to select the correct options in your printer driver. If you've ever been frustrated trying to figure out your printer driver options or you just couldn't get a print that looked right, this chapter is for you.

Printer Profile Basics

The printing process is perhaps one of the most complicated steps of the digital workflow. After all, you're going from a completely different medium—pixels on your screen lit by an electric charge—to ink on a page viewed by light reflecting off the paper. Not only is the light source completely different, but the method of creating the color is too (**Figure 4.1**). Consider this—your monitor uses only three colors to create the image on your screen: red, green, and blue. Your printer, on the other hand, uses at least four colors: cyan, magenta, yellow, and black. That's right; none of the printer colors are the same as your monitor colors. See why this conversion process is so complicated? Not only does your printer need to know how to make a

> **Note**
>
> Although most printers are CMYK (cyan, magenta, yellow, black), they expect to have RGB (red, green, blue) data sent to them. Even if your printer uses six, seven, eight, or nine colors, it's still a CMYK printer. It might use more shades of CMYK, or in some cases, add additional ink colors like red and green to create more accurate tones.

particular shade of, say, green, it usually needs to know how to make that green with no green ink!

In Chapter 3, "Keeping an Eye on Color," I talked about how monitor profiles interact with printer profiles to create the closest match possible, sort of like using an English-to-Spanish translation dictionary.

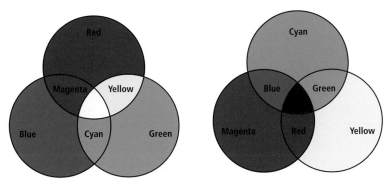

Figure 4.1 Monitors work with colors in the RGB model, but printers typically work in the CMYK model. As you can see, the two approaches are very different; when you mix all the RGB colors they become white, but mixing all CMYK colors produces black.

Your monitor only needs one profile to be accurate but because of the way ink is absorbed and reflected on paper, printers need a different profile for each and every paper that you print on. And, to take it one step further, for the best results, each paper should have a different profile for each lighting condition it will be displayed in. The same photograph printed on a luster finish paper will look very different under daylight conditions than it will under tungsten or fluorescent lighting.

Depending on the model printer you have, multiple versions of the same paper profile may be available too. It's common for manufacturers to provide profiles for the various print modes, such as Normal and Best, because these modes use different densities of ink. It's all sounding pretty complicated, isn't it? The good news is that once you know the major pieces of printer color management, it becomes a simple matter to select the right settings and get the results you want. Going beyond that does require some effort on your part, and later in this chapter I'll show you how to create your own printer profiles for use with special lighting conditions, or new paper types that aren't supported by the manufacturer.

Because Macs and Windows systems handle printing so differently, I've broken their printer settings into two separate sections. If you use only one of these computers, feel free to skip over to that section unless you have a burning curiosity about how the other half lives.

Through Adobe Photoshop or Photoshop Elements and their Print With Preview dialog boxes, you have the most control over which printer profiles are used and how they are used. Other applications give you access to some color management, but it will be more limited or only echo what you can do within the printer driver itself. So, although Photoshop isn't a requirement for good prints, if you're serious about image quality, I recommend upgrading to the full version of Photoshop.

> **Note**
>
> I'm not picking sides here. When it comes to Photoshop and printing, you can't go wrong with either platform.

Windows Printer Drivers

In Windows, you can access your printer driver in two ways: Either select Start > Printers and Faxes, or open the printer's Properties dialog box from within your application. This chapter uses the Printers and Faxes approach. In Chapter 7, "Printing Your Files," I'll show you how to access these settings from within Photoshop.

To get started, select Start > Printers and Faxes. Next, right-click on the printer you want to work with and choose Properties from the context menu. You'll see the default dialog box with basic printer information (**Figure 4.2**) and tabs for specific features, such as Sharing, Color Management, and Maintenance.

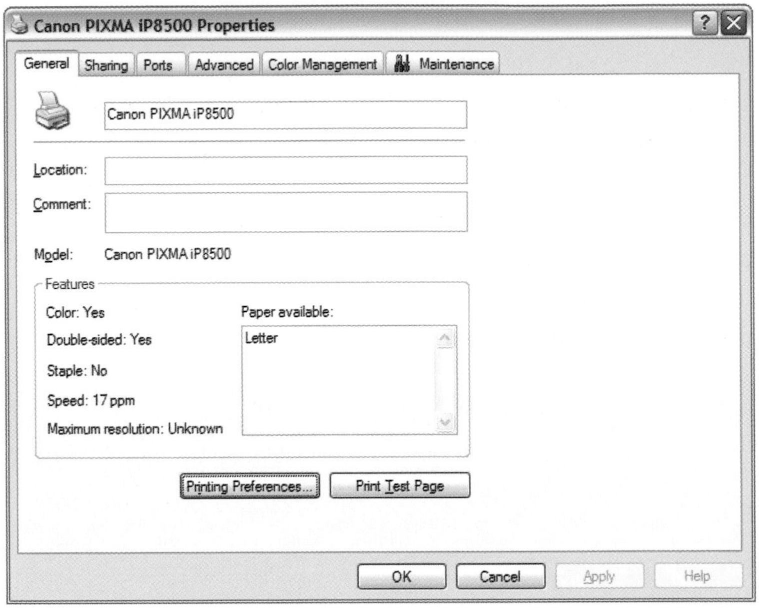

Figure 4.2 *Windows users can select Printers and Faxes in the Control Panel, then right-click on the printer and select Properties to see the default Preferences dialog box. Here you have access to system- and printer-specific settings.*

Note

I've limited the discussion to Canon, Epson, and HP because most people use a photo printer made by one of these companies. If you don't have one of these three, you can still follow along. The general steps will be the same, although your dialog boxes will look different, with more or fewer options.

From here on out, it gets specific, because every printer manufacturer has different options for their printers. To make it simpler for you, I've separated the details by printer type. Feel free to jump straight to the appropriate section—Canon, Epson, or HP.

Canon printers

To illustrate Canon printer settings, I'll use the Pixma iP8500; most current Canon photo printers have the same options available, however. To get started, click the Printing Preferences button in the Properties dialog box to open the Printing Preferences dialog box, which is the main control center for the printer driver.

To give you an idea of the available options and how to use them for the best results when printing different types of images, I'll cover each tab in the dialog box.

Main tab

First up is the Main tab (**Figure 4.3**). Here you specify the Media Type and Paper Source settings (if available). Media Type is one of the most important settings you'll make in the printer driver. A wrong selection here most likely will result in a print that needs to be redone—even when everything else is set properly. This is because the printer driver decides how much ink to use based on the type of paper chosen. Selecting Photo Paper Plus Glossy when you have plain paper inserted will give you a nice, soggy print.

Note

Not all printers have multiple paper paths or sources, so some of these options may not be available on your printer.

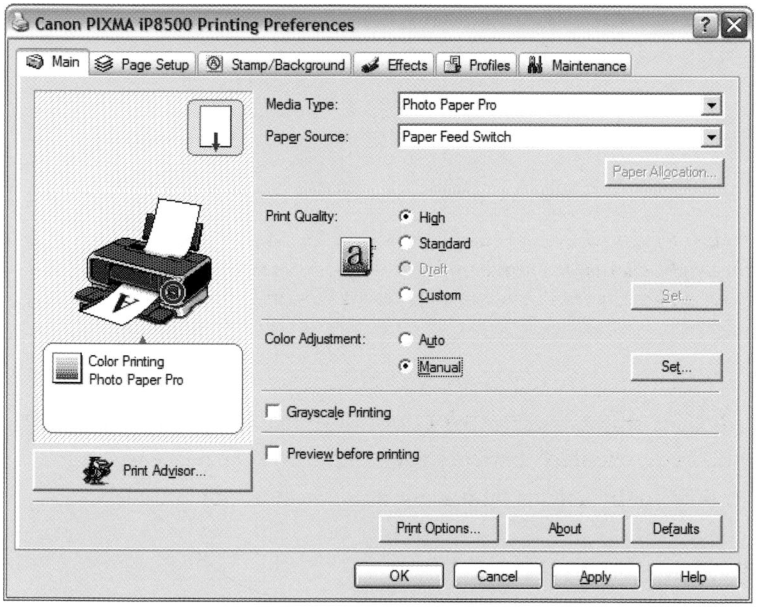

Figure 4.3 *The Main tab for the Canon printer driver provides the same options for most models.*

Next in the dialog box are the Print Quality settings. Unless you're printing on plain paper, your choices are High, Standard, and Custom. For most prints, Standard works fine and uses less ink while printing faster than High. For critical prints, the High setting is your best choice. Custom enables the Set button, which opens the Set Print Quality dialog box (**Figure 4.4**), where you can set the quality level and type of halftoning used. For photos, Fine quality and Diffusion halftoning will give you the best results (which, coincidentally, is the same setting you'll get by selecting High for the Print Quality setting). Why use Custom then? You probably won't need to, but the best use for Custom is to change the halftoning method to something other than the default. Dither can produce some interesting effects, especially when used with black-and-white prints, giving the print a harder look, similar to a newspaper photo. Clicking OK returns you to the Printing Properties dialog box.

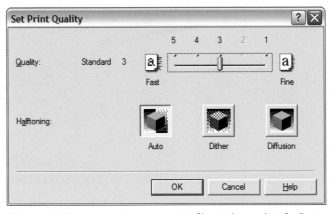

Figure 4.4 *You can create your own quality settings using the Set Print Quality dialog box, which contains settings for the print quality and type of halftoning used.*

Along with the proper media type, the Color Adjustment setting in the Printing Properties dialog box has a major impact on the quality of your prints. The Auto setting works well when you just want a quick print and don't care about fine-tuning. For the best results and full control, select Manual and click the Set button to open the Manual Color Adjustment dialog box (**Figure 4.5**).

The first settings in this dialog box are the Color Balance and Intensity sliders. If your image-editing application doesn't offer color management control, these sliders can be used to adjust any color tint and brightness problems. Sadly, this is a trial-and-error method that requires printing, adjusting, and reprinting until you get the results you're looking for. You'll be much better off skipping these and going straight to the next set of options.

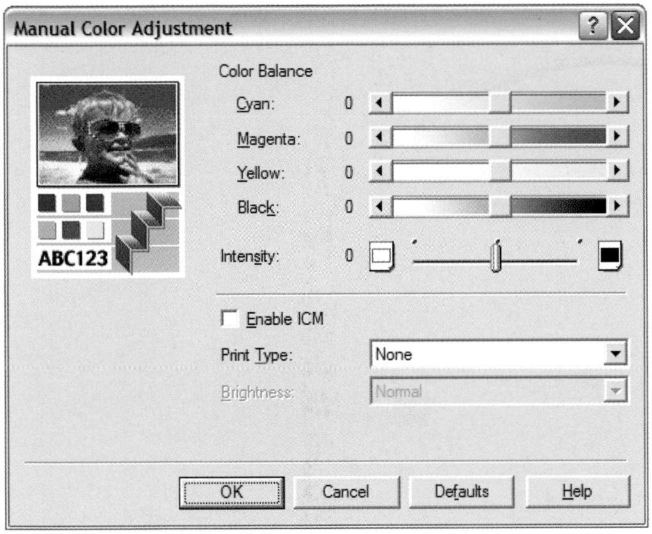

Figure 4.5 *The options in the Manual Color Adjustment dialog box have more impact on the accuracy of your prints than any other settings. These options control how color is managed by the printer.*

The Enable ICM (Image Color Management) check box controls whether the printer or the application handles the translation from screen colors to printer colors. It might seem to make sense to select this option; after all, you're probably thinking "Well, *of course* I want to manage color!" And, if your application doesn't support color management options, then you will be best served by checking this box. If, however, you use Photoshop, do *not* check this box. Enabling ICM in the printer driver and in Photoshop will result in applying color profiles twice—something your mother may not have warned you about but that's a bad idea nonetheless.

The Canon driver also includes settings for typical style prints, which you select by choosing the appropriate option from the Print Type drop-down list. The thumbnail in the upper-left corner shows a preview your choice. When using Photoshop, be sure to pick None. Again, this is because you want Photoshop to control all aspects of the printing process.

Back in the Main tab of the Printing Preferences dialog box, the next option is Grayscale Printing. Checking this box forces the printer to use only black ink, which removes any color cast from your black-and-white prints. The tonal range is also more restricted, and prints will have a grainy look to them. Because of this, I recommend not enabling the Grayscale or Black Only settings for most prints.

You can also select Preview Before Printing, which when checked opens a window showing you what paper size, type, and source you selected along with a preview of how the print will look before you commit it to real paper.

Finally, you can click the Print Advisor button, which gives you the opportunity to learn how to select options with the help of a goofy bird. But, when you've got me, do you really need a goofy bird too?

Page Setup tab

The Page Setup tab is where you set the paper size and orientation (**Figure 4.6**). You can also choose borderless printing and such page layout options as poster prints of up to 16 pages, as well as other specialty layouts that likely won't be of much interest to photographers.

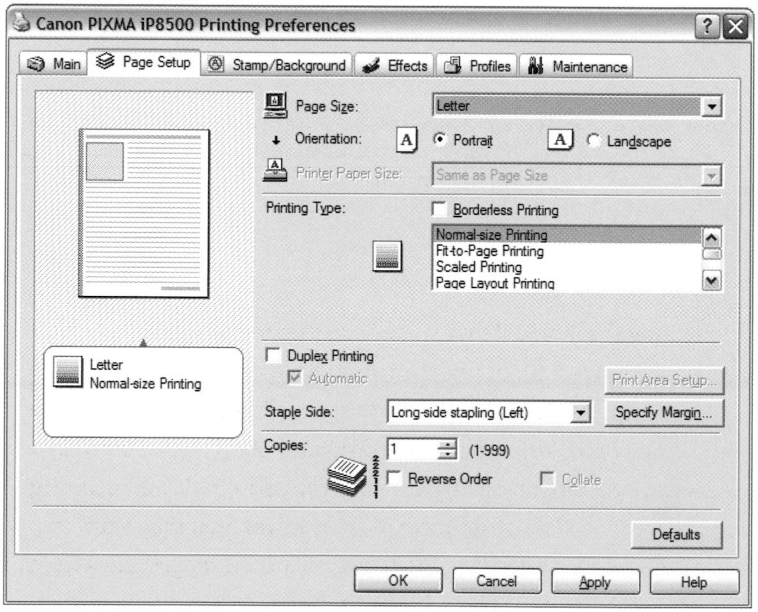

Figure 4.6 *The Page Setup tab has options for paper size, layout, borderless printing, and special projects such as multipage posters.*

Stamp/Background tab

The Stamp/Background tab contains options to print watermarks on your documents, which can be useful when you're printing proof sheets for customers. You can use one of the several predefined stamps, or click the Define Stamp button to create your own with either text or graphics and choose the placement on the page (**Figures 4.7a** and **b**). Background is useful for text documents, but I can't imagine using this with a photo print.

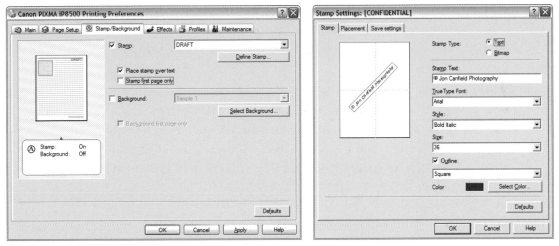

Figures 4.7a and b *The Stamp/Background tab probably won't see much use in your photo printing but can be useful for creating watermarks on prints sent out as samples. By clicking Define Stamp, you can create your own text and position it on the page wherever you like.*

Effects tab

In the Effects tab you'll find options to create toning effects, such as Sepia (**Figure 4.8**), or make auto-adjustments to image files, which can be useful when you're printing directly from a camera or memory card. When printing with Photoshop and color management, you won't be using any of these settings. When printing enlargements of low-resolution files, however, you may want to check the Image Optimizer check box to reduce jagged lines in your images. The next check box, Photo Optimizer PRO, compensates for color casts and exposure problems, and Photo Noise Reduction

Tip

I strongly recommend that you do your image optimization and other editing tasks, such as noise reduction, in Photoshop where you have control over how the effects are applied.

is useful for cleaning up images shot at high ISO settings on your digital camera where noise is obvious. Checking this box results in softer images, however, so use with caution.

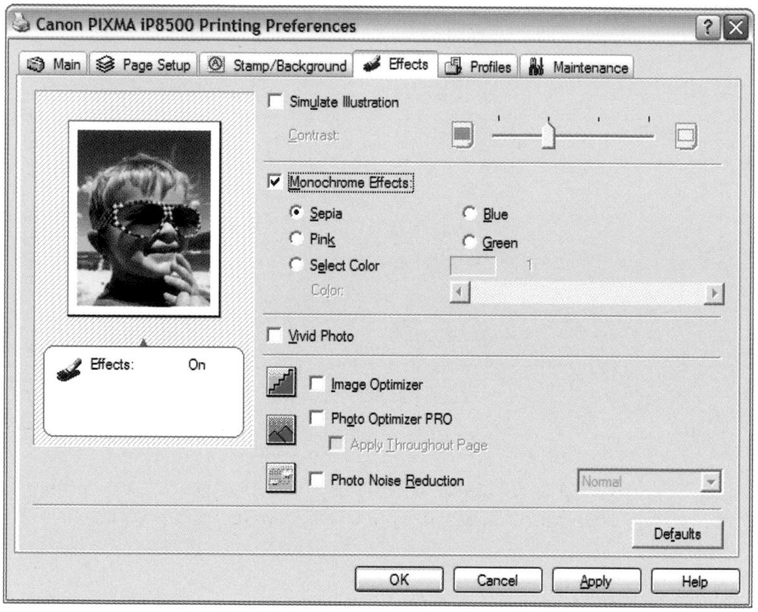

Figure 4.8 The Effects tab offers a number of options that are useful for printing from applications that don't support color management, or for just making quick prints that need a little improvement such as noise reduction, color correction, or toning.

Profiles tab

The Profiles tab (**Figure 4.9**) has a somewhat misleading name. A better title would be Saved Settings, because that's what you really do here. After making a series of changes to options in the Printing Properties dialog box, you can save them here by clicking Add to Profiles. Once these settings are saved, you can recall them for future use.

Maintenance tab

In the final tab, Maintenance, you'll find head cleaning and nozzle check functions along with printhead alignment controls and other settings (**Figure 4.10**). If you notice problems in your prints, such as streaks, banding, or missing colors, a quick stop here for cleaning and a nozzle check will often fix you right up.

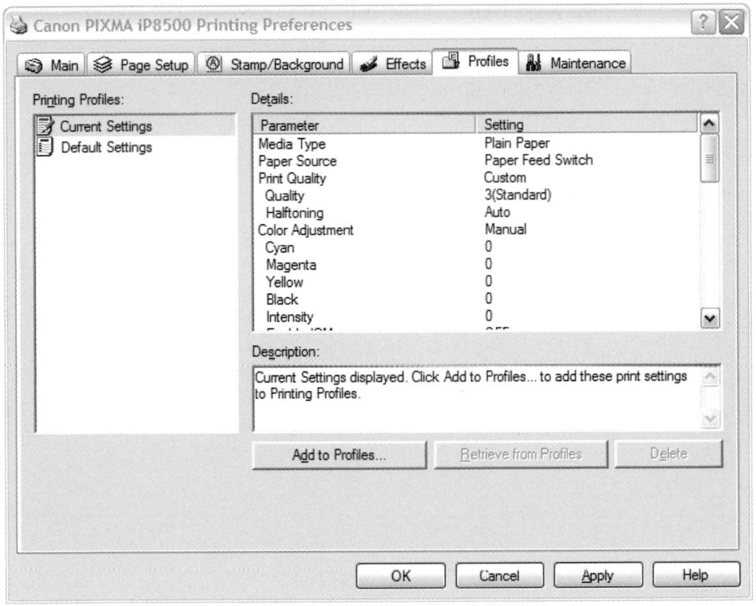

Figure 4.9 *The Profiles tab doesn't actually have anything to do with profiles. You can save and restore settings for different print tasks from this tab.*

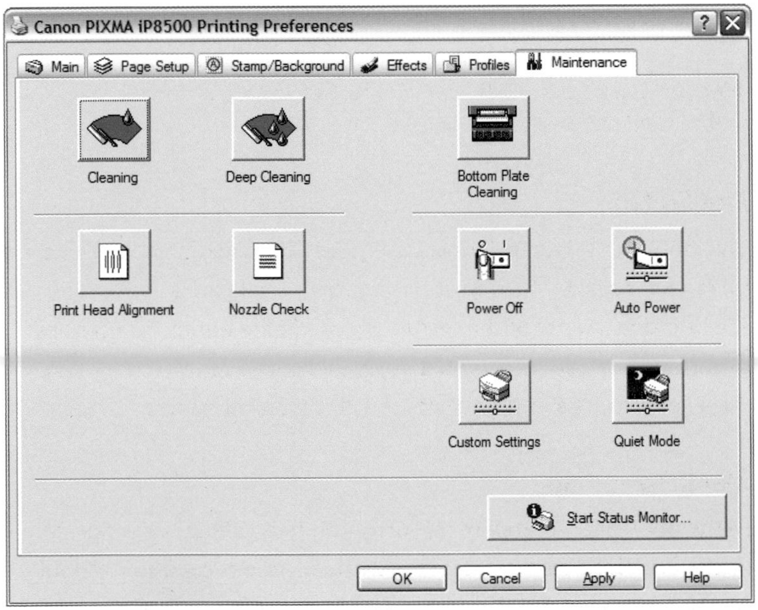

Figure 4.10 *Hopefully you won't be visiting the Maintenance tab often. If you do see problems in your prints, a nozzle check and head cleaning will probably get you back up and running.*

Epson printers

Because the dialog boxes for various Epson models are very different, I'm going to show you the options for both the Epson 4000 and R2400. I'll start with the Epson 4000.

Epson 4000

To begin, click on Printing Preferences to open the main printer dialog box (**Figure 4.11**). In the Printing Preferences dialog box, Epson places most of the important and frequently used options directly on the Main tab, including quality settings, paper type, and access to color management options. Again, one of the most important settings is Media Type. This setting determines how much ink is placed on the paper, and a wrong choice here almost always means a reprint, translating into lost time, paper, and ink. The Ink settings determine whether your print will use all colors or only black ink. Although selecting Black when doing a black-and-white photo is tempting, doing so greatly reduces the tonal range available and gives you a lower-quality print.

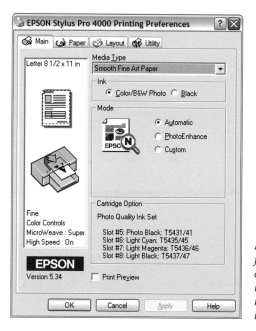

Figure 4.11 The Main tab for the Epson 4000 includes common printer options, as well as access to some of the more advanced features of the printer.

In the dialog box's Mode area, you set the color management options. Automatic lets the printer driver decide what is needed and is the best choice for quick prints or for applications that don't support color management. PhotoEnhance attempts to optimize your images for color and exposure, and includes preset options for several common types of photographs, such as Nature, People, and automatic Sepia conversion. The most important option here when you want full control over the quality of your print is Custom. Selecting Custom activates the Advanced button. Clicking Advanced opens a new dialog box with a number of settings, the most important of these being the Printer Color Management options (**Figure 4.12**).

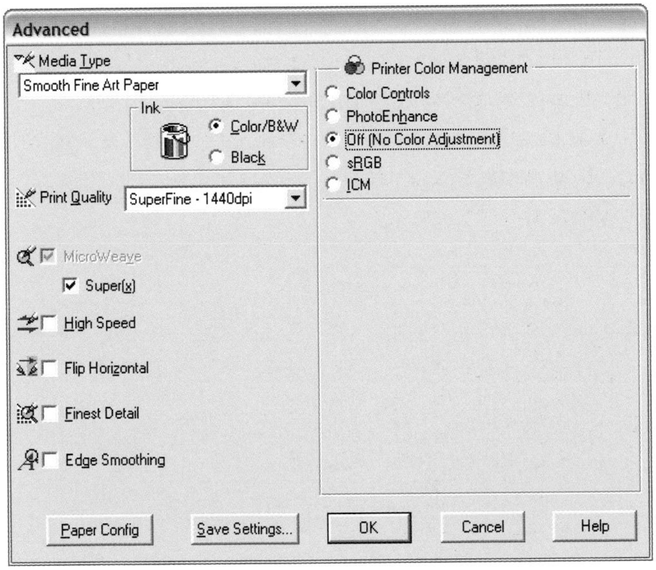

Figure 4.12 *Clicking Advanced in the Main tab of Epson's Printing Preferences dialog opens a new window with several options, the most important of which control how color management options are handled.*

Along with repeating the Media Type and Ink options from the Main tab, this dialog box gives you a Print Quality drop-down list with Fine and SuperFine choices. For draft prints and quick checks on your printing options, Fine, with a printer resolution of 720 dpi, is a good choice. For final prints I recommend choosing SuperFine, with its 1440 dpi printer resolution, for the best possible output.

Other options in this portion of the dialog box control how the ink is laid down on the paper. MicroWeave moves the printheads in finer increments and reduces banding. High Speed enables bidirectional printing, which will speed up the prints at the risk of lower quality. If you're having problems with print quality, particularly fine vertical lines showing up in your prints, turn off High Speed. Flip Horizontal is useful when you need to print in reverse for projects such as iron-on transfers and your application doesn't support reversing the image. Finest Detail is useful when you're printing line art and vector graphics but it isn't needed for photo printing. Edge Smoothing can help reduce jagged edges when you're printing low-resolution images.

Printer Color Management options include Color Controls (**Figure 4.13**) for manually adjusting colors in your prints for brightness, contrast, saturation, and individual color channels. The Mode drop-down list has several preset options.

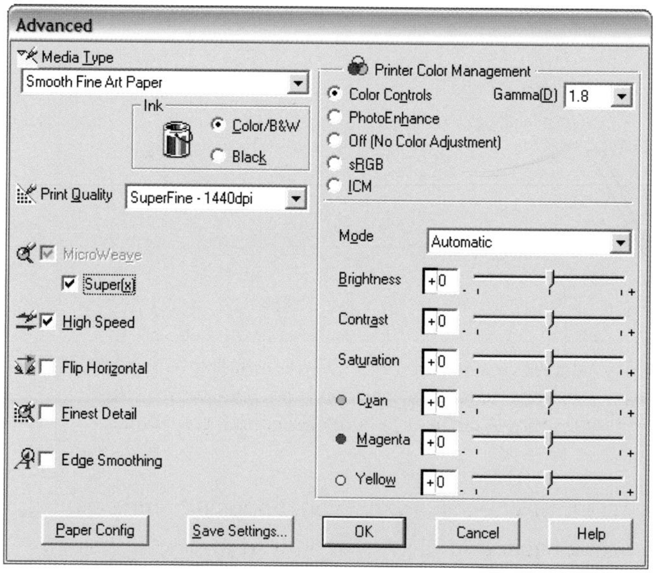

Figure 4.13 *The Color Controls option has sliders to adjust each color as well as brightness, contrast, and saturation. If your image-editing application has no color management options, this setting will give you the ability to fine-tune your prints for accuracy.*

PhotoEnhance (**Figure 4.14**) is for quick correction of such common digital image problems as exposure and color balance, and includes a sharpening function. Off (No Color Adjustment) is the correct choice when you're printing from Photoshop or any other application that gives you full control over color management. Selecting Off ensures that your printer receives only one set of color instructions. sRGB works well when you're printing JPEG files directly from a digital camera and no correction is needed. Because sRGB is a smaller color space than Adobe RGB, it isn't the optimal setting for photographs but does ensure that the printer and the camera are using the same set of color values when printing with no other color management support.

Figure 4.14 *PhotoEnhance works best with photos that just need a quick correction or conversion to black and white or sepia. If you're printing JPEG images directly from the camera, PhotoEnhance is a good option.*

ICM is the best choice to make when your application doesn't support color management (**Figure 4.15**). ICM gives you most of the control that printing from Photoshop does, including profile selection and rendering intents. Selecting ICM tells the printer which profile to use based on your Media Type setting. When more than one profile for the media exists, you can select which one to use from the ICC/ICM Profile drop-down list. (I'll cover rendering intents in Chapter 7).

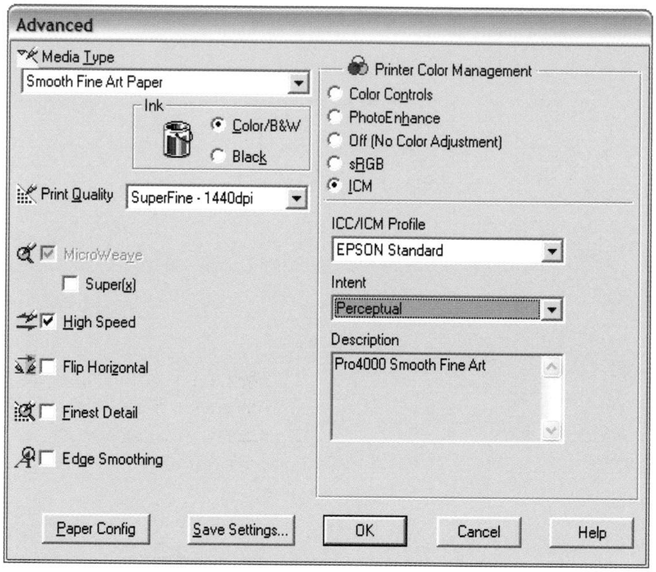

Figure 4.15 *The ICM option is the best choice to make when your imaging application doesn't support color management but you still want to have the most control possible over your output.*

The Paper tab (**Figure 4.16**) options include setting Paper Source, such as tray, roll, or manual; whether to use borderless printing; Paper Size; Orientation; and Printable Area.

The remaining tabs in the Printing Preferences dialog box are Layout (**Figure 4.17**), which has settings for selecting whether to print double-sided or multiple images per page and whether to reduce or enlarge prints, and Utility (**Figure 4.18**). Utility is where you'll head if you see problems such as missing colors or lines in your prints. Nozzle Check and Head Cleaning are normally all it takes to get your printer back in working order.

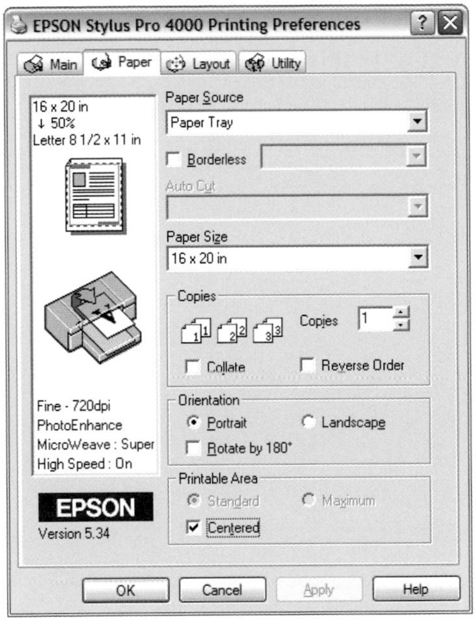

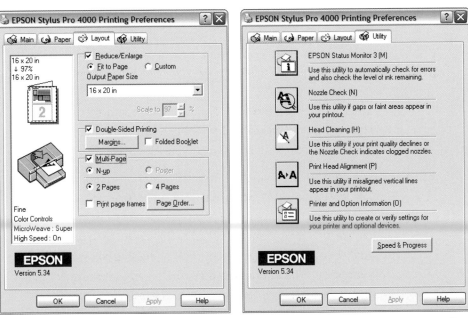

Figure 4.16 *The Paper tab includes settings to control paper source, size, and orientation.*

Figure 4.17 *The Layout tab contains the settings for number of copies and page size.*

Figure 4.18 *If your print quality starts to suffer, the Utility tab has options to clean printheads and check nozzles.*

Tip

There is very little difference between Best Photo and Photo RPM, other than time. Choosing Photo RPM will slow your printing speed to less than half that of Photo. For 98 percent of your printing, I recommend using Best Photo. For the other 2 percent where you might have someone critically examining your print with a loupe, by all means choose Photo RPM. To find it, click the Advanced button, then Photo Enhance and go to Paper & Quality Options.

Epson R2400

In the R2400 Main tab of the Printing Preferences dialog box (**Figure 4.19**), the Quality Option controls how your image is printed. For most photographs, I recommend using Best Photo. Photo is a good option when you want a lower-quality draft, or proof, print. Under Paper Options you'll find the Borderless print setting and the Source, Type, and Size drop-down lists. Size includes both preset paper sizes and a user-defined option for creating specific paper settings. When you use roll paper, the Custom setting lets you set both the width and length to conserve paper use. The Print Options section includes PhotoEnhance and a toggle for Print Preview, to verify your settings are correct before committing them to paper. The big feature in the R2400 (and all of the new Epsons with K3 inks) is hidden behind the Advanced button.

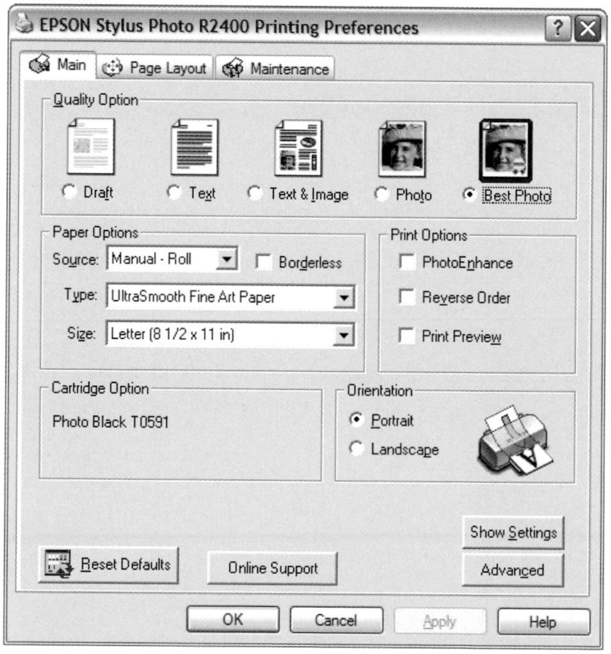

Figure 4.19 The Main tab of Printing Preferences for the R2400 and similar printers has most of the controls needed to set print quality and other options. Clicking the Advanced button takes you to the color management controls.

When you click Advanced, you get four main choices: Color Controls, PhotoEnhance, Advanced B&W Photo, and ICM (or Image Color Management). With Color Controls, you can set individual color sliders (**Figure 4.20a**). PhotoEnhance (**Figure 4.20b**) performs common image corrections, Advanced B&W Photo gives you total control over your black and white prints, and ICM (**Figure 4.20c**) controls how color is translated from screen to printer. The most important of these settings is ICM. If you print from Photoshop, you'll absolutely want to select ICM and then choose Off (No Color Adjustment) to avoid having two profiles applied to your prints (always interesting but seldom what you'd expect!). If your application doesn't support color management, then select Applied by Printer Software to let the printer driver handle color translation.

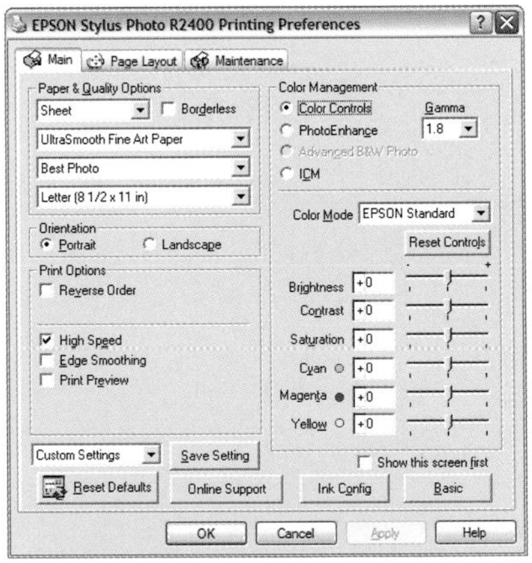

Figure 4.20a

Figure 4.20b

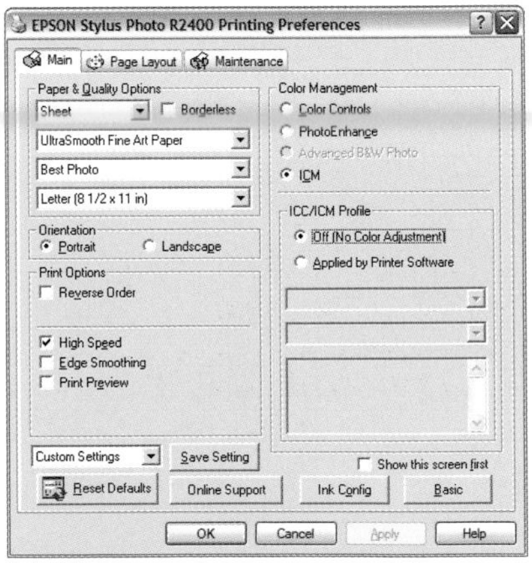

Figure 4.20c

Figures 4.20a, b, and c You can edit individual colors, brightness, contrast, and saturation by selecting Color Controls (a). For automatic adjustment of images, choose PhotoEnhance (b), or pick ICM (c) for complete control over how your printer and applications handle color translation.

The exciting feature in the R2400 and other new Epson printers that use the UltraChrome II K3 inks is the Advance B&W Photo option (**Figure 4.21**). This features gives you control over monochrome prints in a way that used be available only in a RIP (Raster Image Processor) that cost hundreds of dollars extra. Along with choosing such presets as Neutral, Cool, and Warm, you can completely control color, shadow and highlight tonality as well as Optical Destiny. The color wheel lets you select a custom color tone to use, making it possible to simulate such traditional darkroom printing techniques as platinum and selenium toned prints. As you make adjustments to the pointer within the color wheel, the preview window updates to show you what the tone will look like.

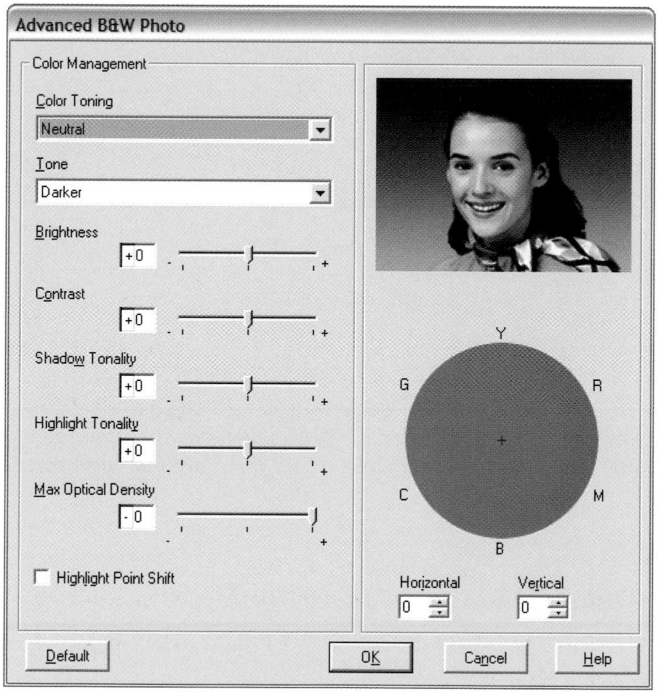

Figure 4.21 *Selecting Advanced B&W Photo opens up a new world for printing black-and-white images. You can apply one of the preset tones of Cool, Neutral, or Warm, or you can set your own custom values with total control over image tones, contrast, shadows and highlights, and density of blacks. Dragging the pointer around the color wheel shows you a preview of how your color toning looks.*

The remaining tabs in the Epson R2400 Printing Preferences dialog are Page Layout (**Figure 4.22**), which has options to control the number of copies, add watermarks, and scale images, and Maintenance (**Figure 4.23**). If you see problems such as missing colors, or lines in your prints, a stop here can clear up many problems. Nozzle Check and Head Cleaning are normally all it takes to get your printer back in working order.

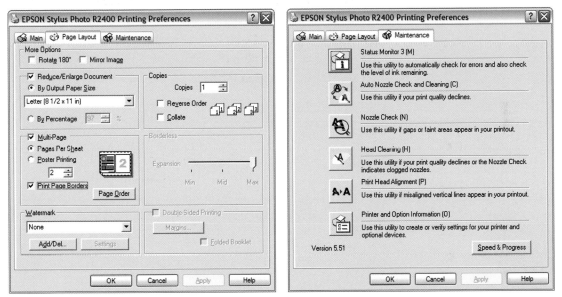

Figure 4.22 The Page Layout tab has options that let you adjust page size, specify the number of copies, reduce and enlarge your prints, or add watermarks.

Figure 4.23 If you're having any trouble with print quality, running a nozzle check and head cleaning from the Maintenance tab will normally correct the problem.

HP printers

To get started fine-tuning your HP printer's settings, click Printing Preferences to open the main printer driver dialog box. You'll start off in the Printing Shortcuts tab.

Printing Shortcuts tab

Most of the features of the HP driver are available from the Printing Shortcuts tab (**Figure 4.24**), with the options changing based on the type of print job you want to perform.

Figure 4.24 *The HP starts out with the rather austere Printing Shortcuts tab.*

Select either Photo Printing-Borderless or Photo Printing-with White Borders to display the photo options for the printer as a series of drop-down list boxes. For Print Quality, I recommend either Best for general photo printing or Maximum dpi for those prints where quality is critical, such as submissions for galleries or contests.

Paper Type is one of the critical choices for accurate prints. By selecting the proper paper type, you'll ensure that the printer uses the correct amount of ink for your prints. The HP 8250 shown here uses a new setting, HP Advanced Paper, which includes special coding information on the back of the paper. When this paper and setting is used, the printer automatically sets the proper type for you to prevent accidental errors.

Paper Size provides all the possible paper choices supported by the printer, including common photo sizes and several options for panorama prints. Paper Source lets you select between the various options supported on your printer, such as tray or manual feed.

Orientation has options for Landscape or Portrait layouts.

Clicking the Real Life Digital Photography button opens a new dialog box (**Figure 4.25**) with quick fix options for many common digital photo problems. One very cool feature with the HP implementation of quick fixes is the Off to High slider, which gives you the ability to control how strong the effect is applied to your image. As you make adjustments to slides or radio buttons, the small preview image above the control is updated to give you an idea of how the effect will look.

Tip

You can also change orientation by clicking on the page sample to the right of the options drop-downs.

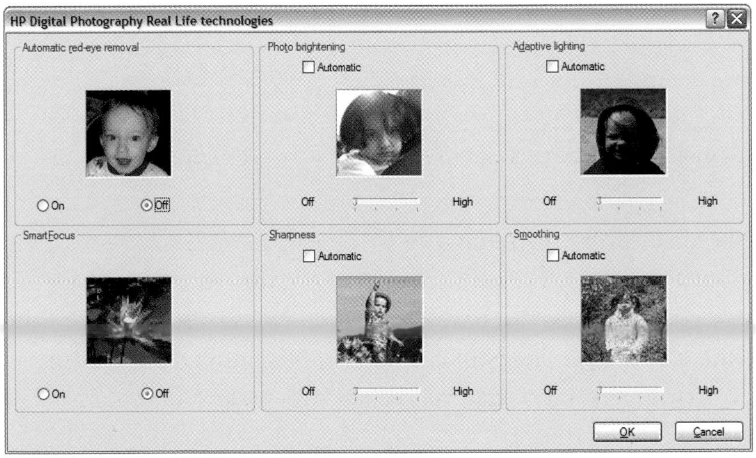

Figure 4.25 *HP's Real Life Digital Photography options give you a great deal of control over common image problems.*

Paper/Quality tab

The Paper/Quality tab (**Figure 4.26**) repeats some of the options available on the Printing Shortcuts tab but offers the additional benefit of allowing you to create custom page sizes and use the Borderless Auto Fit feature. You can also save custom settings here for quick access in the future by using the Print Task Quick Sets list.

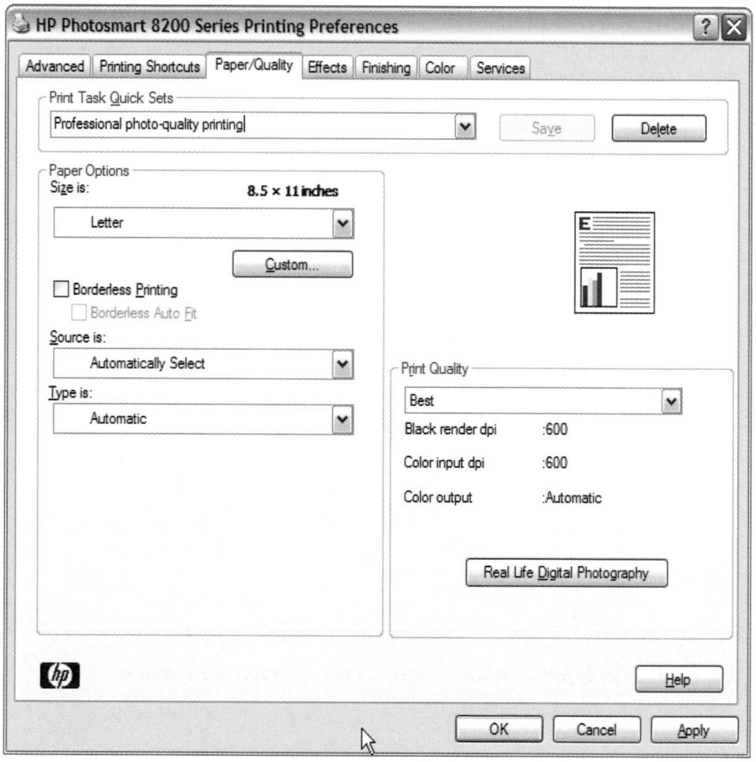

Figure 4.26 *The main benefits to the Paper/Quality tab are the ability to set custom page sizes, auto-fit borderless prints, and save settings for future use as a Quick Set.*

Effects tab

The Effects tab (**Figure 4.27**) has settings for resizing, centering on the page, and adding watermarks. As an added bonus, you can add a Quick Set on this tab if you forgot to do it in the Paper/Quality tab.

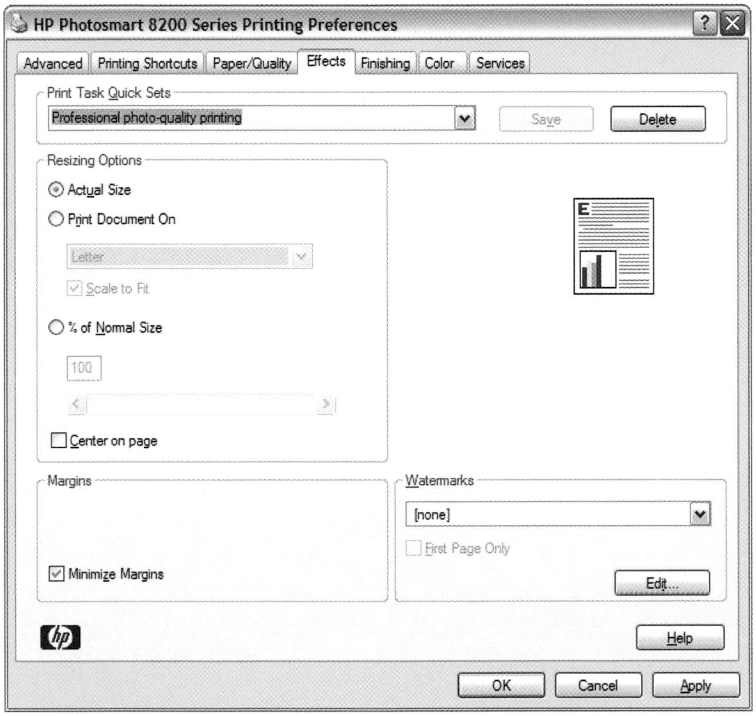

Figure 4.27 *The Effects tab has options for resizing and watermarks.*

Finishing tab

The Finishing tab (**Figure 4.28**) options let you use duplex, or double-sided printing, along with specifying how the pages will print, which is useful for scrapbooks or other double-sided jobs and settings for multiple pages per sheet of paper or multiple page posters. And, in a recurring theme, you can save your settings as a

Quick Set here too. Although I don't personally use Print Preview, it is available here and when checked will show you a rough estimate of how your photo will look on the page before you commit to actually printing it.

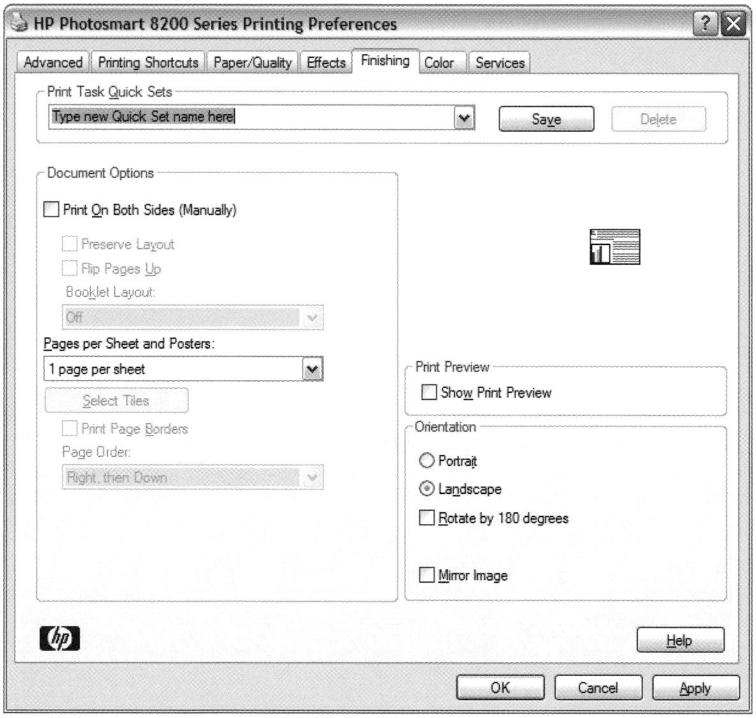

Figure 4.28 *The Finishing tab options include duplex, poster, and page orientation settings, along with Print Preview.*

Color tab

The Color tab (**Figure 4.29**) is where you set color management options, which determine whether your application or the printer driver controls color translation. These, along with the paper settings, are the most important choices you'll make with the HP printers. A wrong choice in the Color tab will likely result in having to reprint a photo with new settings. Choosing Print in Grayscale forces the printer to use only the different shades of gray inks on printers that use multiple grays, such as the nine-color Photosmart 8750. Selecting Black Only forces the printer to use only the black ink on other printers, resulting in a neutral print but one with less tonal range than a regular print will provide.

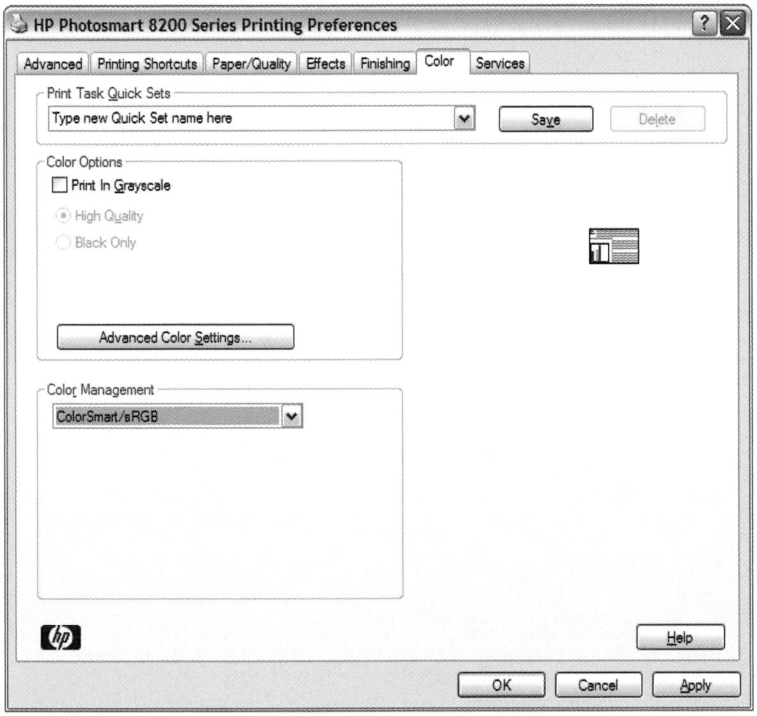

Figure 4.29 *The Color tab is where you'll set the all-important color management options for your prints.*

For complete control over individual colors, Brightness, Saturation, and Color Tone, click the Advanced Color Settings button. This opens a new dialog box (**Figure 4.30**), which features slider controls for each setting. A before and after preview shows you what your changes will look like. This is an effective way to create special effect monochrome images such as sepia toning.

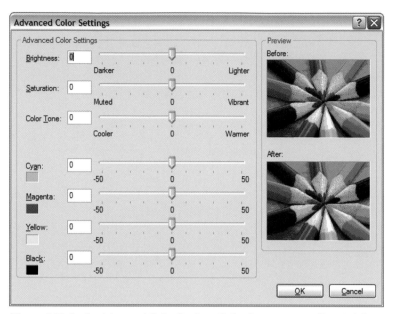

Figure 4.30 *In the Advanced Color Settings dialog box, you can adjust Brightness, Saturation, Color Tone, and individual color channels for special needs such as sepia or color balance correction.*

Back in the Color tab, look in the Color Management drop-down list to find options that control whether the printer or the application handles color translation tasks. If you're printing from Photoshop, you'll want to select Managed by Application for best results. ICM lets your printer handle color, while ColorSmart/sRGB and AdobeRGB are appropriate choices when you know what color space your images are in and no color management is available in your application. And, surprise, there's another chance to save your settings in the Quick Sets list!

Services tab

The final tab in the HP Printing Preferences dialog is Services, which contains one button. Click it to open the Toolbox for maintenance options, including printhead alignment, cleaning, and color calibration (**Figure 4.31**). Why HP chose to put this into a separate dialog box is beyond me, but they did.

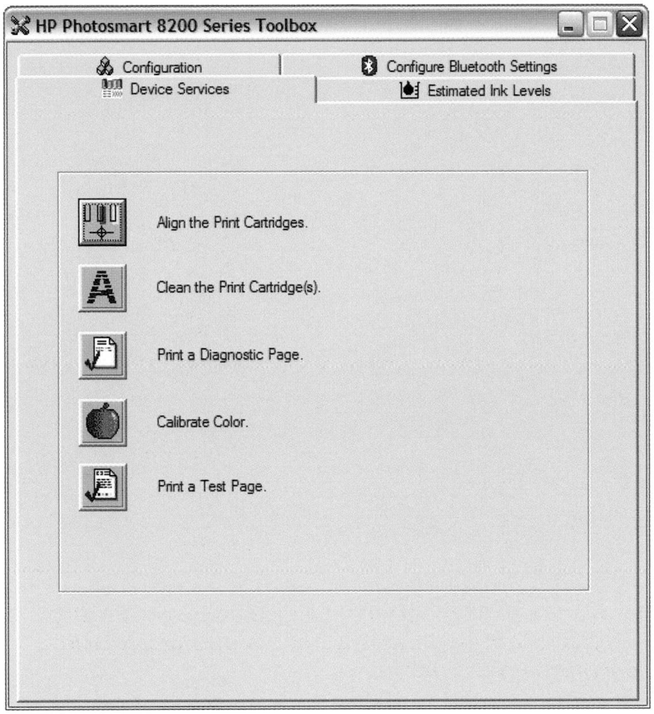

Figure 4.31 *The Toolbox has options for cleaning and adjusting printheads, calibrating color, and setting printer-specific options such as Bluetooth wireless settings.*

Macintosh Printer Drivers

To get started with setting printer options for your Mac, open your image file from within your imaging applications, such as Photoshop or iPhoto, and choose Print (**Figure 4.32**).

In the resulting dialog box, you can select the printer you want to use and any saved settings for that printer from the Presets list. All options for printer settings on the Mac are accessed through the pop-up menu below Presets. The first set of options is Copies & Pages, which controls how many copies to print, and what page range to print if multiple pages are present.

Note

For these examples, I'll be using OS X. If you aren't using it yet, I highly recommend upgrading to OS X.

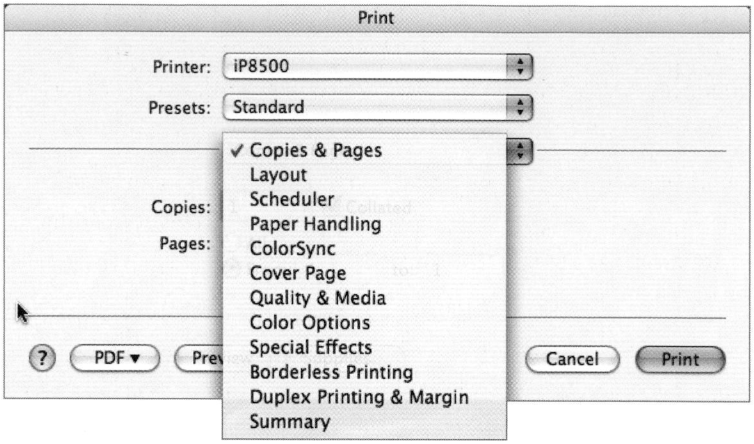

Figure 4.32 *The Print dialog box in Macintosh OS X is the entry point for all printer settings. The available options will change depending on which printer is selected.*

Selecting Layout (**Figure 4.33**) from the pop-up menu gives you options to set how many pages are on a single sheet of paper, what direction the pages flow onto the paper, and whether to use borders.

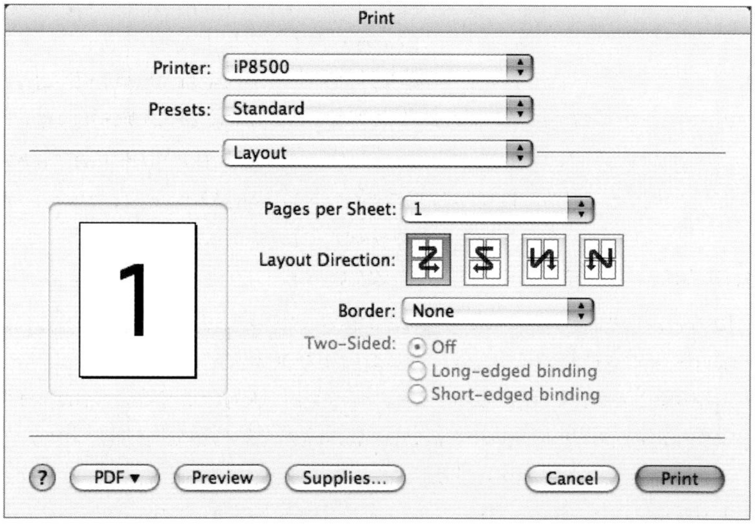

Figure 4.33 *The Layout options let you select how many pages are printed to a physical sheet of paper and in what order to print them.*

Scheduler allows you to set when the print will be done, and what priority to give the job. If you have several prints to do, this is a great way to have them print at a time when you're not using the computer for other things.

Choose Paper Handling from the pop-up menu for options to set page order, page size, and scaling, as well as to print all, odd-numbered only, or even-numbered only pages.

When you select the pop-up menu's ColorSync, you can then set Color Conversion to Standard or In Printer and turn on Quartz Filter. The default settings here are normally the best choice—Color Conversion left at Standard, and Quartz Filter left at None, especially if you're printing from Photoshop or any other application that supports color management. If you want to apply special effects to your prints without using an application that includes that support, the Quartz Filters have several tone controls for black-and-white or other monochrome prints and an overall way to increase and decrease image brightness.

The settings associated with the Cover Page choice probably won't be of interest to photographers unless you share a printer in a network environment and want to have an identifying sheet between print jobs.

Below Cover Page are the specific choices your printer adds to the pop-up menu list. In the next sections, I'll cover the options added by two popular brands of printers: Canon and Epson.

Canon printer options

Choosing Quality & Media (**Figure 4.34**), the first Canon-specific choice in the Print dialog box's pop-up menu, takes you to the important settings for photographic prints. Be careful to select the proper media type to avoid problems with print quality. The paper type you select will control how much ink the printer places on the page, and a wrong selection can, and likely will, lead to a wasted print. Paper Source lets you select which paper path to use if your printer supports multiple paths, and Print Mode sets the quality of print. For photos, you'll want to select Printing a Top-Quality Photo (kind of obvious, isn't it?). Finally, Grayscale Printing forces the printer to use only black ink. Although this does remove problems with color casts, black-only prints have less tonal range and usually result in lower-quality prints.

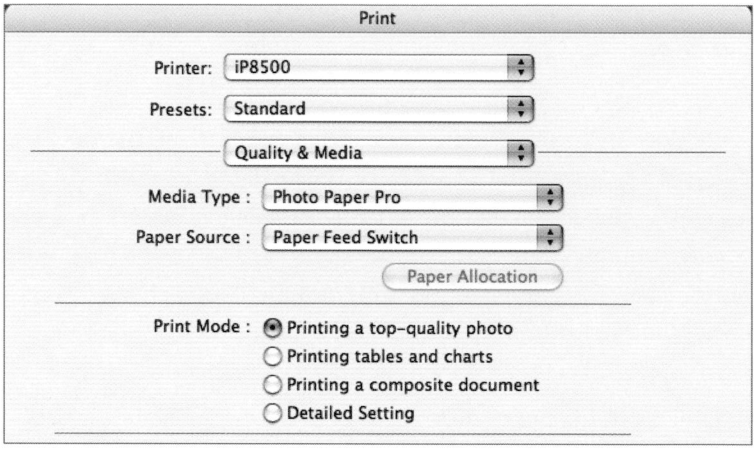

Figure 4.34 *Quality & Media contains the all-important options for selecting the proper paper type as well as what quality level you want your print to be.*

The next choice in the Print dialog box's pop-up is Color Options (**Figure 4.35**). The other critical set of controls, Color Options settings determine the type of color management used by the printer. Color Correction gives you the choice of using the printer's color management, ColorSync, or None. When printing from Photoshop you'll want to select None to avoid having profiles applied to your print twice when using Photoshop to manage color. I'll cover the proper print settings in Photoshop in Chapter 7. If you select None as the Color Correction method, the Print Type and Brightness controls will be disabled and you should leave the Color Balance and Intensity sliders at their midpoint default values, unless you need to correct a color cast problem. When using printer color management, the try setting Print Type to Photo and Brightness to Normal.

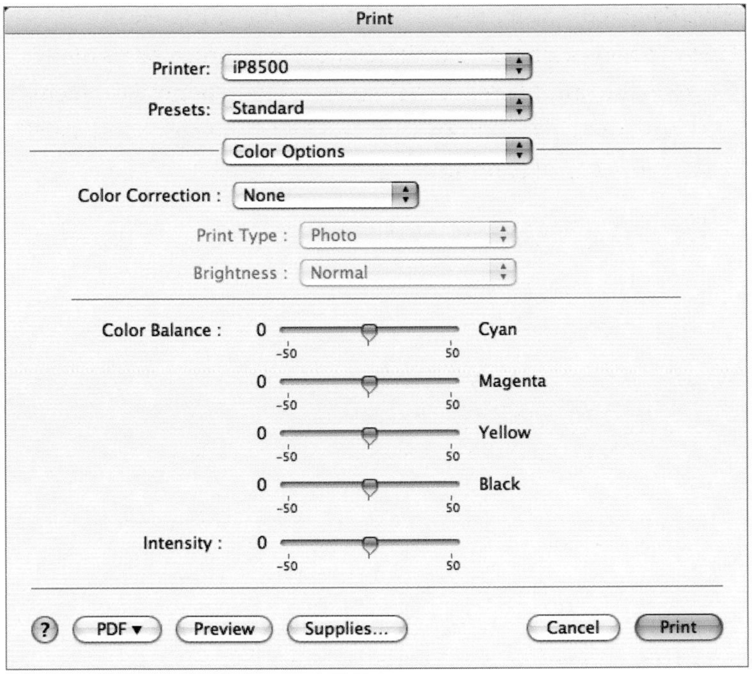

Figure 4.35 *Color Options contains the settings for color management. If you print from Photoshop, select None for the best results.*

Next on the Print dialog's pop-up menu list is Special Effects (**Figure 4.36**). You can set such monochrome effects as sepia and have the printer driver boost color saturation and reduce noise. The Simulate Illustration control turns your photo into line art. All settings are shown in the preview to give you a better idea of what the changes will look like.

Borderless Printing is a puzzle to me. I have yet to figure out why you have an option to set how much of an extension there is to a border that doesn't exist. And, to make things even more confusing, the control is always disabled! If you figure this one out, please e-mail me and explain it!

Duplex Printing & Margin controls the print area used and how double-sided prints are laid out.

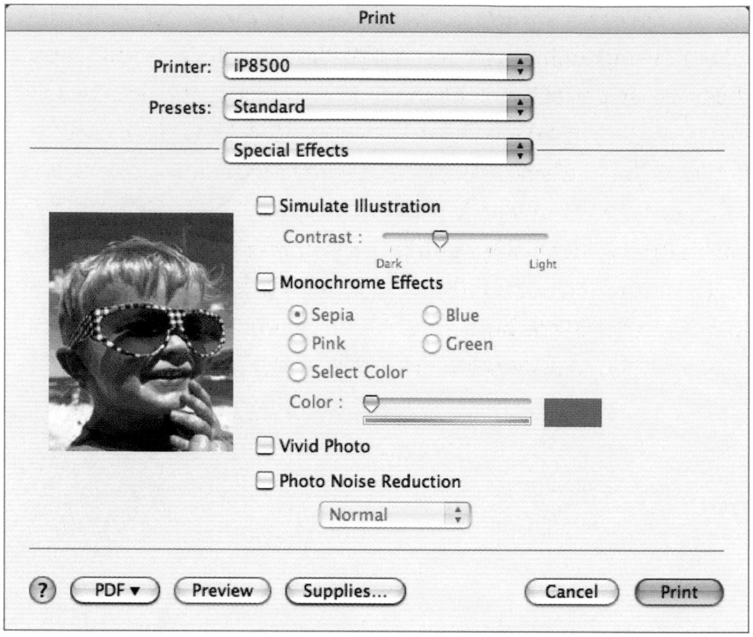

Figure 4.36 *Special Effects has controls for printing toned images and automatic color correction and enhancement.*

Epson printer options

The Epson-specific settings in the Print dialog box's pop-up menu start out with the Print Settings group. Because the newest Epsons that use the UltraChrome II K3 inks are significantly different in a couple of areas, I'll show you the controls for the R2400 and the standard UltraChrome Stylus Pro 4000.

R2400 pop-up menu choices

With the R2400 (**Figure 4.37**), the Print Settings control group starts with Page Setup options for either standard or roll paper. The options available under Media Type change depending on your Page Setup choice. Some papers, such as Velvet Fine Art and UltraSmooth Fine Art, can't use the sheet feeder and must be manually fed. For Color, you can choose Color, Advanced B&W Photo, and Black. Color produces the obvious results, and Black prints using only the black ink. This reduces the tonal range in your images and isn't a good choice, especially now that Epson has added the incredible Advanced B&W Photo mode. This setting uses the three shades of black ink to produce amazing black-and-white prints. Mode is disabled when Advanced B&W Photo is selected, but for Color or Black settings you use the Mode slider to specify whether speed or quality is your top priority. Clicking Advanced enables the Print Quality settings. I recommend using Best Photo for most prints, and for those really critical print jobs, I select Photo RPM, which uses the highest resolution. It slows the print time drastically, but does produce a higher-quality print.

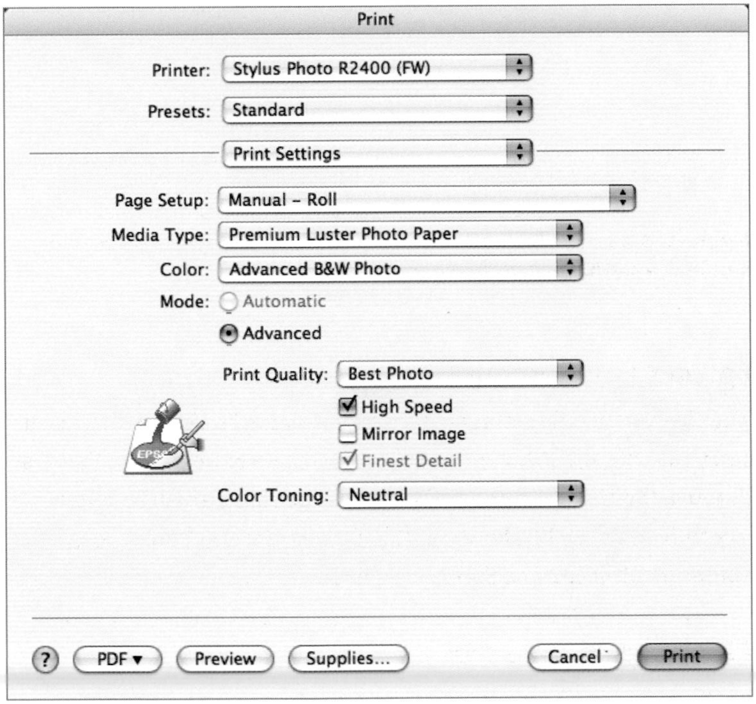

Figure 4.37 The Print Settings control group for the R2400 and other Epson UltraChrome K3 printers contains the options for selecting media type and print quality.

When Advanced B&W Photo is selected, the Mac displays an additional pop-up menu: Color Toning. From this you can choose Neutral, Cool, Warm, and Sepia.

The Color Management control group looks very different based on your Color setting. If you chose Advanced B&W Photo in Print Settings, Color Management will contain controls for toning your black-and-white prints, including Brightness, Contrast, Shadow and Highlight Tonality, and Optical Density settings (**Figure 4.38**). An image preview area displays any changes made, and if you don't like what you've done, a quick click on Defaults restores the original settings. You can fine-tune color toning options by dragging the pointer around the color wheel for exactly the look you want.

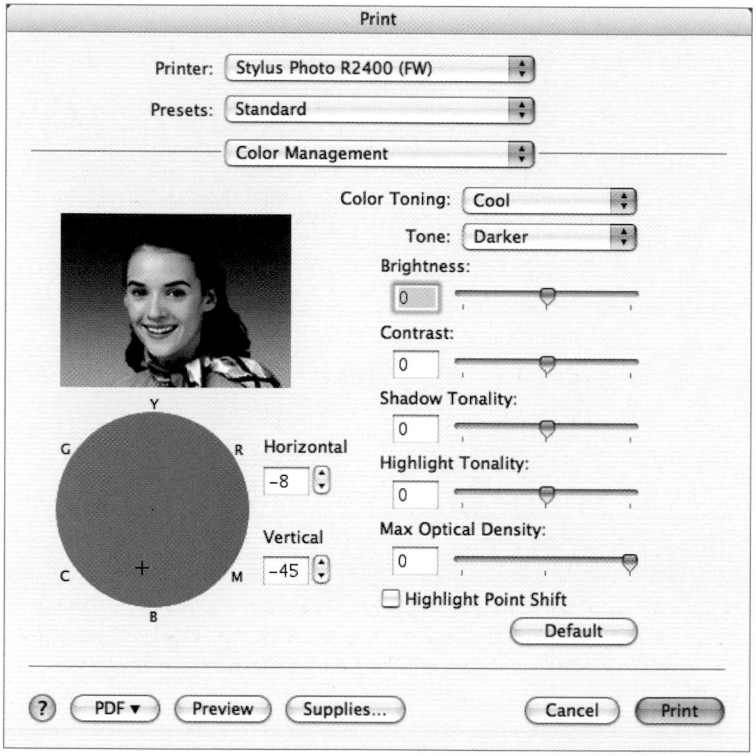

Figure 4.38 *Advanced B&W Photo offers you amazing quality and control over black-and-white and toned prints.*

When you specify Color as the output type, the Color Management controls switch to radio buttons that let you specify the type of color management you want to use (**Figure 4.39**). Select Color

Controls to make adjustments to Brightness, Contrast, Saturation, and colors. Selecting ColorSync lets the printer handle all color translation, while selecting Off (No Color Adjustment) gives all color control to your application. If you use Photoshop, this is the choice you'll want to make.

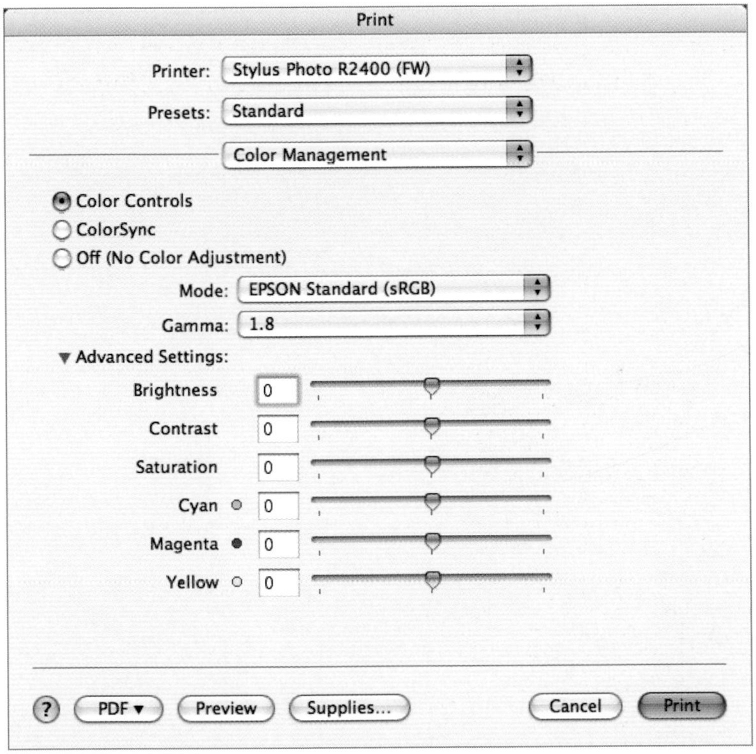

Figure 4.39 *Selecting Color as the output type gives you access to color management settings that will determine how your prints are handled. If you print from Photoshop, however, select Off (No Color Adjustment) instead for best results.*

Ink Configuration and Extension Settings control groups enable you to adjust the density of ink, the ink's drying time, and the paper thickness. Under most circumstances you won't need to make adjustments to these settings. When using special fine art papers from other manufacturers, you might need to experiment a bit if print quality isn't what you expect.

4000 pop-up menu choices

The Epson 4000 Print Settings (**Figure 4.40**) control group includes pop-up menus for the paper source (Paper Tray or Manual Feed) and the media type. Depending on the paper source you specified, some paper options may not be available because certain papers are too thick to use in the paper tray and must be fed using the manual feed slot or by roll paper. Media types with (250) in the name indicate roll papers.

For Ink, you can choose Color/B&W Photo or Black. Because using black only results in lower-quality photos, I suggest leaving Ink set for Color/B&W Photo.

Set Mode to Advanced Settings for the best control over your prints. For Print Quality, I suggest using SuperFine – 1440dpi for most prints. The SuperPhoto – 2880dpi setting doesn't really improve quality but does slow things down and uses more ink.

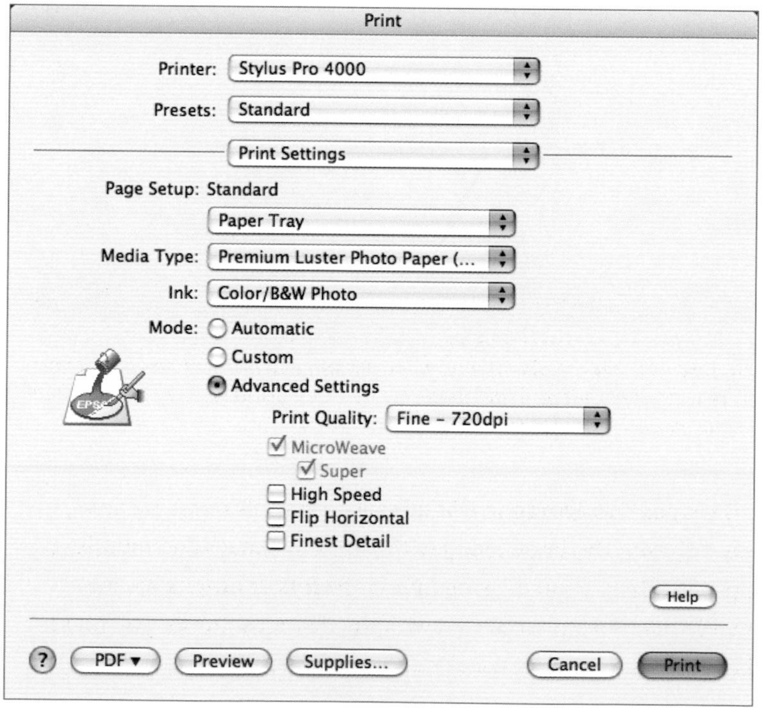

Figure 4.40 *The Epson 4000 Print Settings control group contains the media type options and quality settings. For general printing, I suggest using Fine.*

Printer Color Management (**Figure 4.41**) is, along with setting
the proper media, the most important setting you'll make before
printing. When using Photoshop, the best choice is Off (No Color
Adjustment), which lets Photoshop handle all color management.
I'll discuss how to do this in Chapter 7. The other settings groups,
Color Controls and ColorSync, let you make adjustments to printer
settings, or give color management to the printer driver.

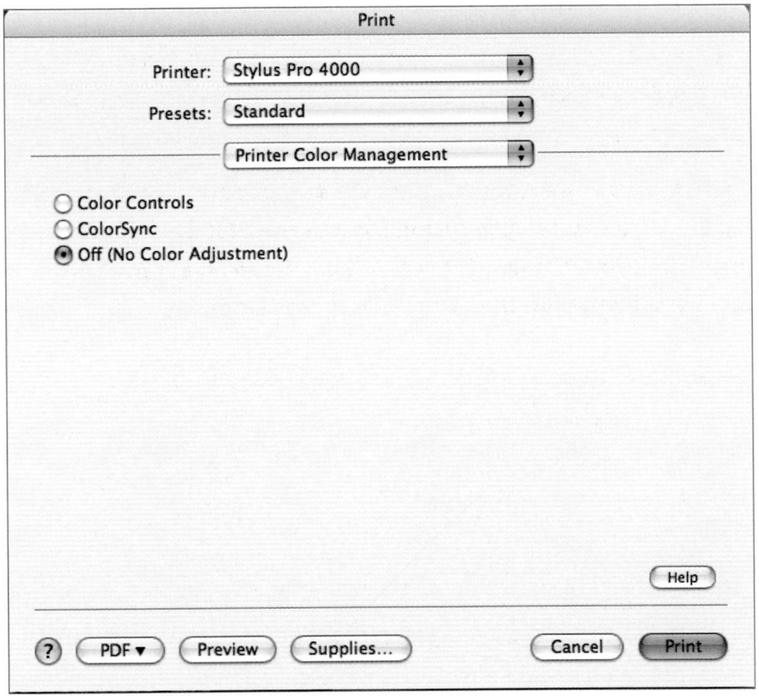

*Figure 4.41 Printer Color Management options will make or break the qual-
ity of your prints. Along with selecting the proper media type, nothing in the
printer driver is more critical to successful prints.*

The Paper Configuration (**Figure 4.42**) controls fine-tune ink
density and dry times, along with paper thickness and handling
options. Unless you're using fine art papers or other specialty
media that doesn't work well with the default settings, you most
likely won't need to make any changes here.

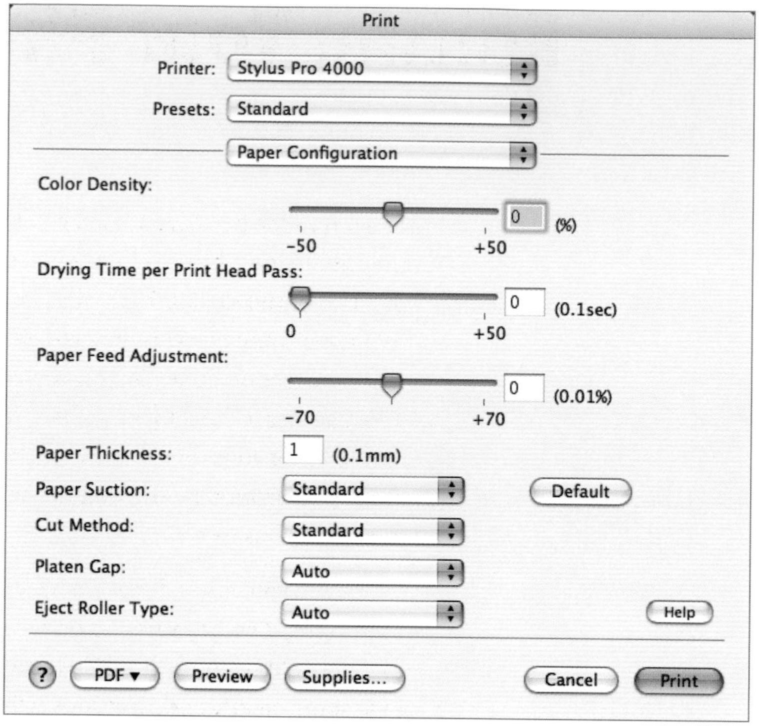

Figure 4.42 *The Paper Configuration controls will be useful if you have problems with specialty papers that don't print well with the default settings.*

Moving On

When you select the correct settings for your printer, the results are likely to be at least close to what you intended. Getting the right settings in multiple places can be confusing, but the steps in this chapter will help you quickly get your printer and software speaking to each other.

Now that your monitor and printer are speaking the same color language, you're ready to turn your attention to optimizing your images for printing. In Chapter 7, I'll build on what you've learned here to show you how to use custom profiles and printer settings to get the absolute best prints. If you're interested in how to optimize your images for printing or making creative adjustments, head on into Chapter 5, "Editing Your Photos." If you just want to print what you have, jump right into Chapter 6, "Resizing and Sharpening Your Images."

5 | Editing Your Photos

You found the perfect subject, you knew just how you wanted the shot to look, but the image you got doesn't quite match the one in your head. That's where Adobe Photoshop and Photoshop Elements come in. With the help of their layers, curves, levels, and color-correction controls, you can tweak your image to perfection. This chapter will help you sort out which tool is best for the kind of doctoring your image needs and identify how much is enough, saving you from crossing that delicate boundary between amazing and disastrous results.

Or maybe you've got a great image, but you want something more than straight color prints—if only your photo was more like a painting, it would be incredible. This chapter will also show you how to take some creative license: converting to black and white, hand-coloring images, adding borders and edges, and more.

With these techniques you can finally print that image you see in your mind. After all, if photography was just about snapping the picture, it wouldn't have the same appeal to most of us.

Layers Basics

One of the most useful features of Adobe Photoshop and Photoshop Elements for editing digital images is the ability to work with layers. With layers, you can selectively correct or enhance areas of the image while protecting the original image data from change.

Photoshop has five types of layers: image, adjustment, fill, new, and text. The two most important layer types for digital photography are image and adjustment. Because these two types of layers are so fundamental to image editing, we'll take a close look at each.

Image layers

Image layers are simply exact copies of the image—essentially the same result you'd get if you chose the Copy and Paste commands. You have an extra copy of image data that you can blend into the original layer or modify as you wish. The hand-coloring demonstration a bit later in this chapter is an example of using image layers.

The drawback to using image layers is that it increases the size of your file by the same amount as the original file. In other words, if you start with a 50 MB TIFF file and add one image layer, you will then have a 100 MB file to manipulate. As you can see, using multiple image layers can quickly add up and slow your computer to a crawl.

Adjustment layers

The real power comes with adjustment layers. These don't contain any image data but work to apply a nondestructive edit to the image below. A common use for adjustment layers is color correction. By using an adjustment layer, you can make changes to the color balance or the curves of your image without actually modifying the image itself. If you change your mind later, just hide the layer or delete it and you're back to where you started.

Adjustment layers are also great for working on particular areas of an image. By using layer masks with the adjustment, you can selectively apply corrections to only the area of your image that you wish to change.

Note

The topic of layers can fill entire books. One of the best out there on adjustment layers is Tim Grey's *Photoshop CS2 Workflow: The Digital Photographer's Guide* (Sybex, 2005).

Protecting the Master Image

Before doing anything to your image, you want to be sure that you're working on a backup copy of the master, or original, image. The easiest way to do this is by selecting Image > Duplicate Image, which creates a new copy of your image (**Figure 5.1**). Before you do anything else, close the original to avoid accidentally making changes to it.

Figure 5.1 *Use Photoshop's Duplicate Image command to work on a copy of your master image, protecting the master against accidental changes.*

Optimizing Your Image

Odds are your image isn't going to be perfect straight from the camera. Especially for printing, some image adjustment and optimization should be expected for best results.

You can do some amazing things with Photoshop and Elements to correct common problems like lighting and contrast corrections. These tools can't rescue a fundamentally flawed image, but when your images need a little boost to reach their true glory, the features are there to help you.

Adjusting Curves and Levels

One of the most powerful correction tools at your disposal in Photoshop is the Curves control. Because of its reputation for being difficult to master, this tool instills fear into many digital imagers. Keep in mind that the time you invest in learning how to use the Curves control will pay for itself many times over.

The Curves control is available in Photoshop only. The closest counterpart in Elements is the Levels control, which can make similar corrections but with nowhere near the same degree of control. I'll show you how each feature works, starting with Curves.

Using Curves

I recommend using Curves on an adjustment layer, so to begin select Layer > New Adjustment Layer > Curves. In the dialog box that appears, give your layer a descriptive name and click OK.

Note

For the adjustment levels work we'll be doing here, leave the Mode option set to Normal. The different blending modes are useful for special effects, but for the Curves and Levels adjustments, Normal is typically your best choice.

Tip

If your Curves dialog box doesn't show the small grid as shown in Figure 5.2, hold Alt/Option and click on the grid to toggle between the large and small grid. The small grid is easier to use for fine adjustments.

When the Curves dialog box first opens, you'll see a diagonal line running from lower left to upper right across a grid (**Figure 5.2**). The line represents the current distribution of tonal values, and you adjust it by clicking on the curve line and dragging it up or down.

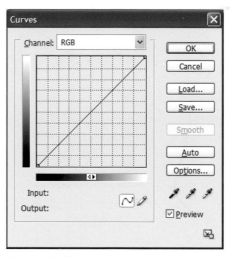

Figure 5.2 *The Curves control is the most powerful method of making image adjustments in Photoshop.*

In the lower-right corner of the Curves dialog box, you'll find an icon that lets you toggle between large and small views of the Curves control. If you need the screen space to see more of your image, the small view might work better for you.

The Curves control makes adjustments by shifting the tonal value of the pixels at the curve location that you select. Moving the curve up lightens a tonal value, while moving the curve down darkens it.

To make a change, first add an anchor point by clicking on the curve, and then drag the curve to the new value. **Figures 5.3a** and **b** show an image and its curve before and after an adjustment. By dragging the curve up near the midpoint, I have corrected the overall dark tone in the image.

Figures 5.3a and b *The original image is dark overall with washed-out midtones (a). Raising the curve corrects the overall tone of the image and makes the whites more accurate (b).*

One of the most common adjustments made with the Curves control is the *S-curve*. This curve shape increases the contrast in the midtones of an image while retaining highlight and shadow detail. To create an S-curve, move the upper end of the curve to the left and the lower end of the curve to the right, as shown in **Figure 5.4**. Small movements are all that are needed for most adjustments, and you'll quickly see a nice increase in the contrast of your image, giving it more depth.

Note

You may be wondering about using the individual color channels to make corrections. These are useful for making corrections to color balance problems, and I'll cover that in a bit.

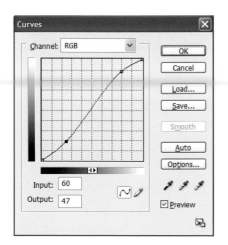

Figure 5.4 *The S-curve is one of the most common adjustments made with the Curves control, adding contrast to the midtones while retaining shadow and highlight detail.*

Figures 5.5a and b *Before applying the S-curve, the image is a little flat (a). After the S-curve, there is more contrast and depth in the image (b).*

Figures 5.5a and **b** show the before and after of applying an S-curve.

Using Levels

You can use the Levels control, available in both Photoshop and Elements, to make similar adjustments, but it doesn't give you the same amount of control over the changes as Curves do. To begin, create an adjustment layer by selecting Layer > New Adjustment Layer > Levels. Give your new layer a descriptive name, like Levels (how original!), and click OK. You'll see the dialog box shown in **Figure 5.6**.

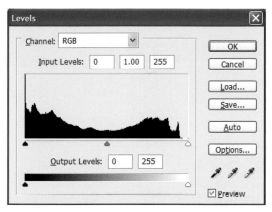

Figure 5.6 *The Levels control is available to Photoshop and Elements users. It doesn't give the same amount of control over adjustments, but it is a valuable tool for setting shadow, highlight, and midtone levels.*

The Levels control has three sliders below the histogram. The left slider controls the black point, the center slider controls midtones or overall lightness and darkness of the image, and the right slider controls the white point.

Under normal circumstances, your goal when using the Levels control is to get the maximum range of values possible. To do this, drag the black slider to the start of histogram data and the white slider to the end of the histogram data. You then adjust the overall tone of the image by moving the center slider left to lighten and right to darken. All of the current settings are also shown as numeric values in the Input Levels boxes. The range of 0 to 255 is the maximum, with 0 representing black and 255 representing white. The 1.00 value indicates a midtone exactly in the center of the histogram. As you move the sliders, these numbers will update to show the new values. **Figures 5.7 a**, **b**, and **c** show the difference a slight adjustment to the midtone slider can make on the overall image.

Note

I say "normal circumstances" because there are always exceptions to the rule. High-key images will have most of the image data on the highlight end of the histogram with nothing in the shadows, while low-key images will be just the opposite. If that's the look you're going for, you obviously don't want to spread that data across the entire histogram and ruin the look.

Figure 5.7a

Figure 5.7b

Figure 5.7c

Figures 5.7a, b, and c *Small adjustments to the midtone slider can make a large difference in the overall look of your image.*

 One feature that you might find very useful as you make your adjustments in the Levels control is to hold down the Alt/Option key while adjusting the black point or white point slider. This turns your image into a preview of where the data will begin to clip, or lose detail. When you're adjusting the black point slider, the screen will turn white for all areas within range. As you move the slider to the right, the screen will begin to show image detail, indicating that those areas of the image will be displayed as black. On the other side, dragging the white point slider with the Alt/Option key pressed will turn the screen black. As you drag the slider to the left, image detail will begin to display, indicating that those areas will be displayed as white. The goal is to adjust both sliders until clipping begins and then back off just a bit, maximizing the range of information in your image. **Figures 5.8a**, **b**, and **c** show how this feature works.

You can also set the black and white points for your image by using the eyedroppers in the Levels control. Selecting the black eyedropper and clicking an area of your image that should be black will set the black point to that value. The white eyedropper works in the same way on the highlights. The gray eyedropper doesn't set the midtones as you might expect. It actually determines what tonal value in your image should be considered neutral, making it a good tool to correct for color casts.

Figure 5.8a

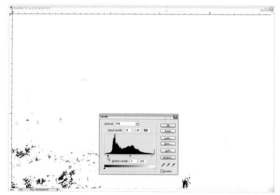

Figure 5.8b

Figures 5.8a, b, and c By holding down the Alt/Option key while adjusting the black and white point sliders in the Levels control, you can preview the changes to see where your shadows and highlights will begin clipping. Figure 5.8a shows the image I'm working with; 5.8b shows the preview when adjusting the black point; and 5.8c shows the preview when adjusting the white point..

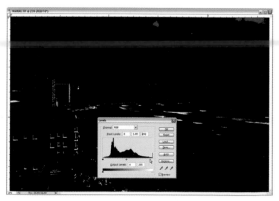

Figure 5.8c

The Output Levels slider below the histogram controls where your printer sets black and white points. I'll cover those in depth later in the chapter.

Color correction

At times, you might notice that your image isn't quite right. The colors seem a little off; perhaps the white areas have a blue tone that you don't like. If this is the case, there are a couple of easy ways to correct the color.

Note

Neutral doesn't mean gray; it means that each color is equal in value, which means that each color has close to the same amount of red, green, and blue. If you don't see an obvious possibility in your image, clicking different areas will update the preview to show the effect the current selection will have.

The first of these is through the Levels control. Create a new adjustment layer by selecting Layer > New Adjustment Layer > Levels. Now, select the gray eyedropper and then click an area in your image that should be neutral in tone.

The second method of correcting a color cast is to modify individual color channels in the Levels dialog box. Starting with a levels adjustment layer as you did in the previous example, select a color channel from the pop-up menu above the histogram (**Figure 5.9**).

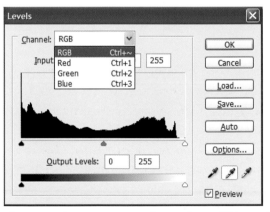

Figure 5.9 *You can correct a color cast by modifying each color channel in the Levels control.*

Starting with the Red channel, move the midtone slider to correct any color cast between red and cyan. Next, select the Green channel and move the midtone slider to correct any color cast between green and magenta. Finally, select the Blue channel and adjust the midtone slider to correct any color cast between blue and yellow.

The third method uses the Color Balance control (**Figure 5.10**), which is available in Photoshop only. This is perhaps the easiest method for many people because the controls and relationship to color are so clear.

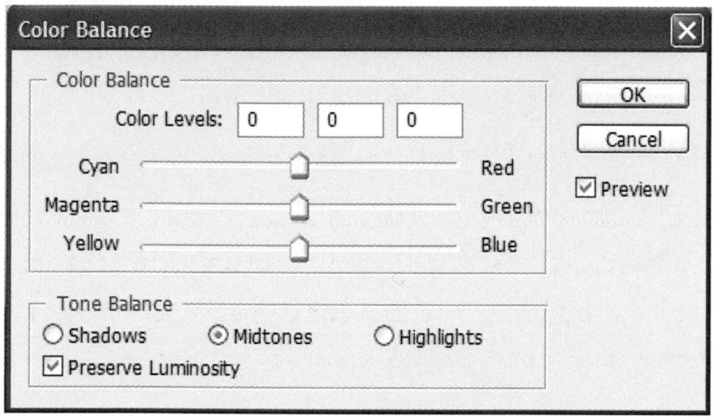

Figure 5.10 *The Color Balance control is an easy-to-use method of correcting color problems in your image.*

To get started, create an adjustment layer by selecting Layer > New Adjustment Layer > Color Balance. There are three sliders, one for each primary color. Dragging a slider toward its respective color will add that color and remove its complement. Moving the slider toward Red adds red and removes cyan; moving it toward Green adds green and removes magenta; and so on. **Figures 5.11a** and **b** show examples of adjustments to the color sliders. In this example, I needed to reduce the red by moving the slider toward Cyan. I also added green and blue to the image to further correct the color cast.

Figures 5.11 a and b *The original image shows a strong color cast, the result of a tinted filter not being removed prior to shooting. The after image shows the adjustments made with the Color Balance control to correct the color cast.*

The Tone Balance controls limit where the adjustments to color balance are made. By default, the midtones will be affected, correcting all but the ends of the tonal range. You can restrict the adjustments to either shadows or highlights by selecting the appropriate option.

Elements color correction

If you use Elements, you have a couple of other options available to you. The first of these is Enhance > Adjust Color > Remove Color Cast (**Figure 5.12**). This works like the gray eyedropper in the Levels control. Click an area in your image that should be neutral in tone and Elements will correct the color.

Figure 5.12 *Elements has a simple Remove Color Cast feature that works similarly to the gray eyedropper in the Levels control.*

The second method is great for portraits and other photos of people, but it's only available for Elements 4.0 users. Select Enhance > Adjust Color > Adjust Color for Skin Tone (**Figure 5.13**). Click anywhere on the subject's skin and Elements will correct the image for proper skin tones. If you want to fine-tune the adjustment, you can do so by adjusting the Tan, Blush, and Ambient Light sliders.

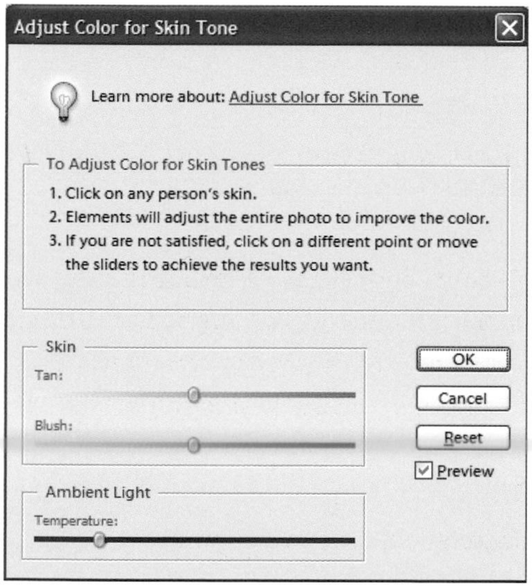

Figure 5.13 *To correct skin tones, the Adjust Color for Skin Tone command makes a tough task very simple.*

Adjusting output levels

There is one simple fact in digital printing: your printer is not capable of reproducing the same range of shadow and highlight detail that your monitor displays. This can be extremely frustrating, especially when you have your image adjusted on screen to be exactly what you want and the print has shadows that are blocked up with little or no detail in the darkest areas.

A fix is close at hand, though, and like many things in Photoshop it's not immediately intuitive until you've used it.

To get started, open the Levels dialog box by selecting Image > Adjustments > Levels (**Figure 5.14**) in Photoshop, or Enhance > Adjust Lighting > Levels in Elements.

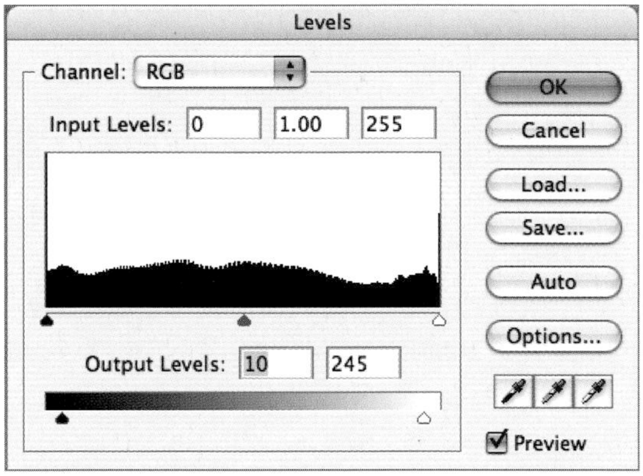

Figure 5.14 *Use the Levels control to adjust output levels for printing that will avoid lost detail in the shadows and highlights.*

Below the histogram, you'll see an Output Levels control that specifies where the black and white points are set. Although the defaults of 0 (black) and 255 (white) may be fine for screen display, you'll want to adjust these settings for print. Because every printer is different, it's impossible for me to assure you that if you use these settings all will be wonderful in your world. Instead, you'll need to do a bit of experimentation for the best results. I can, however, give you a good guideline to go by. Starting with a black level of 10 and a white level of 245 will generally get you close to what the typical inkjet printer can handle. Try these settings and do a print. If you're still seeing shadow or highlight problems on the print that don't show on screen, make further adjustments.

More often than not, your problem areas will be in the shadows. Inkjet printers, particularly those that only use a single black ink, tend to not be able to retain detail in the shadows, *blocking up*, or becoming solid, sooner than your monitor will. If this is happening to you, try increasing the black output setting by small increments until you begin to see detail in the important areas of your shadows. It's important to avoid going overboard, though. Setting the value too high will give you detail all the way through your shadows, but the shadows also begin to look washed out and flat. Rather than getting everything in detail, pick the critical features and let the rest go.

Black-and-White Conversions

Black and white has seen a huge surge in popularity since digital photography became popular. It's kind of ironic that we spend all of this money for digital cameras, computers, and printers to duplicate the look of our old Instamatic with Tri-X film. Still, there's something almost magical about a well-done black-and-white image that just can't be matched by a color print.

Photoshop offers several ways to reach black-and-white nirvana. The easiest, and typically the first method tried, is simply selecting Image > Mode > Grayscale (**Figures 5.15a** and **b**). Sadly, this tends to result in a washed-out image that is less than satisfactory (to be perfectly blunt, it often looks lousy), but for many people it's the only way they know to get a monochrome image.

> **Note**
>
> Different types of paper will have different results, so you may find yourself doing a fair amount of experimenting. Look for blocked-up shadows or missing highlight areas in your image. If you see either of these, you'll need to adjust the matching slider.

Figures 5.15 a and b *Color images converted with a straight Mode > Grayscale conversion tend to look flat and dull.*

A much better approach, but one that requires some experimentation, is to use the Channel Mixer (which is only available with the full version of Photoshop). I'll cover that technique in a bit, but first let's look at some other options that can quickly get you into a black-and-white mood.

Plug-ins

One of the easiest paths to quality black-and-white conversions is through the use of plug-ins, which are available from a number of sources. The best of these, in my experience, are the converters in the nik Color Efex Pro 2.0 package (www.nikmultimedia.com). With several preset options for straight black-and-white conversion or for creating toned images, such as sepia, the nik filters are easy to use and very customizable (**Figure 5.16**). Color Efex is available in several configurations, ranging in price from $80 to $300. All have at least basic black-and-white conversion filters, with even more options available in the complete editions.

Note

nik, as well as most other plug-in makers, offers free trial versions of its software. You can download the trials to see if you like a plug-in before spending your money.

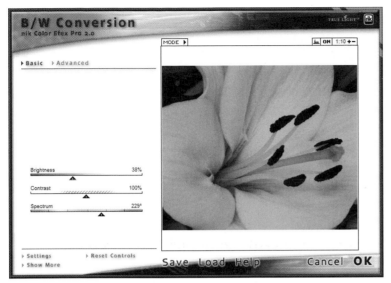

Figure 5.16 *The nik Color Efex Pro 2.0 plug-in has a very good black-and-white conversion filter.*

Advanced conversions

As I mentioned earlier, for full control over black-and-white conversions, the best method is to use the Channel Mixer in Photoshop. To get started, open your image and select Layer > New Adjustment Layer > Channel Mixer. Give your layer a descriptive name and click OK to open the Channel Mixer dialog box (**Figure 5.17**). Here you'll find controls to adjust the amount of color in each color channel.

For black-and-white conversions, start off by clicking the Monochrome check box to desaturate your image (**Figure 5.18**). If you've ever shot black-and-white film with color filters, you'll be familiar with the way Channel Mixer works.

Figure 5.17 *The Channel Mixer (only in Photoshop) gives you complete control over each color channel in your image, similar to using color filters with black-and-white film.*

Figure 5.18 *Selecting the Monochrome check box desaturates the image, but still lets you adjust color values in a way that is similar to using color filters with black-and-white film.*

When you move a slider to the right, it's just like using a stronger version of the filter. Each source channel works by enhancing its own color. In other words, higher numbers on the Red channel enhance the red tones in your image and darken the opposite color, which is blue.

For the lily example, I wanted to enhance the whites and greens. Using a mix of color settings, I decided that 44% Red, 46% Green, and 10% Blue gave me the results I was looking for (**Figure 5.19**). The total values in Channel Mixer should add up to 100 in order to maintain tonality. Higher or lower numbers, while they can be used, will give you mixed results.

Figure 5.19 *Using the Source Channel sliders, I was able to come up with a much better-looking black-and-white image than was possible with a simple grayscale conversion.*

It might help to compare the three converted images side by side. **Figures 5.20a**, **b**, and **c** show the differences between Convert to Grayscale, the nik Black and White filter, and the Channel Mixer.

Figures 5.20a, b, and c
The three conversion methods discussed show very different results. Grayscale (a) looks flat compared to the other two, while the nik Black and White conversion (b) has more contrast. I think the best results come from the Channel Mixer conversion (c), but it took the most effort too.

Figure 5.20a

Figure 5.20b

Figure 5.20c

In my mind, the Channel Mixer will give you the best results with conversions but it does require more effort on your part. If you use Elements, this option isn't available to you.

Duotones, Tritones, and Quadtones

As the names imply, these are monochrome images with additional color applied. A duotone has one additional color, a tritone has two, and a quadtone has three additional colors.

To create a tone image, you'll first need to convert to grayscale by selecting Image > Mode > Grayscale.

Next, select Image > Mode > Duotone and you'll see the Duotone Options dialog box.

By default, the Type option will be set to Duotone and only the first two inks will be active. The first ink defaults to Black. Clicking on the white square for Ink 2 opens a Color Libraries dialog box (**Figure 5.21**). You can choose from several color books, but PANTONE solid coated is the most commonly used book. (Feel free to experiment with the others. The vertical scroll bar will show you the range of colors in that book.) Use the scroll bar to move through the color samples; when you find one you like, select it from the list and click OK.

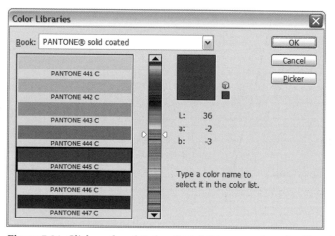

Figure 5.21 *Click on the white box for Ink 2 to access the color libraries where you'll select the color you want to use in your toned image.*

If you selected Duotone, you'll only be able to add one color to your image. Selecting the other options activates those Inks. **Figures 5.22a**, **b**, and **c** show samples of duotone, tritone, and quadtone images along with the colors selected to create the tone.

Figure 5.22a

Figure 5.22b

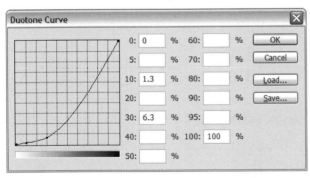

Figures 5.22a, b, and c You can achieve a range of tone effects by selecting Duotone, Tritone, or Quadtone.

Figure 5.22c

Finally, by selecting the Curve check box for any of the Inks, you can adjust the curve for that color, just like you would with the Curves control (**Figure 5.23**).

Figure 5.23 Click the Curve check box for any ink color to adjust the curve for that ink. The control works like the standard Curves control.

For example, I adjusted the curves for both Black (Ink 1) and PANTONE 436 C (Ink 3) to give **Figure 5.24** a more open look in the shadows.

Figure 5.24 *After I make adjustments to Ink 1 and Ink 3, the quadtone image takes on a new look that I think is more pleasing.*

Toned images are fun to experiment with, and can give your black-and-white prints an added appeal.

Hand-Coloring Images

Whether you add all-over color or selective color elements on a black-and-white image, hand-coloring images can be very effective with some subjects. In particular, portrait and wedding photography lend themselves well to the hand-colored treatment.

To understand how the technique works, take a look at an example.

1. Start by adding a copy of the background layer to a color image (**Figure 5.25**). The easiest way to do this is to select the Background layer and drag it to the folded page icon at the bottom of the Layers palette, creating a new layer named Background copy (**Figure 5.26**).

Figure 5.25 *Here's the original image in color.*

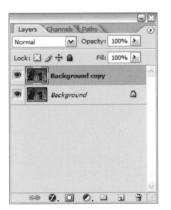

Figure 5.26 *Add a copy of the background layer to your photo by dragging the Background layer onto the new layer icon.*

2. With the Background copy layer selected, create a new adjustment layer by selecting Layer > New Adjustment Layer > Channel Mixer. (Elements users will need to create a Hue/ Saturation adjustment layer because Channel Mixer isn't part of Elements. In the Hue/Saturation control, adjust Saturation to −100 for monochrome.) Click the Monochrome check box, and adjust the color channel sliders until you see a black-and-white image you like (remember the tips you learned earlier). Your image will now look like a black-and-white conversion, but it's

Tip

You can increase the size of a brush or eraser by pressing the] key. Pressing [decreases the brush size.

ready for the magic to begin (**Figure 5.27**). Before you can work on this layer, though, you'll need to select Layer > Merge Down to apply the adjustment to the Background copy layer.

Figure 5.27 With a black-and-white version of the image on the Background copy layer, the photo is ready for you to begin hand-coloring.

3. Select the Erase tool and set it to a size that matches the area you want to have color showing through. Begin selectively erasing those areas. In the example, I want the tree to be in color while the rest of the scene remains black and white, so erase the tree leaves and branches (**Figure 5.28**).

4. Continue erasing until you're satisfied with the result. If you want to get really creative, you can adjust the opacity of the eraser to give the image a washed-out color look, similar to some old hand-colored images.

Tip

Photoshop users can eliminate the need to use a background layer. By adding a layer mask to the Channel Mixer layer, painting in black will reveal color. Changing the brush opacity will let you control the strength of the color effect.

The result is a unique-looking image that would have been extremely difficult to reproduce with conventional paints and film (**Figure 5.29**).

Figure 5.28 *As you erase the black-and-white layer, the color layer below begins to show through.*

Figure 5.29 *The final image with a colorful tree against a black-and-white background.*

This is a fun effect to play with, and one that will have you wishing you owned a graphics tablet for more control.

Creating Border and Edge Treatments

Sometimes a plain-old straight edge isn't quite what an image needs to bring it to life. When your photo is begging for that little something extra, a border or edge treatment might be just what you're looking for.

Photoshop Elements includes a selection of frame effects that you can drag and drop onto your image (**Figure 5.30**).

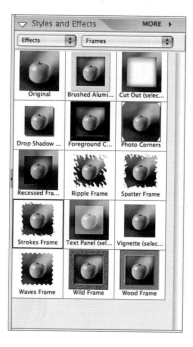

Figure 5.30 *Elements includes a number of ready-to-use frame effects that you simply drag and drop onto your image.*

To use these frames, select Effects from the Styles and Effects palette and then choose Frames. Drag the frame you want to use onto your image, and Elements will apply the effect as a new layer (**Figure 5.31**).

Figure 5.31 *After you drop the strokes frame onto the image, the edge has a custom look to it.*

Photoshop doesn't include the same frames, but you can still easily create custom borders and edges for your images. My preferred method of creating borders is to paint using a mask. To begin, make sure that you're working on a copy of the Background layer by dragging the Background layer onto the Create New Layer icon at the bottom of the Layers palette (**Figure 5.32**).

Figure 5.32 *Start off with a duplicate of your Background layer by dragging the layer to the Create New Layer icon in the Layers palette.*

Create a layer mask for the new layer by clicking the Add Layer Mask icon at the bottom of the Layers palette. Now, select the Brush tool and from the Brush palette (**Figure 5.33**), select a brush shape and size for your border.

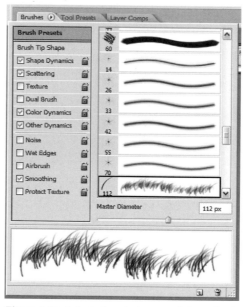

Figure 5.33 *Select a brush shape and size to begin painting your border.*

Make sure that black is the foreground color and start painting where you want your border treatment to appear. When finished, you should see something similar to **Figure 5.34**.

Another option is to add a fill layer over your image by selecting Layer > New Fill Layer > Solid Color. Click OK, and then select a color in the Color Picker dialog box that opens. Now, using the Eraser with a brush shape that you like, paint over the fill layer to reveal the image below (**Figure 5.35**). You can see the effect in the layer mask thumbnail in the Layers palette (**Figure 5.36**).

Figure 5.34 *Paint your border using black, and the result will look similar to this.*

Figure 5.35 *Add a fill layer to your image and erase parts to reveal the image below for another interesting effect.*

Figure 5.36 *As you paint your border effect, the layer mask thumbnail will update to show the areas being affected.*

Several plug-ins are also available for creating border and edge effects that give you thousands of options for customizing and creating unique borders. One of the best of these is PhotoFrame from onOne Software ($149.95, www.ononesoftware.com). PhotoFrame (**Figure 5.37**) lets you apply multiple effects to an image, control the size and color, and more.

The other plug-in that I use frequently is Photo/Graphic Edges 6.0 from Auto FX Software ($179, www.autofx.com). Photo/Graphic Edges can be used as either a plug-in, or as a stand-alone program, which makes it useful to anyone, whether or not they use Photoshop (**Figure 5.38**).

***Figure* 5.37** *PhotoFrame has thousands of options for creating frames and borders. You can use multiple frames to create your own custom effects.*

***Figure* 5.38** *Photo/Graphic Edges from Auto FX Software is another excellent option for creating borders and edge effects.*

The program includes over 10,000 effects that you can customize, and features a number of presets to show you how the effect will look. For the image in **Figure 5.39**, I selected a burned edge to complement the old feel of the barn.

You won't want to use these effects on every image, but there are times when you'll find that adding a creative border or edge treatment can improve the photo and give it a little extra pop.

Figure 5.39 *The finished border looks great and was easy to create.*

Turning a Photograph into a Painting

If you ever wished you'd learned to paint (or, in my case, wish you had the talent to paint), you're in luck. Photoshop and Elements can help you out, and such programs as Corel Painter that can do amazing things with a digital image.

Photoshop and Elements include a number of filters that you can use to give your images a more "painterly" look with very little effort. The easiest way to begin is to select Filter > Filter Gallery. Elements users can also select Filters from the Styles and Effects palette, but I recommend using Filter Gallery for easier viewing of filters and their effect (**Figure 5.40**).

I find the filters under Artistic and Brush Strokes to be the most useful for this type of effect. Selecting any filter updates the preview area to show you how the filter will look when applied to your image. Most filters have a number of sliders that you can use to control how the effect is applied.

Note

Filter Gallery does not show all of the filters included with Photoshop or any of the third-party filters you may have installed. For a complete list of filters, look in the Filters menu.

Figure 5.40 Filter Gallery in Photoshop and Elements will let you quickly turn a normal photograph into something much more "painterly."

When you have the effect you're looking for, click OK to apply it to your image. **Figures 5.41a** and **b** show examples of what's possible with the Filter Gallery.

Tip

You can apply multiple filters by clicking the New Effect Layer icon at the lower right of the Filter Gallery (it looks like a folded page). If you don't like the way a filter looks, select it and click the trash icon to delete it.

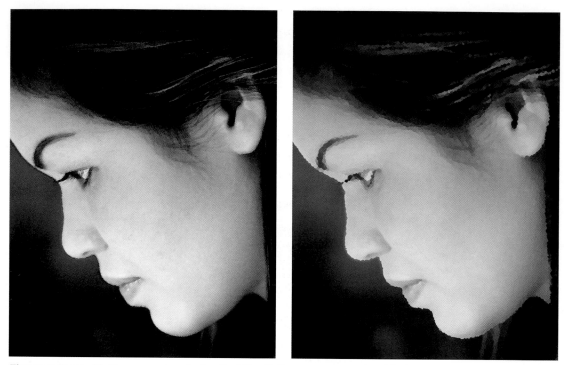

Figures 5.41a and b *Two examples of using the Filter Gallery to create a painted look. 5.41a uses the Watercolor brush, and 5.41b uses the Palette Knife brush.*

An alternative method

For really creative looks and total control over the photo-to-painting process, it's impossible to beat Painter from Corel (www.corel.com). Available in two versions, Painter Essentials (about $100) and Painter IX (about $400), this product is designed from the ground up to let you create digital paintings. The program includes a number of brushes that mimic natural artist brushes, and give you an innovative way to paint over your existing image file.

Using Painter Essentials, I'll step you through the process of creating a painting from a photograph. To give you a better idea of how much more realistic Painter can be, I'll use the same image used in the Photoshop examples.

Tip

Painting with a graphics tablet and pen works best. It's hard to beat the Wacom tablets, and as an added bonus, they include Painter Essentials with the tablet.

In Painter Essentials, select File > Open and open the photo you'll be converting. Next, select File > Quick Clone to create a copy of your image in a new window (**Figure 5.42**). The cloned image will be much lighter than your original and serves as a guide for tracing with your paintbrush.

A new feature with Essentials 3.0 is Auto-Paint, which is perfect for someone like me with little artistic talent. Click on the Cloners brush options in the upper-right corner of the window (**Figure 5.43**) and select a brush style. For this example, I selected Bristle Oil Cloner.

Figure 5.42 *Choosing Quick Clone opens a copy of your image ready to be traced over for painting.*

Figure 5.43 *Select a clone brush to begin the Auto-Paint process.*

Next, select a stroke from the Auto-Painting palette. I used Scribble Large for the example. You can also modify the stroke pressure, length, and rotation if desired, but I left these options at their defaults for the example. Finally, set the Brush Size option to the desired amount and click the Play button. Essentials will begin to

Tip

You can see how the painting is turning out by clicking the Stop button and selecting Canvas > Tracing Paper. Click Play to resume the painting process.

paint over your clone image with the brush strokes (**Figure 5.44**). When you're satisfied with the results, click the Stop button.

As Auto-Paint does its job, your clone image will fill in with brush strokes. If you decide that you want more brush strokes applied to your painting, you can click the Play button again to fill in with more strokes.

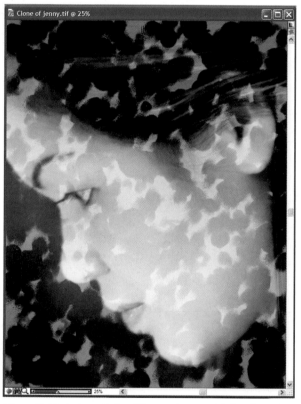

Figure 5.44 *As Auto-Paint fills your image with brush strokes, you can see the painted effect take shape.*

The finished painting, shown in **Figure 5.45**, has a very traditional look to it that you'd be hard-pressed to duplicate in another program.

Figure 5.45 *The completed painting looks very much like a traditional oil painting. When printed on canvas, it would be hard to tell this started out as a digital photograph.*

Note

For an excellent resource on using Painter, check out *The Painter IX WOW! Book* by Cher Threinen-Pendarvis (Peachpit Press, 2005).

I've only touched on what Painter and Essentials is capable of here, but if you have any interest in this type of effect, either of these programs will be a fantastic addition to your digital toolkit.

Typical Image Workflow

With so many adjustments and enhancements possible, it's easy to get overwhelmed. Where do you start? Should certain adjustments always be performed before others? When your head starts to spin, consult this typical outline of image workflow:

1. Copy your images from camera to computer.

2. Rename the image and add metadata (keywords, and so on) to your images.

3. Create a backup copy of your images on CD, DVD, or an external hard drive.

4. Open the image for editing in Photoshop or Elements.

5. Make any needed adjustments to the overall image by using Curves or Levels.

6. Correct for any color cast problems using the Levels, Color Balance, or Enhance controls.

7. Make adjustments to brightness, contrast, and saturation if needed.

8. Make adjustments to the output levels.

9. Perform any creative editing tasks such as converting to black and white, adding filters, or adding frames. Save your image as a copy to be used as the master edited file.

10. Resize your image for output (See Chapter 6).

11. Sharpen your image for output (See Chapter 6).

12. Select the proper paper profile in the Print with Preview dialog box.

13. Print your image (Chapter 7). Save your image as a print version if desired. I prefer to include the image size in the name, like "awesome_image_11x14.tif]".

14. Mount, mat, and frame as desired (Chapter 10).

Pat yourself on the back. Well done!

Moving On

You're almost ready to print! This chapter showed you how to optimize your images to prepare them for printing. The last two steps prior to printing are still ahead, though. And because they're so important, I've given them a separate chapter. To learn how to properly resize and sharpen your images, turn the page!

6 | Resizing and Sharpening Your Images

A perfect photo is a rare thing—especially straight out of the camera. Maybe the size isn't exactly as you'd like, or that branch protruding awkwardly into the frame needs to be cropped out, or the details lack sharpness. In Chapter 5, you learned some editing techniques that will improve your prints, but they won't do the whole job. You still need to properly resize and then sharpen your image.

Resizing and sharpening have a major impact on the final quality of your prints. I've seen far too many prints that suffered from poor resizing or sharpening techniques—prints with jagged edges, blurry features, and obvious sharpening artifacts. The examples in this chapter will show you how to choose the best settings for your images. You'll see the results of various settings so that you'll know how to avoid common mistakes in your own prints.

Using Image Size

Adobe Photoshop and most other image-editing programs can handle the majority of image-sizing operations with ease. I'll focus on the popular Adobe software for the examples, but other programs offer similar settings. The first stop for resizing in Photoshop and Photoshop Elements is the Image Size dialog box. In Photoshop select Image > Image Size (**Figure 6.1**) to get there; in Elements choose Image > Resize > Image Size. In both cases, the keys to good results when using Image Size are to know what to expect and how to choose the right settings.

Figure 6.1 *For most of your resizing needs, the Image Size dialog box available in Photoshop and Photoshop Elements will give you excellent results when used properly. Many other image-editing programs have similar features.*

Dimension versus Size

One of the most confusing aspects of image sizing is the difference between document size and pixel dimensions. After all, the Image Size dialog box has two sets of Width and Height fields.

The Pixel Dimensions settings refer to how large the physical image is. For example, a file that is 4500×3000 pixels will always be 4500×3000 regardless of what resolution you choose.

The Document Size settings, however, change when you change the Resolution setting. With pixel dimensions of 4500×3000, your 300 ppi image will be 15×10 inches when printed. Change Resolution to 72 ppi, which is a common screen size, and you now have a document that measures 62.5×41.667 inches!

There are still exactly the same number of pixels in the image—they are just spread out over a much larger area.

Selecting the right resolution

Of all the controls in the Image Size dialog box, Resolution will have the biggest visual impact on the quality of your prints. Screen resolution, which is also often the resolution used by digital cameras for JPEG captures, is 72 pixels per inch (ppi). This is great for on-screen viewing, but it doesn't make for a very pretty print, as you may recall from Chapter 1, "Understanding Digital Reproduction."

So how do you know what the *right* resolution is? All printers have optimal image resolutions, but in general, inkjet printers work best when using a setting of 300 ppi, or a number that is evenly divisible, such as 240 ppi, 180 ppi, 360 ppi, and so on. Knowing your printer's most effective setting can help you find a good balance between the best resolution and size for your print to get the size print you want. For high-quality prints of 8×10 inches or smaller, 300 ppi generally gives you the best results. Going up from here, some people swear they can tell the difference between a print done at 300 ppi and one done at 360 ppi. Those people are either fooling themselves or have amazing eyesight. Unless I use a loop, I can't see a quality difference between the two.

For larger prints, you need less resolution. This may sound rather odd until you realize that large prints are typically viewed from a greater distance than small ones. The increased distance gives your image the appearance of higher resolution. For 11×14-inch prints, I often go with 240 ppi, and for larger than 20×30 I may choose to print as low as 180 ppi.

Paper type can also play a role in how much resolution you need for quality results. Traditional smooth-surface papers, such as gloss or luster, need a higher resolution than a textured fine art paper, such as Moab Entrada.

Why is all of this important anyway? For once I have a simple answer! The less resizing your image needs, the higher your image quality will be when printed. Resizing the dimensions of your print means adding or subtracting pixels, which always means some image degradation.

> **Note**
>
> Believe it or not, the average billboard uses less than 72 ppi. Distance has its advantages!

Table 6.1: Print Sizes and Resolution

Print Size	Resolution (ppi)
Up to 8×10″	300 to 360
Up to 16×20″	240 to 300
20×30″ and larger	180 to 240

When you use Image Size, you'll have the best results by setting Resolution first without changing the pixel dimensions. To do this, open the Image Size dialog box and clear the Resample Image check box (**Figure 6.2**). Now enter your desired Resolution for printing. For this example, I selected 300.

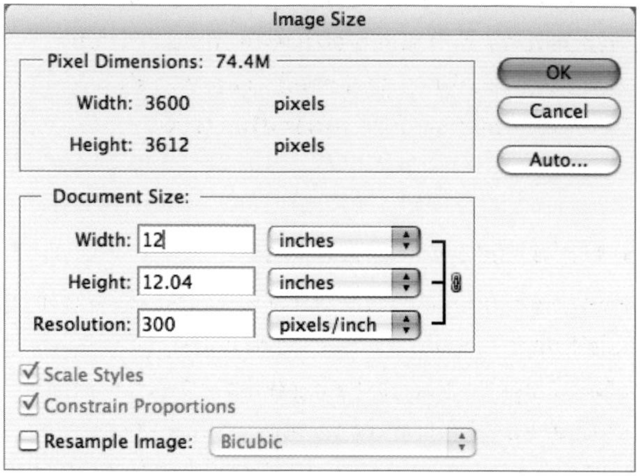

Figure 6.2 *Set your desired printing resolution first by clearing the Resample Image check box.*

With the new resolution set, click the Resample Image check box and enter the desired Width or Height in the Document Size fields (**Figure 6.3**). When you do this, you'll notice that the Pixel Dimensions settings change to reflect the new size and resolution you've selected. In the next section, I'll cover which of the Resample options to use and how each helps you.

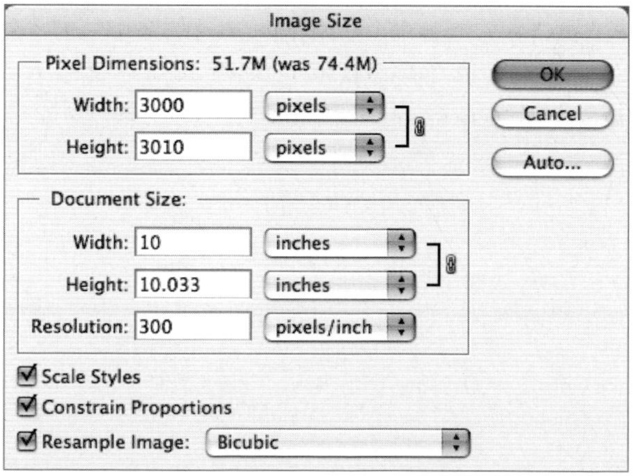

Figure 6.3 *With the desired resolution set, click the Resample Image check box and enter the document width and height for your print.*

Be sure to keep the Constrain Proportions check box selected to avoid image distortion when you resize your image. When Constrain Proportions is enabled, you need to enter only a width or a height. Photoshop sets the other dimension automatically.

Selecting the right resample options

If you need to change the pixel dimensions of your image, you must click the Resample Image check box, which provides a pop-up menu of *interpolation* options. Resampling is done by examining the pixels in your image and determining where and how to add pixels (if you're enlarging) or remove pixels (if you're reducing) to achieve the new size. If your image is 8×10 with no resizing and you want to print at 11×14, Photoshop (and any other program) needs to add pixels to fill in the space. This is where resampling and interpolation come in—depending on which option you choose, Photoshop will fill in the spaces with new pixels in an attempt to make the new size look good.

Which of the five interpolation options will work best for you? It depends on what kind of resize you're doing. For photographs, the safest choice when resizing, either larger or smaller, is Bicubic. This method works by examining the color values of surrounding pixels. Bicubic (**Figure 6.4a**) uses a set of calculations to produce smoother tonal gradations, which are applied to the image when adding or removing pixels to produce the new size.

Tip

If you've made a mistake, there's no need to click Cancel to recover. Holding the Alt key (Windows) or Option key (Mac) changes the Cancel button to Reset. This restores all the settings without closing the dialog box like Cancel does.

So that you can make an educated decision on which will work best for you and your image, here are the other options:

- **Nearest Neighbor.** The fastest interpolation method, this gets you speed by simply replicating pixels in an image. It works best with line art and illustrations and is usually a quick way to make a good photo look bad (**Figure 6.4b**).

- **Bilinear.** A more advanced method, this option averages the colors of surrounding pixels to determine the color of the new pixels. It's faster than Bicubic, but the results are not as good, particularly if you make significant changes to the image (**Figure 6.4c**).

- **Bicubic Smoother.** Designed to be used when enlarging images, this option uses the same type of interpolation as standard Bicubic but produces smoother results that work well with enlargements (**Figure 6.4d**).

- **Bicubic Sharper.** The reducing counterpart to Bicubic Smoother, this option is designed to maintain the detail in an image that is being reduced in size. Although it works well in many cases, it can oversharpen an image (**Figure 6.4e**).

For most uses, I recommend using Bicubic. If you're in a hurry, the Bicubic Smoother and Bicubic Sharper options are worth trying and often do a very good job. There is no simple rule for when these options work well, but I often find that Bicubic Sharper tends to oversharpen many images, particularly photos with people. Bicubic Smoother often does well with most enlargements, but being the control freak that I am, I prefer to leave the sharpening portion of my image editing to the right tools and with my own settings.

Tip

Although I'm a control freak, you might be perfectly content with the automatic smoothing and sharpening Bicubic Smoother and Bicubic Sharpener can give you. They're certainly worth a try; after all, you can always choose Undo and try something different!

Figure 6.4a

Figure 6.4b

Figure 6.4c

Figure 6.4d

Figure 6.4e

Figure 6.4 a through e *Compare the different interpolation methods in Photoshop's Image Size dialog box. Bicubic (a), Nearest Neighbor (b), Bilinear (c), Bicubic Smoother (d), and Bicubic Sharper (e) can produce results that are very different from each other. For most photo work, I recommend using Bicubic.*

The ten percent solution

Before Photoshop offered Bicubic Smoother for image enlargement, one of the "insider" tricks was to resample your image 10%
at a time. For reasons unknown to me, resampling an image in 10%
increments consistently gives better results when large increases
are needed.

To use this method, go to Image > Image Size, and in the Pixel
Dimension section enter **110** in either the pixel Width or pixel
Height field of the Image Size dialog box. Then, select percent from
the pop-up to change the measurement type (**Figure 6.5**). Click OK
and repeat until you've reached the size you need.

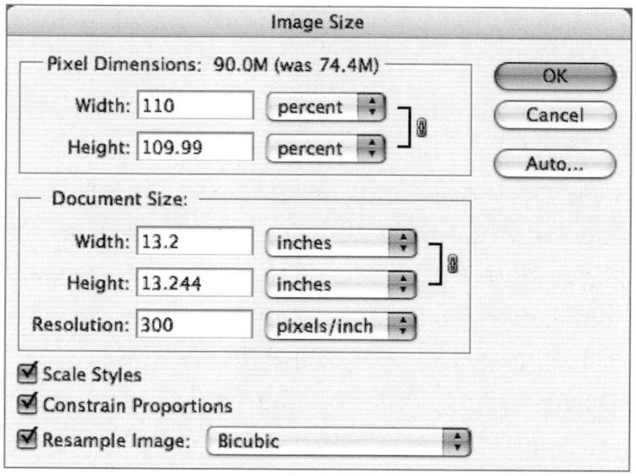

Figure 6.5 *Increasing your image in 10% increments will give
you better results than a single image size operation when you're
going for a large image.*

The difference between the two methods isn't as apparent in
Figures 6.6a and **b** as it would be in the full-size print, but you
should be able to see differences in detail levels in the fur and the
nose. This resize took the image from 12 inches all the way up to
31 inches.

Figures 6.6a and b *By resizing 10% at a time (a), you can go very large with better results than if you had done the resize in one step (b). 6.6a is the result of resizing 10% for a total of ten times.*

Using Auto Resolution

You can automatically set the resolution for your prints by selecting Auto Resolution in the Image Resize dialog box. This will open a new dialog box (**Figure 6.7**) that calculates the resolution after you enter the number of lines per inch (lpi), or *screen*, that your printer delivers as well as the quality you desire. You'd think a setting named Auto would make things easier, but the reality is that you'll need to know more about your printer than most people (and some manufacturers) can tell you.

Figure 6.7 *The Auto Resolution command works by calculating the best resolution for the number of lines per inch your printer uses.*

If you do know what the printer's screen is, what will Auto Resolution do for you? Following the established rule of thumb, it calculates resolution at 1.5 or 2 times the number of pixels per inch more than your printer's lines per inch rating. In other words, a 133 lpi screen would use a setting of 200 or 266 ppi. High-quality magazines typically use screens with 133 lpi, while a high-end fine art book might use a screen of 200 lpi. Conversely, a newspaper may only use a screen of 85 lpi.

For most uses, I recommend skipping the Auto Resolution setting and instead using the resolution guidelines in Table 6.1. If you're sending your photos to be done on an imagesetter, the printer screen might be useful information to have. In most cases the print shop should be able to tell you what resolution they want your files to be in order to get the best results from their printing process (if they can't tell you this, it's time to look for another print shop).

Other ways to resize in Photoshop

Like everything in Photoshop, there is more than one way to accomplish a resizing task. As an alternative to the Image Size dialog box, you can use the Crop tool or the Resize Image Assistant.

Tip

Clicking the double arrows between the Width and Height fields swaps the two numbers, which is great when you're switching from portrait to landscape mode.

The Crop tool is one of the quickest ways to get an exact size. When the Crop tool is selected, the toolbar updates to show Width, Height, and Resolution fields that can be set (**Figure 6.8a**). When values are entered here, any crop that you make on your image will be scaled to the exact size and resolution specified. For example, the active crop area in **Figure 6.8b** will give me exactly 8×10 inches at 300 ppi.

Figures 6.8a and b *The Crop toolbar has options to set a specific size for your image. Any crop that you create will automatically be sized to those dimensions and resolution.*

Found on the Help menu, the Resize Image Assistant (or Wizard on a PC) (**Figure 6.9**) takes you step by step through the image-sizing process. First, specify whether you'll be using the image online or in print and click Next. Photoshop will then duplicate the image.

Enter the desired document size (**Figure 6.10**), and click Next
again. The next step asks what your screen will be in lines per inch.
Choose one of the several standard options (**Figure 6.11**) or enter
a custom setting, then click Next. Finally, select the quality level
(**Figure 6.12**) you'd like. This time when you click Next Photoshop
will resize the image.

Figure 6.9 *The Resize Image Assistant, found under Photoshop's
Help menu, walks you through the process of resizing your image. The
first step is to specify whether the final result is for online or print use.*

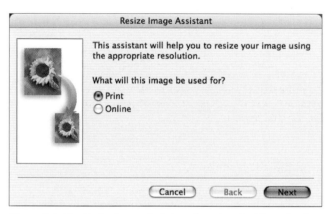

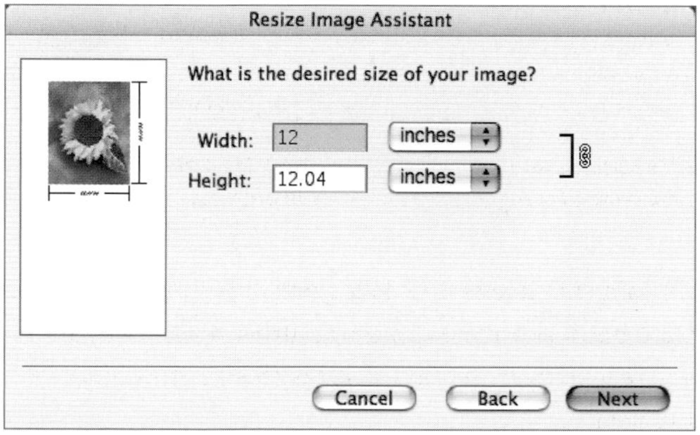

Figure 6.10 *The second step in the Resize Image Assistant asks for a
finished document size. Enter either a width or height here, and the
Assistant will provide the other dimension.*

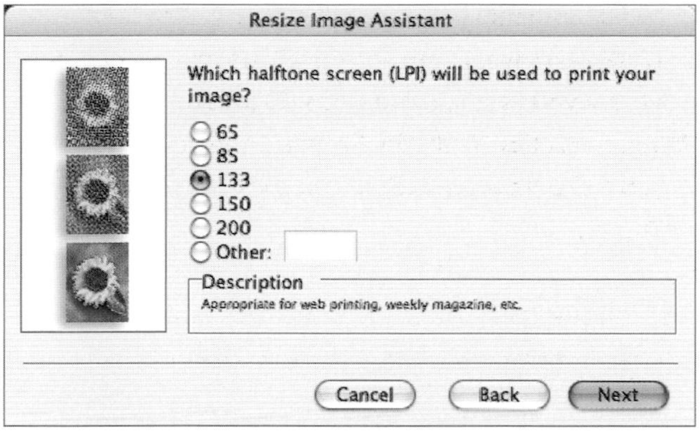

Figure 6.11 *There are several preset options for screens, or you can enter a custom value if needed. Each preset gives you feedback on what the typical use is for that setting.*

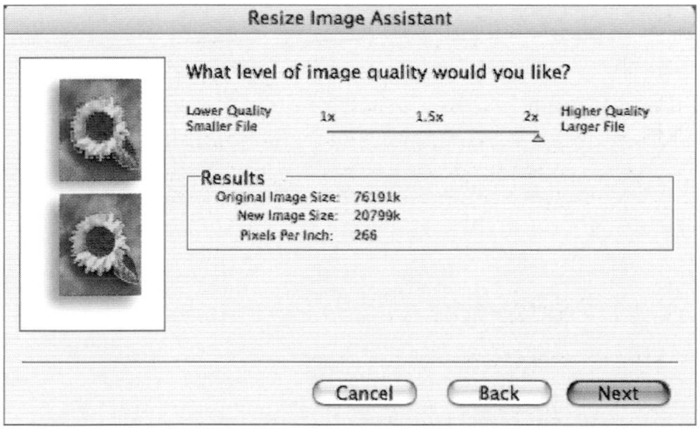

Figure 6.12 *After setting the desired quality, click Next. Photoshop will resize your document using the information you provided.*

I recommend using the Image Size dialog box rather than the Resize Image Assistant because you have more control over individual settings. If you're looking for a quick and easy resize, the Crop tool method works well.

Note

When you use the Crop tool or the Resize Image Assistant, Photoshop will perform any necessary resampling using the default setting. Normally this is Bicubic, but you can change that by selecting Edit > Preferences > General (Windows) or Photoshop > Preferences > General (Mac) and choosing a different option for Image Interpolation. I don't recommend changing from Bicubic as a default, however.

Other Sizing Techniques

Although the resizing features of Photoshop do an excellent job, especially for those times when your resizing is in what I'd consider the "normal" range of up to three or four times the original size, sometimes you just want to go big. And not just any kind of big, but *BIG* big. For those times, several specialized tools are available that can do an amazing job.

pxl SmartScale

Available from onOne Software (www.ononesoftware.com) for about $200, pxl SmartScale is a Photoshop (and compatible programs) plug-in that claims to handle enlargements of up to 1,600%. Personally I've never had an image that I wanted to enlarge that much, but it does do an excellent job at poster size and larger sizes.

You load the plug-in by selecting it from the Filters menu in Photoshop or Photoshop Elements. If you're using a different program that supports Adobe plug-in files, check your software for information on installing and using plug-ins. You can either work on an open image or let pxl SmartScale open the image for you. After the image opens into the plug-in, you'll see a very simple window with a few controls (**Figure 6.13**) that looks familiar to anyone with Photoshop experience.

Controls are available to set an exact image size, such as the 30×45 inches I used in Figure 6.13, or you can drag the scale slider to whatever size you like. For print use, I prefer to use the Document Size settings and enter my desired size here, along with the resolution.

pxl SmartScale also includes a Detail palette with controls that let you specify how you want sharpening applied to the image. Overall Sharpness controls how much sharpening or blurring is done to your image; Edge Contrast controls how strong a contrast level is applied. Extreme Edges is good for line art but should be avoided for photographs because of the unnaturally strong edges it creates.

Tip

Large images don't need as much resolution to look good. Because you will very seldom view a poster size image at the same distance as an 8×10 or smaller size, using a lower resolution means less actual resampling needs to be done. You'll likely find that using half the resolution you normally would is sufficient for a high-quality print.

Edge Detail controls how much detail is retained along edges. For most resizing operations, I recommend leaving the Details off by deselecting the Adjust Scaled Image check box. You'll typically have better results by using Unsharp Mask or Smart Sharpen in Photoshop.

One drawback to pxl SmartScale, at least in the current version (1.0.4 as I write this), is that it only works with 8-bit images. Because image resizing is typically one of the last steps in the editing process, this isn't a huge issue, but I do prefer to work in 16-bit as much as possible for the best image quality.

Figure 6.13 *pxl SmartScale has an easy-to-learn interface with plenty of power for huge enlargements. In this example, I've enlarged the image from 8×12 to 30×45 with virtually no visible loss in resolution or sharpness.*

Genuine Fractals

Genuine Fractals, now in version 4.0, has been around forever (okay, just years, but it seems like forever). The latest version has finally corrected what I always felt was a serious flaw in the program: You had to save your images in a proprietary format. You can now resize your image directly into Photoshop and avoid the entire image-conversion issue. The interface (**Figure 6.14**) is easy to use and learn, with a large preview area taking up most of the screen.

Figure 6.14 *Genuine Fractals is one of the original enlarging tools. Now in version 4, it's much more integrated with Photoshop and does a very good job with big enlargements.*

To resize, you simply enter new numbers for width or height and the desired resolution for the finished image. You can crop within Genuine Fractals if you wish, and there are tools for zooming (also available with the Navigation control) and moving around in the preview area. Once you have specified your size, click Apply to complete the resize.

Available from onOne Software for around $100, Genuine Fractals 4 works with 16-bit images and generates high-quality enlargements. It's the slowest of the options listed here, but it does a very good job.

Fred Miranda's Resize Pro

Fred Miranda (www.fredmiranda.com) offers some of the best values around in Photoshop plug-ins, and his Resize Pro plug-in is a great example of this. Where the two previous examples will each set you back $100 or more, Resize Pro is a modest $30. Resize Pro (**Figure 6.15**) offers several unique features. For example, it is available in several versions that are customized for specific camera to achieve best results. Of course, the downside to this is that you'll need separate versions if you use multiple types of cameras. Fred has versions available for most Nikon and Canon digital SLRs, as well as a few other cameras. Other special features include the ability to the sizing method: Paper, Image Size, or Percentage. Resize Pro also includes color noise reduction; although I've found this feature works well, I prefer to leave color noise reduction for a separate task in order to fine-tune my results. Resize Pro works fine with 16-bit images and lets you save your settings for future use.

Figure 6.15 *Fred Miranda's Resize Pro plug-in is a bargain and does a great job. Several versions are available, each customized to work with a specific type of camera.*

Tip

Select High ISO File if your image is a portrait, particularly with female subjects. This option keeps skin tones smoother.

To get started with Resize Pro, open your image and choose File > Automate > Resize Pro (the name will include your camera model, such as Canon 1Dm2 Resize Pro).

The Low and High ISO File settings are pretty straightforward. For most images shot at ISO 400 or lower, you should select Low ISO File.

Select the Interpolation Level based on the image type. Photos with high levels of detail should use Level 3, whereas portraits work best with Level 1. For most images, the default setting of Level 2 is fine.

As I mentioned earlier, I prefer to leave noise reduction to a separate editing task, but if you don't want to deal with it directly, Resize Pro does a good job (at the expense of slowing down the resize operation, however).

Sizing Method is a great help for preparing your images for printing. If you select Size for Paper, you can choose from a number of preset page sizes, or enter your own custom page size. If you want to maintain a border on your print, simply enter the Margin amount, and Resize Pro will handle the math to give you the size you want.

Setting Sizing Method to Image Size is useful when you're resizing for the screen or when you're working with a custom printing service that requires that any images you submit be a particular size.

PhotoZoom Professional

Formerly known as S-Spline, PhotoZoom Professional is one of the most highly regarded image resizing tools available. Available from Shortcut (www.trulyphotomagic.com) for $129, PhotoZoom Professional still uses S-Spline, which does an extremely good job of scaling images. Unlike Genuine Fractals and pxl SmartScale, PhotoZoom gives you a number of options for determining the type of resizing method used and includes presets for specific types of files such as Photo - Portrait, Photo - Detailed, and others (**Figure 6.16**).

Figure 6.16 *PhotoZoom Professional does a better job of resizing than pxl SmartScale or Genuine Fractals, but forces you to save your document and reopen it for output.*

The plug-in (a standalone application is also included) offers a number of useful options, such as preset sizes for both screen and print use and the only Unsharp Mask feature that I would use in a resizing tool. Unsharp masking in PhotoZoom Professional rivals Photoshop itself for control over the end result.

To run PhotoZoom Professional, select File > Export > PhotoZoom Professional. The right side of the window features a Preview area that is big enough to be useful, while the left side contains all the settings for the program.

By clicking the > button to the right of the size options, you can select from a number of preset print sizes. For most of us metric-phobic Americans, the preset sizes for the photo prints will be less useful. I certainly don't know what a 50×70 cm print is going to look like without converting it into inches.

Several Resize methods are available, but for best results I recommend using S-Spline. And, if you choose to use the Unsharp Mask feature, you'll find presets included for different file types.

The biggest disadvantage to using PhotoZoom Professional is that you don't just resize your image—you have to save the new image and then reopen it to complete work and print.

The bottom line on resizing

Of all the options covered here, Fred Miranda's Resize Pro does the best job with most images, providing more detail than the other options. It's also one of the fastest options. On my tests Resize Pro was over 15 times faster than Genuine Fractals 4.0, and nearly 10 times faster than pxl SmartScale. But before you go out and buy any additional resizing tools, I recommend using Photoshop's own Image Size feature. If you're not happy with the results, then check out the other options.

Once the photo has been resized to the correct dimensions, it's ready for the final step prior to printing: sharpening. If you thought there were lots of options for resizing, wait until you see what sharpening has in store! Ready?

Sharpening

Sharp details and a crisp focus are two key ingredients for a stunning photograph, but they can be very hard to achieve, especially when technology is conspiring against you. (Admit it; how many disappointments have you passed off as "I was trying for that soft focus look?") Most digital images need at least some level of sharpening help due in large part to the anti-aliasing filter most digital cameras use to help prevent jagged lines in your captures. Complications await your photo at the other end of the digital workflow too: when you print your image, some softness occurs when the ink is placed on paper. A varying amount of ink spreading, or *dot gain*, happens, giving each dot of ink a slightly soft edge. The degree of dot gain will depend on the type of ink and paper you're printing to; fine art papers are more susceptible to dot gain than the traditional style of photographic papers.

All of this comes down to recognizing that your digital images will need some degree of sharpening for the best possible output.

> **Tip**
>
> The sharpening tools covered here can do some pretty amazing things, but one thing that is beyond the capability of software is creating a well-focused image from a blurry one. If you want the best results, use the proper techniques. In other words, quit being lazy and use your tripod!

Knowing how much and when to apply that sharpening can make the difference between a good and bad print.

When sharpening is applied to an image, you are actually increasing the contrast along edges in your image, creating a halo. The ultimate goal with sharpening is to find the balance between an acceptable halo and too much (**Figures 6.17a** and **b**).

For most sharpening, I prefer to use Unsharp Mask (found in Photoshop CS2 and Photoshop Elements) or Smart Sharpen (found in CS2 only) filters, but sometimes a third-party plug-in can do a better job, or make a very difficult sharpening task much easier. In the next sections I'll walk you through how each solution works and the situations for which they're best suited.

Note

One thing you will notice is that I don't cover Photoshop's Sharpen, Sharpen More, and Sharpen Edges filters. Why? Because these options give you no control over how much sharpening is applied. Because sharpening can have such a huge impact on perceived image quality, I can't recommend using any of those options.

Figures 6.17a and b *Sharpening works by enhancing the contrast along edges in your image, creating a halo. Too much sharpening, as in 6.17a, results in a bright ugly halo that immediately screams oversharpened. In contrast, 6.17b uses the correct settings. The halo is still there, but when done properly it enhances the image rather than ruining it.*

Tip

Remember that there is no single correct setting for sharpening all images. If there were, you could just select Filter > Sharpen > Sharpen and be done with it. It would also reduce the size of this chapter by quite a bit!

Unsharp Mask filter settings

Photoshop's Unsharp Mask filter (**Figure 6.18**) is the most popular way to make sharpening adjustments to a digital image and offers a great deal of control over the way edges are enhanced. I hear you out there. "Why is it called Unsharp Mask, and why do I want to *un*sharpen my image?" The name comes from an old traditional darkroom technique in which you produced a new print by combining the original negative with a duplicate negative that was slightly out of focus. The out-of-focus, or unsharp, negative served as a mask that increased the contrast along the edges of the resulting print, giving the appearance of greater sharpness.

Figure 6.18 *The Unsharp Mask filter gives you the most control over how your image is sharpened. It's worth every bit of your time to master this filter for the best results with different printing needs.*

The digital version of Unsharp Mask (Filter > Sharpen > Unsharp Mask) works by increasing the apparent contrast between edges in your image. To use Unsharp Mask correctly, it's important to understand how each of its three slider controls—Amount, Radius, and Threshold—work and interact with each other to apply contrast to the edges. You'll find that making adjustments to the sliders is often an iterative task, with slight tweaks to one control requiring a change to one or more of the others.

Subject matter also has a huge impact on how you handle sharpening. Images with lots of fine details will be able to handle higher amounts of Unsharp Mask than a low-detail image or portrait will.

With that in mind, I'll start off with a brief description of what each control does and then go into detail on how to optimize those settings for different subject types.

Amount

The Amount slider controls how strongly the contrast effect is applied. As you increase the setting, the contrast grows stronger resulting in brighter halos. **Figures 6.19a**, **b**, and **c** show how much difference the Amount slider can make on an image.

Figures 6.19 a, b, and c Consider the difference between an unsharpened image (a), the correct Amount setting (b), and an Amount setting that's too high (c). Your ultimate goal is to enhance the edges without making the halos obvious.

Radius

The Radius slider determines the width of the halo. I feel that this is the most critical setting in Unsharp Mask and should be set first. Higher numbers work best with low-detail images and portraits, and low numbers are best for images with high levels of detail (**Figures 6.20a**, **b**, and **c**).

Figures 6.20 a, b, and c The Radius slider has more impact on a quality sharpening job than the other controls. The unsharpened image (a) has no Radius setting applied. When the correct amount is applied (b) the edges are well defined, but when the Radius is too high (c), it ruins the appearance of the image.

Threshold

The Threshold slider specifies the difference between pixel tones. The higher the number, the more contrast Photoshop requires before applying sharpening to an edge. This is an excellent way to control what portions of your image are sharpened (**Figures 6.21a** and **b**).

Figures 6.21a and b *The Threshold slider controls how much difference Photoshop must find between pixel values before considering them an edge. 6.21a has a high Threshold setting applied, which means that very few edges will be found. This is a good choice for skin tones. The low setting in 6.21b causes almost everything in the image to be considered an edge, resulting in a very contrasty image.*

Examples of Unsharp Mask in action

You've got the theory; now take a look at how to use Unsharp Mask to sharpen some real examples of different subject types: a portrait, a landscape, and a macro image. With all of these examples, I start out by estimating the Radius and then setting the Amount. I use Threshold last to fine-tune the sharpening effect. The first step is to open the Unsharp Mask filter by selecting Filter > Sharpen > Unsharp Mask.

The portrait

For the first example, consider the portrait in **Figure 6.22**. The typical portrait has less contrast than many other subjects, with large areas of skin that you'll want to keep smooth and natural looking.

Tip

When using Unsharp Mask, always work with your image at 100% size. Using a smaller-than-actual-size view to make these adjustments is nearly impossible.

Tip

Clicking on the actual image (not the preview) centers that point in the Preview window of the Unsharp Mask dialog box. This is much easier than dragging the image around in the preview.

Figure 6.22 *Portraits don't need to be sharp everywhere. In fact, you'll want to keep skin areas looking smooth, which means using higher Radius and Threshold settings with lower Amount settings.*

I knew that I wanted to keep the skin areas looking smooth to avoid making blemishes and other features too prominent. To do this, I used a higher Radius setting to spread the effect out over a wider area and make it less obvious (**Figure 6.23**).

Portraits are normally in the 2.0 to 3.5 range for Radius. After some experimentation, a setting of 2.6 gave me the result I was looking for. Next I turned my attention to Amount. Remember that Amount controls how strong the contrast effect is, with higher numbers giving you a stronger effect. Because I wanted to avoid strong contrast, I kept the Amount setting relatively low (**Figure 6.24**).

Figure 6.23 *First adjust Unsharp Mask's Radius slider for the portrait. I'm using a higher setting here to keep the effect from being too obvious.*

Figure 6.24 *Next set Amount. If you don't want a strong effect, a lower number here is best.*

The final Amount setting I used for the example was 90%. You'll typically find that settings in the range of 70% to 130% are good for portraits.

The last setting is Threshold. Because I wanted the sharpening to be applied very selectively, I used a high number here (**Figure 6.25**).

Figure 6.25 *The last adjustment to my portrait is with the Threshold slider. Using a higher number keeps the sharpening from being applied to areas that should look smooth.*

Threshold will vary quite a bit depending on the look you're after. On average, though, a setting in the 6 to 12 range is good for most subjects.

Figures 26a and **b** provide a before-and-after comparison with my final sharpening settings.

Figures 6.26a and b *Before sharpening, the entire image looks a little soft (a). After the correct Unsharp Mask settings are applied, there is a good balance between areas of sharpness and smooth skin tones (b).*

The landscape

Landscape and nature photographs often have large areas that should contain well-defined edges combined with other areas, such as sky or water, where you want to maintain smooth tones. For **Figure 6.27**, for example, I wanted to have as much detail as possible in the rocks and trees while leaving the sky and water smooth.

Figure 6.27 *The first adjustment to my landscape is with the Radius slider. I'm using a middle setting here to keep the effect from being too obvious in the sky while still providing enough contrast to the edges in the other areas to increase sharpness.*

For this image, a setting of 1.2 gave me a good balance between detail on the ground and sky. A typical setting for this style of image is in the 0.8 to 2.0 range. Lower numbers are best for more contrast, and you'll want to use a higher setting when larger areas of your image need less contrast.

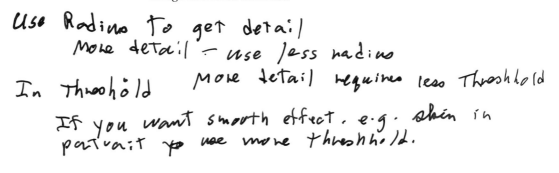

Use Radius to get detail
    More detail — use less radius
In Threshold   More detail requires less Threshold
    If you want smooth effect. e.g. skin in
    portrait to use more threshhold.

The Amount setting is higher than what I used for portraits because I wanted the effect to be more obvious, giving the image a higher degree of apparent detail (**Figure 6.28**).

Figure 6.28 *A higher Amount setting gives the image more apparent sharpness in areas of fine detail.*

This image worked best with an Amount setting of 160%. On average, a setting between 120% and 200% works well for landscapes.

The Threshold setting for my landscape is a much lower number than I used for portraits because I wanted the filter to find more edges, especially in the rocks and trees (**Figure 6.29**).

Figure 6.29 *The final adjustment to the landscape is with the Threshold slider. I use a fairly low number to maximize the sharpness in the rocks and trees.*

A setting of 3 added the detail I was looking for to the image without causing problems in the sky areas. In general, a range of 0 to 6 is appropriate for this type of image; use higher numbers when you need less detail, such as a scene with large amounts of sky or smooth water.

Figures 6.30a and **b** provides a before-and-after comparison with my final sharpening settings.

Figures 6.30a and b *Before sharpening, the entire image looks a little soft (a). After the correct settings have been used in Unsharp Mask, a good balance exists between areas of detail and the sky (b).*

The macro image

The final example is a macro image where I want the most detail possible. For this image, I used a very small Radius setting of 0.5 because there are so many edges in the scene (**Figure 6.31**).

Figure 6.31 *A low setting for the Radius slider keeps my edges smaller, which is important in a photo like this with a high level of detail.*

After setting the Radius, I moved to Amount to further enhance the photo's high detail level. A setting of 300% was the best choice (**Figure 6.32**).

Figure 6.32 *A high Amount setting works well for this type of image to enhance the edges as much as possible.*

I often use settings above 200% for images like this one, and occasionally as high as 375%.

The final setting was to Threshold. Again, because of the high level of detail in the image, I wanted to have as many edges defined as possible. This meant a low setting for Threshold—in this case a setting of 1 worked best (**Figure 6.33**).

Figure 6.33 *A very low Threshold setting increases the number of edges that will be sharpened.*

You'll often find that macros and other highly detailed images have a Threshold setting of 0 to 3.

Figures 6.34a and **b** provide a before-and-after comparison with my final sharpening settings.

Figures 6.34a and b *Before sharpening the entire image looks a little soft. After the correct settings have been used in Unsharp Mask, the entire image looks sharper, with much better definition.*

Using Smart Sharpen

Smart Sharpen (Filter > Sharpen > Smart Sharpen) is new to Photoshop CS2. It includes some excellent features that offer more control than you get with Unsharp Mask. Smart Sharpen is especially helpful for controlling how shadows and highlights are sharpened. The filter also has a couple of features (**Figure 6.35**) that improve its usefulness. The most obvious of these is the larger preview area, which defaults to 100%, thus making it easier to see what effect your settings have on the image. The other major difference from other Sharpen filters is the option to work in Basic or Advanced mode. Let's take a closer look at Smart Sharpen's settings.

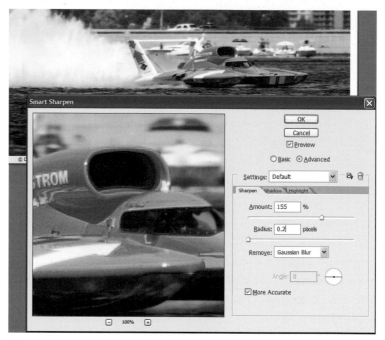

Figure 6.35 *New to Photoshop CS2, Smart Sharpen offers a number of features that have made it a good replacement choice for many sharpening tasks.*

Amount and Radius

These two sliders operate exactly the same as Amount and Radius do in Unsharp Mask. Rather than repeat myself, I'll spare you and just refer back to the previous topic.

Remove

Below the Amount and Radius sliders lives a new control, Remove. This controls how the sharpening is applied to your image and has three options. The default setting of Gaussian Blur is the same method used by Unsharp Mask. Lens Blur optimizes the sharpening method to maintain fine detail while minimizing the size of halos. The third option is Motion Blur. Don't get your hopes up thinking this is going to correct those images where you didn't hold the camera steady, but for very minor problems, Motion Blur can help you out. When you select this option, the Angle control becomes active, letting you specify the direction of the blur. You can make changes by clicking anywhere on the circle, dragging the line, or entering a value in the field next to the control.

More Accurate

This one's real simple. Use it. Period. Selecting this check box does slow the performance some but it also gives you better results with the final sharpening. And if you're going to take the time to sharpen your image, don't you want the best results you can get?

Advanced Options

The Advanced Options, activated by selecting the Advanced Radio button, give you access to the features that help make Smart Sharpen so compelling (**Figure 6.36**). The Shadow and Highlight tabs both have the same set of controls to determine how much or how little sharpening should be applied to these areas of your image. The difference is where the Fade, Tonal Width, and Radius will be applied.

Figure 6.36 *The Advanced Options in Smart Sharpen are the main reason to use this new feature. From here you can control how much sharpening is applied to shadow and highlight areas of your image.*

Tip

Clicking on the Edit field will let you adjust the amount with the up and down arrows on your keyboard for more control.

The Fade Amount controls how strongly the sharpening is reduced. Lower values mean less reduction while higher values result in more reduction, or less sharpening, in those areas. It works best to start out at 0% and slowly increase the amount until the effect is reduced by the desired amount.

Tonal Width sets how wide a range of tones will be affected by the Fade Amount. Lower values affect only the extreme ends of the tonal range (dark pixels for shadows, bright pixels for highlights). Higher numbers expand the range of tonal values that will be affected. I have never used a value above 40.

Radius determines how far the filter should look to determine if a pixel is part of the shadow or highlight area. I don't find this setting to be particularly useful—I see very little difference between the minimum and maximum settings—so I just leave it at the default.

Luminance sharpening

Lots of experts recommend using Photoshop CS's Lab mode and sharpening the Lightness channel, affecting only the luminance of the image while leaving the color channels alone. The method works fine, but I don't feel that any real benefit is gained even though I've tried many times to make it a better solution. Still, if you'd like to try it for yourself, it's easy enough to do. This feature is a Photoshop-only option.

The first step is to convert your image by selecting Image > Mode > Lab Color. Now select the Channels palette (**Figure 6.37**) and click on the Lightness channel.

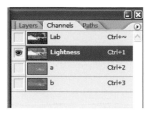

Figure 6.37
You'll need to convert your image to the Lab color space before trying Luminance sharpening.

The image is displayed in grayscale. You're then ready to begin the actual sharpening with Unsharp Mask or Smart Sharpen.

Selective sharpening

There will be times when no single method is just right for your image. Perhaps it's a portrait where you want a soft, dreamy feeling to everything but the eyes and lips. No combination of Radius, Amount, and Threshold is going to work for what you're trying to do. It's time to bring layer masks and selective sharpening to the rescue.

You might recall that I spent a great deal of time in Chapter 5, "Editing Your Photos," talking about adjustment layers and layer masks as part of the image-editing process. They work very well for sharpening too.

To begin with, open your image and duplicate the background layer (**Figure 6.38**) by either dragging it to the New Layer button at the bottom of the Layers palette, or by selecting Ctrl+J/Cmd+J (Windows/Mac).

Figure 6.38
Duplicate the background layer to begin creating a selective sharpening layer.

Now apply the sharpening you want to the copy of your background layer, concentrating on the areas you want to sharpen, such as the eyes in **Figure 6.39**.

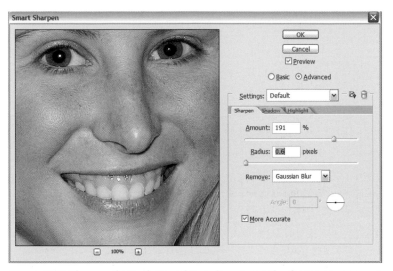

Figure 6.39 *Sharpen the Background Copy layer to get the sharpness you want in the critical areas, ignoring the rest of the image for now.*

Now it's time to make the adjustments that will confine your sharpening to only those areas you wish to retain. You can either start off by making a selection, such as the lips or eyes, or go straight to a layer mask. I find that it's easier for me to work with a selection first whenever possible (**Figure 6.40**). You should also feather the selection to create a softer edge for the transition between the sharpened layer and the original layer. You can do this by choosing Select > Feather (Alt+Ctrl+D/Option+Cmd+D) and choose a number that gives you a smooth transition between the soft and sharp areas. For this sample, I selected 3 pixels.

Tip

You can create multiple selections like the ones around the eyes in Figure 6.40 by holding down the Shift key and drawing a new selection.

Figure 6.40 *Select the areas in which you want to retain sharpness and then create a layer mask.*

Regardless of your choice (to select first or to mask first), the next step is to create a layer mask by clicking the Add Layer Mask button at the bottom of the Layers palette. If you started with a selection, you'll see it rendered in the layer mask thumbnail next to the image thumbnail (**Figure 6.41**).

Figure 6.41
After creating your layer mask with a selection, you'll see an additional thumbnail next to the image thumbnail in the Layers palette. Make sure the layer mask is active before continuing.

That's it! The layer mask has hidden everything except your selection, in this example the eyes. Compare the starting and ending versions, and you can see that along with smoothing out the skin tones, the new version has eyes that are in better focus (**Figures 6.42a** and **b**).

Figures 6.42a and b *The before image (a) needs a little correction, but softening the skin will also soften the eyes. The after image (b) shows the end result after using a selection and layer mask to create sharper eyes.*

You might not be able to start out with a selection, though, or you might need to clean up your selection after creating the mask. For this work, you'll use the Paintbrush tool to hide or reveal detail in your masking layer. Before starting out, be sure that the colors are set to the default black and white. You can do this by either pressing the D key or by clicking the small icon in the lower-left corner below the color squares.

The important thing to remember when painting selections is that black hides and white reveals the contents or effect of that layer. To get started, copy your Background layer as you did in the previous example, by dragging it to the New Layer button at the bottom of the Layers palette.

Apply the Unsharp Mask or Smart Sharpen filter on the Background Copy layer as you did in the previous example, again focusing on the eyes as the main area of sharpness.

Now create a layer mask by clicking the Layer Mask button at the bottom of the Layers palette. For large areas that I want to keep hidden, I use the Paint Bucket and fill the entire layer with black, then switch to white and reveal the areas I want sharpened. Select a brush size that works well for the area you want to reveal, and set the Hardness of the brush to a low number in order to create a soft transition between the layers.

Make sure that white is the active color and paint over the eyes with the brush tool. As you paint, you'll see the eyes becoming sharper while the rest of the image retains the soft look of the Background layer. If you want to see what you've made visible, click the eye icon next to the Background layer to hide that layer (**Figure 6.43**).

Tip

You can quickly change the brush size by using the left and right bracket keys ([and]).

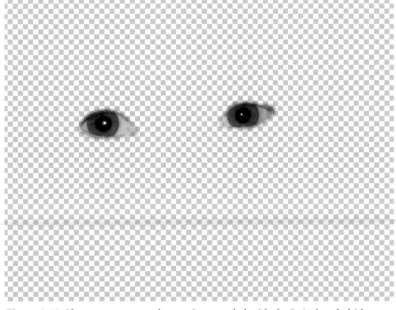

Figure 6.43 *If you want to see what you've revealed with the Paintbrush, hide the Background layer. Only those areas that have been painted in white will be visible.*

By using various settings for Opacity and brush hardness, you have total control over what is revealed with a layer mask, making this an ideal solution for selective sharpening.

Other sharpening methods

Although you can handle any sharpening task with Photoshop's own tools, sometimes it's easier to use a plug-in that can handle advanced selection and sharpening needs much quicker, and often with better accuracy. Two of the best options available are PhotoKit Sharpener and nik Sharpener Pro 2.0. And although both do excellent work, they take entirely different approaches to the task.

PhotoKit Sharpener

Available for about $100, PhotoKit Sharpener from PixelGenius (www.pixelgenius.com) has a number of options geared toward various sharpening needs. It's not the most intuitive or user-friendly tool available, but the results are hard to beat (**Figure 6.44**). One very nice feature is that all of the layers used to create the sharpening effect are retained, making it easy to modify individual settings if needed, or just learn how the program works to apply the techniques on your own. PhotoKit Sharpener isn't a filter but a set of scripts. You launch it by selecting File > Automate > PhotoKit Output Sharpener (there are other options here for capture and scanning, as well as creative effects, but because this is a book on printing, we want the Output Sharpener).

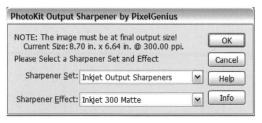

Figure 6.44 *PhotoKit Sharpener has a number of options for different sharpening needs. The tool works extremely well and is useful for learning how advanced sharpening tasks can be done.*

There are two sets of options in the Output Sharpener. Sharpener Set selects the output device type, whether continuous tone, halftone, inkjet, or screen use, and Sharpener Effect has settings for each output type. In the example image, I've selected the Inkjet Output Sharpeners as the Set, and 300 Matte as the Effect. This effect is optimized for printing a 300 ppi on matte finish paper. It's important to select the correct printer type and print resolution to get the best results.

nik Sharpener Pro2

nik Sharpener Pro 2.0 (nik Multimedia, www.nikmultimedia.com) works as a plug-in and has a more traditional look to it. By default, it starts out with its own floating window, but it's also available from the Filters menu. The Complete Pro version ($329.95) includes sharpening filters for every type of output device you might encounter (there is also an Inkjet edition for $160 less). With Sharpener Pro, once you specify the type of output device you'll be using a window opens with optimized settings for that printer (**Figure 6.45**). You make adjustments to how the sharpening is done by setting the image size, viewing distance, paper type, and printer resolution.

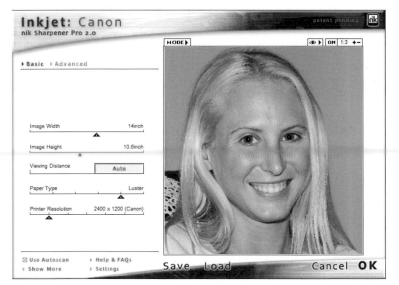

Figure 6.45 *The Sharpener Pro interface is easy to use and offers a number of controls tuned to the chosen output device.*

If you want total control over the sharpening, you can select Advanced to access sliders that enable control over the amount of sharpening applied to different color ranges. You also have the option to selectively apply the effects by painting or erasing them from areas of your image, making this an alternative approach to the selective sharpening technique covered a bit earlier in the chapter.

Moving On

This chapter may have only covered two subjects, but when it comes to printing, there are few subjects more important than proper image sizing and sharpening. Without the proper techniques, you can easily create a print that has you headed straight for the trash can.

I recommend working on your image sizing and sharpening tasks in the order discussed in this chapter. Resizing your image should come after your other editing tasks, and sharpening should be done only after your image is resized, and only for the intended output.

Now that we've dispensed with all of the image-editing and preparation tasks, it's time to go on to Chapter 7 where the magic happens: printing your images.

7 | Printing Your Files

Everything up to this point has been in preparation for the main event—printing your digital photos. With color management options correctly set, and your image editing complete, it's time to let your printer generate that masterpiece. Whether it's a family vacation snapshot, a formal portrait, or a fine art landscape, it's not enough to simply make your image corrections and hit the Print button. Choosing the correct paper type and printer settings will ensure that your prints match your vision.

In Chapter 4, "Using Printer Settings," you learned the basics of working with your printer driver. This chapter will build on those concepts to cover the proper settings for printing images from Adobe Photoshop CS2 and Photoshop Elements, as well as discuss when printing from a raster image processor (RIP) is a good option.

Selecting the Media

Outside of color management settings, the media you choose to print on will have the biggest impact on how your photo looks. Although printers used to provide limited paper choices (and all but inkjet printers still do), a wide variety of papers (and in many cases, inks) are available that you can use to get exactly the look your image requires.

Paper choices

Most photos are printed on papers that mimic the look and feel of traditional photo papers, but there are other choices. Resin-coated (RC) papers are available in both gloss and semigloss finishes that are familiar to anyone who has had a roll of film developed and printed. Another common paper type is a matte finish. Not so common are art papers, which are a close cousin to the matte finish papers but have more variety in their weight and surfaces.

The majority of photos will look fine with any of these finishes, but most people prefer the RC papers. Let's take a closer look at each of the paper types and their advantages and disadvantages.

RC papers

Photos printed on resin-coated papers, available in gloss or semi-gloss (also referred to as luster), are the closest approximations you'll find to traditional darkroom style prints. In fact, with few exceptions, when you go to a photo lab or use one of the kiosks for printing your images, gloss and semigloss are likely the only options you have for your prints. Both papers work well for a variety of image types and will do the best job of retaining detail in your photos. So, if you have lots of small details or fine patterns in your photo, choose one of these papers for the best results. The choice between gloss and semigloss is mainly one of personal preference. I tend to favor semigloss for most prints, but I'll often choose a gloss finish for photos with vibrant colors and for some black-and-white portraits.

The drawback to RC papers is their print life. Typically RC will have the shortest display life of any of the paper types due to the way the ink is absorbed by the coating on the paper. Rather than soaking into the paper itself, the ink is contained in the resin coating. This is why images retain more detail—and also explains why they don't last as long.

Matte papers

Matte-finish papers follow closely behind the RC papers in both popularity and wide support. Every inkjet printer manufacturer offers a matte finish. These papers look and feel more like a normal heavy sheet of paper rather than a photo paper, and are well suited to fine art, landscape, and portrait subjects. Matte papers tend to have a more textured surface, which is less favorable to fine details.

Matte papers will typically last at least as long as RC paper prints; depending on the type, they can last even longer.

Note

Regardless of what paper type you select, unless it's properly displayed it isn't going to last as long as it could. Display life for an unframed print is often less than half that of a properly framed print on the same paper. Chapter 10, "Presenting Your Work," shows you how to correctly mount and frame your prints for the best results.

Note

For more details on expected print life, refer to the chart in Chapter 2, "Setting Up a Print Studio."

Fine art papers

Although they may resemble matte paper, fine art papers deserve their own section because they are available in such a huge variety of surfaces, weights, and even color. For many photographers, fine art papers are used for their best work or for limited-edition prints. It takes more work to get a good print on a fine art paper than it does with the normal inkjet papers, but when it's done right the results can be stunning.

Fine art papers tend to be heavier in weight than the typical paper and may not work in some printers, particularly those that have a bent paper path such as some of the HP PhotoSmart or Canon printers. So be sure to check your printer manual to see the thickness of paper it can handle. The best papers are made with 100% rag content, which makes them excellent for archival and long print life.

There are way too many choices to list separately, but one of my favorites is Moab Entrada (www.moabpaper.com), which is available in 190 and 300 grams per square meter (gsm) and in natural and bright-white finishes. I do most of my limited-edition prints on Entrada 300 Natural. Entrada is also a double-sided paper and works well for portfolio prints.

Hahnemühle (www.hahnemuhle.com) is a German company that has been making paper for a few hundred years now. It offers several different fine art papers. Its Torchon and Albrecht Dürer have a textured surface similar to a watercolor paper, and its German Etching features a smooth finish that works well when you want to retain detail in your prints but still have the advantage of a heavy fine art paper.

The disadvantage to these paper types is primarily the cost. Plan on spending over $1.00 a sheet for 8×10 prints and $5.00 or more for a 16×20 print. This is obviously not a paper for trial-and-error experiments!

Note

If you want to make a really strong impression, Hahnemühle has a Certificate of Authenticity and Hologram system that you might be interested in. The package of 100 certificates and matching numbered holograms tie the print together for a true limited-edition series.

Some of the printer manufacturers offer fine art papers as well, most notably Epson with its UltraSmooth Fine Art, Somerset Velvet, and Textured Fine Art. Canon uses Hahnemühle for their wide-format professional series printers.

Another major drawback to using fine art papers, in addition to the cost, is getting accurate profiles. Many of the paper companies provide profiles for the more popular printers, and all of them have suggestions for which settings to use with your printer. But for the cost of this paper you'll want to use the correct profiles—even if it means creating your own, or having one made (see the section "Custom Profiles," later in this chapter).

> **Tip**
>
> Many of the paper companies offer sample packages with one or two sheets of each paper type. This is a great way to try the papers on your printer before investing in a package of 50 sheets or a full roll.

Ink choices

This one is easy. With very few exceptions I suggest sticking with your printer manufacturer's inks. The quality will be consistent, and you know the ink will work properly in your printer. It might seem as if you're paying more for the name-brand ink, but in the long run you'll be much better off. Those cheap replacement inks and refill kits available online and at the office supply stores are not only a waste of money but a waste of time as well. Quality varies widely from one batch to the next, and most printer profiles are useless with these inks. There are a few exceptions to the rule, of course.

Pantone ColorVANTAGE

If anyone knows about color, it should be Pantone, right? After all, Pantone (www.pantone.com) is the standard for color consistency. The company offers the ColorVANTAGE ink set for several printers (currently wide-format Epson models). They offer a wider color gamut than the Epson UltraChrome inks, providing a more saturated and vibrant print with better blacks. I've switched to the ColorVANTAGE inks in my Epson 4000 printer for all my color printing and I've enjoyed consistently excellent results. For best

results, you'll want to download the Pantone-created printer profiles that are available for most popular papers.

Media Street

Media Street (www.mediastreet.com) has a variety of inks for most
printers. Its Generations ink, along with its Niagara Continuous
feed system, is a good replacement for Canon, HP, and Epson inks.
One advantage the Media Street inks give to Canon and HP users
is the longer print life associated with pigment inks. Media Street
features a line of papers as well as a full set of printer profiles for
most common paper types.

Perhaps the most interesting area for specialty inks is the monochrome ink sets such as Media Street's Generations QuadBlack. This
setup uses two black inks along with four shades of gray ink for true
black-and-white print results.

Lyson

Lyson (www.lyson.com) is another well-respected source for black-
and-white ink sets. I've used Lyson's Daylight Darkroom system
with outstanding results. Combining a full set of grayscale inks
along with papers and profiles optimized for its inks, the Daylight
Darkroom system is capable of black-and-white prints that are
indistinguishable from traditional darkroom prints.

Many other specialized ink sets are available as well. You'll find a
listing of some popular ones in Appendix A, "Resources."

Soft proofing

As I mentioned earlier, some of the fine art papers are very pricey,
so getting the right prints on the first try is more important than
ever. Luckily, Adobe Photoshop CS2 has a feature that lets you
check your prints before you hit the Print button. This feature,

Note

Both the Daylight Darkroom
and Generations QuadBlacks
require the use of special print
drivers known as RIPs for best
results. I'll cover this printing
method later in the section
"Selecting and Using a RIP."

known as soft proofing, simulates on screen how the colors in your photo will look on paper with the selected printer profile.

To get started, begin with your image open and select View > Proof Setup > Custom. You'll see the Customize Proof Condition dialog box, shown in **Figure 7.1**.

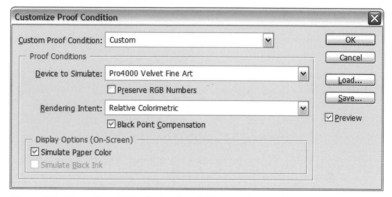

Figure 7.1 Photoshop CS includes the ability to soft-proof, or simulate, the colors of your print before committing it to paper.

The Customize Proof Condition dialog box lets you specify what device to simulate, and typically you'll select your printer and paper profile here. In the example shown, I've told Photoshop to use the Epson Pro 4000 printer and Velvet Fine Art paper. All of your installed profiles are available from the drop-down list, which gives you a nice way to preview what your print will look like on different papers without actually printing (**Figures 7.2a** and **b**).

The Preserve RGB Numbers option simulates how the colors will look without being converted to the output device being simulated. This option is best used when printing to a CMYK device or an application such as Adobe InDesign. For photo printing, I recommend leaving this option off.

Figure 7.2a and b *Using soft proofing lets you see how your photo will look on paper. 7.2a shows the normal view when working in Adobe RGB. When I soft-proof the image for Epson Velvet Fine Art paper (b), the color shift is easy to see and allows me to make adjustments if necessary.*

The Rendering Intent option determines how colors will be converted from one color space to the other. In this example, I'm going from Adobe RGB to Epson Pro 4000 Velvet Fine Art. Because every device interprets color differently, some type of

Note

For more details on color spaces and color management, see Chapter 3, "Keeping an Eye on Color."

color mapping is required to get the best results. Your choices for Rendering Intent are:

- **Perceptual.** Preserves the visual relationship between colors to keep all changes as natural as possible. It's best used with photos that contain out-of-gamut colors since it does the best job of mapping those colors to ones that will fit within the new color space.

- **Saturation.** Sacrifices accuracy for vibrancy. It works great for graphics and charts but isn't appropriate for photos.

- **Relative Colorimetric.** Works by looking at the highlight of the source color space and compares it to what the destination is capable of. All colors are then shifted to the closest reproducible color. Relative Colorimetric is the default for printing in the United States and Europe.

- **Absolute Colorimetric.** Ignores colors that are outside of the destination gamut. It keeps color accuracy as close as possible, but out-of-gamut colors will not be reproduced accurately.

For most printing situations, I prefer to use Relative Colorimetric. Some custom profiles are created with the Perceptual intent. If this is the case for your profiles, then select Perceptual.

The Black Point Compensation option simulates the full dynamic range of the output device. Click this check box to ensure that shadow detail is preserved.

The Simulate Paper Color check box, when supported by the selected profile, enables you to simulate the white color of the paper (it's amazing to see how white some paper isn't).

The final option, Simulate Black Ink, is also available only when supported by the profile. When this option is selected, blacks are rendered with the gray color many printers use in place of a true black ink.

If you find yourself using the same settings frequently, you can save them for future use. Saved settings are available from both the Customize Proof Condition dialog box and from the Proof Setup menu.

Gamut Warning

Photoshop CS2's Gamut Warning option is your other good friend when you're proofing your image prior to print. When colors are out of gamut, they can't be reproduced accurately on the output device. When you print to a CMYK device, the gamut is typically smaller than what the RGB device, whether inkjet or monitor, is capable of. By selecting Gamut Warning (View > Gamut Warning), you can quickly check your image for colors that will be troublemakers during the print process. **Figures 7.3a** and **b** show how Gamut Warning can identify potential problem areas in your image.

Gamut Warning is most useful when you're sending your prints out to a device that you aren't familiar with, such a prepress printer. Choosing this option can save you quite a bit of time and money when you're paying someone else to print your photos.

Figures 7.3a and b *Using Gamut Warning can identify potential problems with colors that might not display properly when the photo is printed. 7.3a shows the normal view, and 7.3b shows the same image with Gamut Warning turned on. The gray areas indicate potential print problems.*

To correct for out-of-gamut colors, you can make adjustments to saturation by selecting Image > Adjustment > Hue/Saturation, or you can quickly make adjustments to specific colors by opening the Color Picker (**Figure 7.4**). With the Color Picker open, clicking an out-of-gamut area in your image displays a warning triangle with a color box that contains the closest match in gamut color. Clicking the color or the triangle replaces the out-of-gamut color with the safe one.

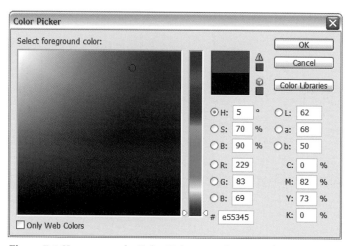

Figure 7.4 *You can use the Color Picker to replace out-of-gamut colors in your image with safe colors. Click an out-of-gamut area in your image to display the closest matching color. Clicking this color replaces the current one.*

Printing

Finally! It's time to print that image that you've been working on. It took a while to get here, but isn't it nice to know that you have the image just as you want it and you are confident that it will print as close to what you see on screen as possible?

Using Print with Preview

Photoshop and Photoshop Elements include multiple ways to print your images. The best method, and the only one that I recommend using, begins with the Print with Preview dialog box, which gives you complete control over the settings that will be used by Photoshop and your printer.

To open Print with Preview from Photoshop, choose File > Print with Preview. (I'll cover the Elements method in a bit). Photoshop's Print with Preview dialog box will most likely look similar to **Figure 7.5**, with options for positioning the image on the page, scaling the image to a particular size, and access to the Print and Page Setup options for your printer. All of the real power is still hidden from view.

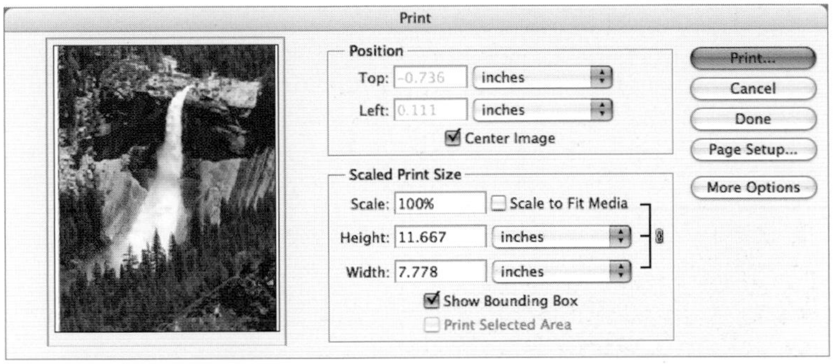

Figure 7.5 *The first time you open Print with Preview, all of the really good stuff is hidden from view. Click More Options to correct this.*

By default, Photoshop turns on Center Image, which, logically enough, centers the image on the page. You might be surprised to select this option and see that your image isn't actually on the center of the printed page, though. Most printers use different margins for the sides, top, and bottom of the page. Selecting Center Image ignores these margins, but when the printer takes over, the image is placed in the center of the printable area of the page.

By turning off Center Image, you can position your image anywhere on the page you want by either entering a Top and Left position or by dragging the preview image to a new location on the page.

Scaled Print Size works well for small changes in size, and is most often used in combination with the Scale to Fit Media check box. The resizing you achieve using this feature isn't as good as you'll get using the resizing options covered in Chapter 6, "Resizing and Sharpening Your Images," so for anything other than slight adjustments to fit the page, I recommend that you not use Scaled Print Size.

You can size your image by checking Show Bounding Box in the Scaled Print Size area and dragging on the corner handles of the image preview.

If your Print with Preview looks like Figure 7.5 on your computer, click the More Options button. This opens up a new set of controls with options for output (**Figure 7.6**) and color management. For photographs, we're interested in the Color Management options (**Figure 7.7**).

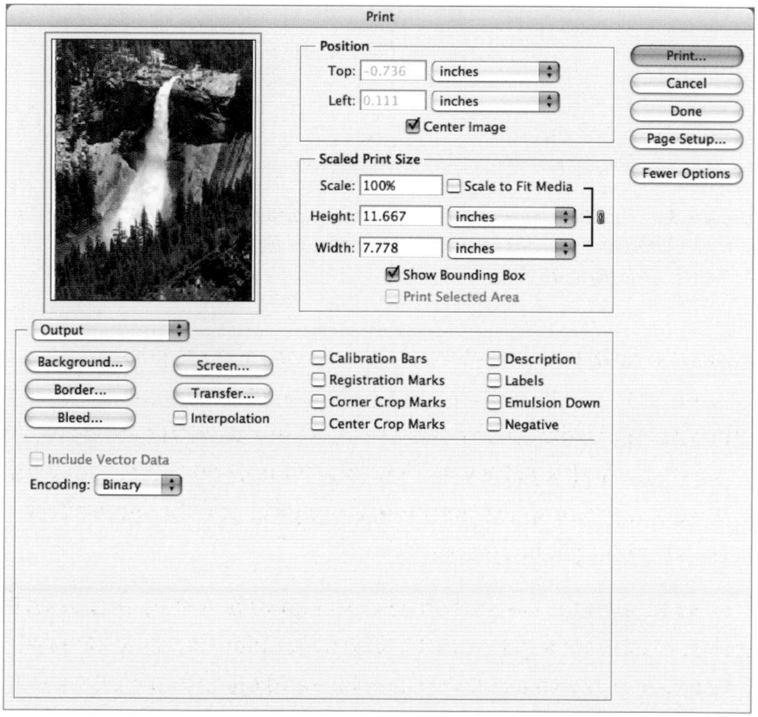

Figure 7.6 *Output options let you select background colors, specify whether to print a border, and choose control options useful for page layout, such as calibration bars and registration marks.*

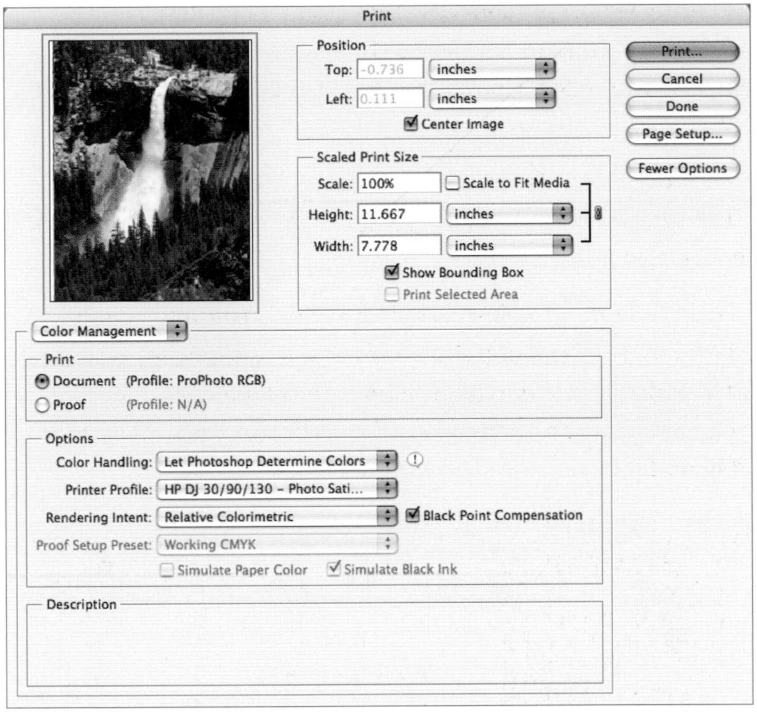

Figure 7.7 *The Color Management options contain the real power when printing from Photoshop. The correct settings here will make all the difference in the world in your print quality.*

Select Color Management from the pop-up menu to get started. Under Print, you'll see the options Document and Proof. This is the color space that you've been working in and should be set at Document. At this point you are telling Photoshop to start out with the working color space. Selecting Proof gives you the same effect as soft proofing but on paper.

The settings in the Options area control how Photoshop handles the colors being sent to your printer. The first, Color Handling, determines where the translation takes place and offers four choices:

- **Let Printer Determine Colors.** Tells Photoshop to do no translation but instructs the printer driver to handle all color conversions. This is normally not the best choice, particularly if you use custom papers and profiles, because the print driver often doesn't include a way to access those profiles.

- **Let Photoshop Determine Colors.** Gives you have full access to all printer profiles installed on your computer. This is the best setting for complete control over your output. In Figure 7.7's example I selected the HP DesignJet 130 Photo Satin profile.

- **No Color Management.** Tells Photoshop to do nothing. No color conversion will be done by either Photoshop or the printer driver.

- **Separations.** Prints each color channel separately. This choice is active only when the document is in the CMYK mode. Use it only when sending files to a press.

Before moving on to Printer Profiles and Rendering Intent, which offer the same pop-up options for Photoshop and Photoshop Elements, let me show you how to find the Print Preview dialog box in Elements.

Print Preview in Elements

Photoshop Elements, as might be expected, has fewer options available in its Print Preview dialog box. Don't worry, the critical settings are there; you just access them a bit differently.

With Elements, you select File > Print. By default you'll see the dialog box shown in **Figure 7.8**. To enable the color management options, click the Show More Options check box, just above the Help button.

Once you've clicked this check box, you'll see options to select Printer Profiles and Rendering Intent (the Mac version calls these settings Print Space and Intent). Click on the Printer Profile/Print Space pop-up menu to select the correct printer profile for your paper type. In **Figure 7.9**, I selected the Canon w6400 printer and Fine Art Photo paper.

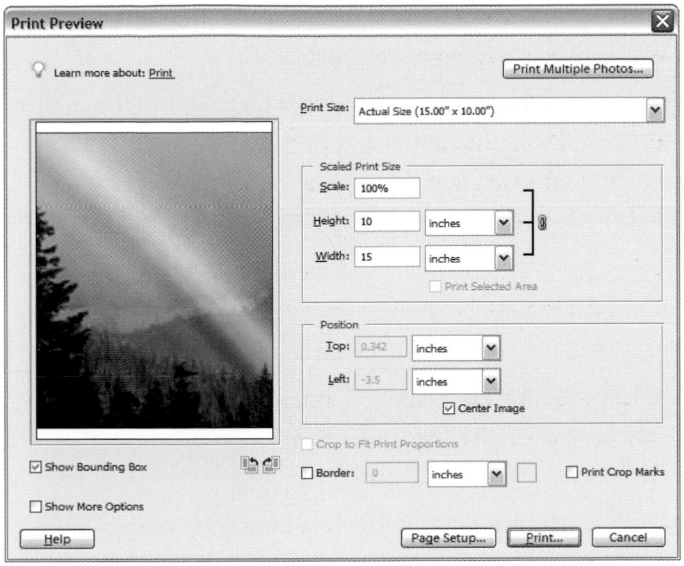

Figure 7.8 *Photoshop Elements includes the critical color management settings for your prints. Click the Show More Options check box to enable these settings.*

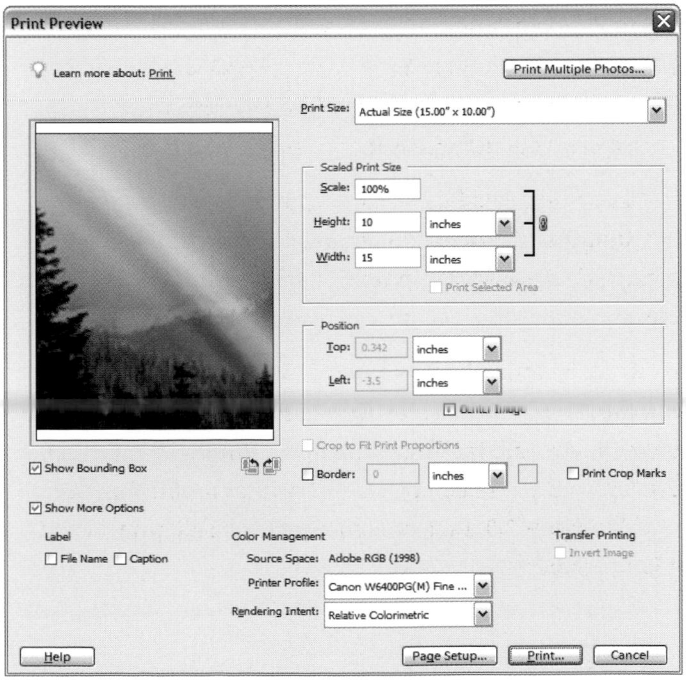

Figure 7.9 *Select the profile for your paper and printer as well as the rendering intent for better quality output from Elements.*

Note

Because Photoshop Elements doesn't support soft proofing like its big brother, the only way to determine whether Perceptual or Relative Colorimetric is the best choice for Rendering Intent (Intent) is to try them both. In most cases, you probably won't be able to see much of a difference. I recommend selecting Relative Colorimetric and then trying Perceptual if you see problems with colors blocking up in your prints.

Rendering Intent

As you may remember from the discussion on soft proofing, Rendering Intent (Intent in Photoshop Elements for the Mac) determines how colors will be converted from one color space to the other. Because every device interprets color differently, some type of color mapping is required to get the best results. Here are your choices:

- **Perceptual.** Preserves the visual relationship between colors to keep all changes as natural as possible. It's best used with photos that contain out-of-gamut colors as it does the best job of mapping those colors to ones that will fit within the new color space.

- **Saturation.** Sacrifices accuracy for vibrancy. It works great for graphics and charts but isn't appropriate for photos.

- **Relative Colorimetric.** Works by looking at the highlight of the source color space and compares it to what the destination is capable of. All colors are then shifted to the closest reproducible color. Relative Colorimetric is the default for printing in the United States and Europe.

- **Absolute Colorimetric.** Ignores colors that are outside of the destination gamut. It keeps color accuracy as close as possible, but out-of-gamut colors will not be reproduced accurately.

For most printing situations, I prefer to use Relative Colorimetric. Some custom profiles are created with the Perceptual intent. If this is the case for your profiles, then select Perceptual.

Photoshop CS2 adds a check box for Black Point Compensation that simulates the full dynamic range of the output device. This option should be selected to ensure that shadow detail is preserved.

Printer Profiles or Print Space

As you remember from Chapter 4, every printer and every paper type uses a different profile. Profiles instruct the printer how to reproduce a particular color on that type of paper. Selecting the wrong profile can lead to some interesting—but usually undesirable—results, such as color problems and too much ink on the page.

When you installed your printer driver, odds are that several profiles were also installed. These profiles, created to work with the typical printer of a particular model, can range from very good to horrendous. If you happen to have a printer that is close to the reference point used by the manufacturer, you're in good shape. Most printers are at least close, but I have seen some that produced prints that were only worth hanging in the trash can. Creating a custom profile for that specific printer normally fixes things up, but it's time consuming and can be expensive.

The good news is that the higher-end photo printers have much tighter quality control with very little variation from one unit to the next. Some, like the HP DesignJet series, include built-in color calibration to optimize the printer for a particular paper type—almost like getting custom profiles every time you print!

You might be surprised when you click Print Preview's Printer Profiles pop-up list (click the list for Print Space in Elements for the Mac). Along with your printer profiles, you'll see a number of options, including display profiles for your monitor, a number of CMYK preset profiles, and all of the standard working spaces such as Adobe RGB and sRGB. If you have multiple printers installed, it's not uncommon to have 50 or more items listed here. With at least one profile for each paper type (**Figure 7.10**), they add up quickly. Some printers come with separate profiles for each print quality as well, so it's not uncommon to have multiple entries for the same type of paper, which makes your choices even more confusing.

Note

If you want to get really serious about your output, it's a good idea to have a profile for the type of lighting the print will be displayed in. Most people aren't willing to go to that extreme (and, to be honest, it's not that big of a difference in most cases). But for critical work, I'll often do my prints tuned for the specific lighting they will be viewed under.

Photoshop doesn't distinguish between printer profiles and other profiles you have installed on your system, so selecting the right option can be a little perplexing. Fortunately, the printer profiles usually include the name of the printer to help identify them. So, what about all those other profiles? Adobe includes a number of standard profiles for prepress devices. These are shown as Euroscale Coated, Japan Color 2001 Coated, US Sheetfed, and US Web as examples. The Dot Gain profiles are designed to work with halftone printers such as those used by newspapers, while the Gray profiles are, not surprisingly, designed for black-and-white output.

Unless you have a specific reason for selecting one of these options, you can safely ignore them when doing your own printing. If on the other hand you send your work out for printing and the service specifies a particular profile, then you would want to take advantage of these options.

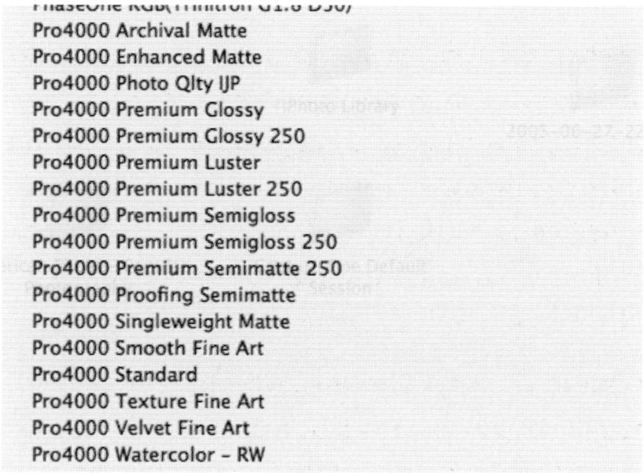

PhaseOne RGB(Trinitron G1.8 D50)
Pro4000 Archival Matte
Pro4000 Enhanced Matte
Pro4000 Photo Qlty IJP
Pro4000 Premium Glossy
Pro4000 Premium Glossy 250
Pro4000 Premium Luster
Pro4000 Premium Luster 250
Pro4000 Premium Semigloss
Pro4000 Premium Semigloss 250
Pro4000 Premium Semimatte 250
Pro4000 Proofing Semimatte
Pro4000 Singleweight Matte
Pro4000 Smooth Fine Art
Pro4000 Standard
Pro4000 Texture Fine Art
Pro4000 Velvet Fine Art
Pro4000 Watercolor – RW

Figure 7.10 *Printer profiles add up quickly, especially when you start adding custom profiles for other paper types. These are just the default profiles for the Epson 4000 printer.*

Custom Profiles

The settings we've discussed will help you improve your prints, but they can take you only so far. The profiles you received with your printer, or that you downloaded from a Web site, were created with a reference printer, not yours. Because printers are all mass-produced, there is some variation to them; not every printer will perform exactly like the next, or like the reference printer. It's more of a problem with the consumer-grade printers (also known as the ones that most of us can afford) but does carry over to the professional models as well. In cases like this, you should investigate having a custom profile created or creating one yourself.

Made-to-order profiles

The best option is to have a custom profile created by one of the many services available.

Alternatively, you can create your own profiles, which I'll cover in a bit, but unless you use a variety of new papers that aren't included in your printer's default list, it's much more cost effective to have custom profiles created than to buy the equipment needed to create your own.

There are plenty of choices when it comes to custom profiling, but the two that continually get high grades from users and are highly recommended are Dry Creek Photo (www.drycreekphoto.com) and Cathy's Profiles (www.cathysprofiles.com). I have yet to hear from anyone disappointed in their work. I also offer custom profiling services, and although I haven't had any complaints either, I certainly wouldn't suggest that you should only come to me.

The specifics of working with any of these services differ, but they all follow the same general process. You'll be required to download a color chart (**Figure 7.11**). The exact chart may vary from one service to the next, but all include a set of color squares that you print on your printer and paper choice using the specific settings provided by the profiling service. This means turning off all color adjustment controls to prevent the printer from making changes that would prevent you from getting an accurate profile.

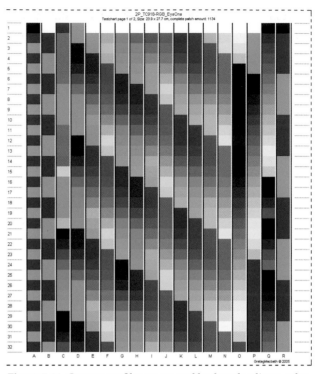

Figure 7.11 *Custom profiles are created by downloading a color chart that you then print on your printer and selected paper. Subsequently, you send the output to the profiling service to create a custom profile.*

After printing out your profiles, you mail them back (via regular old-fashioned mail—e-mail is not an option here) to the profiling service, which will use special equipment known as a *spectrophotometer* to read and measure the color values for each patch on your color chart. For best results, each patch is read three times and the results are averaged for accuracy. The measurements are then saved as a profile that is e-mailed to you along with instructions on how to install it.

Prices vary, in some cases dramatically, from one service to the next. Cathy's Profiles run $40 each, while Dry Creek Photo charges

$50 for a single profile and offers an annual plan for an additional fee. I charge $50 but offer discounts for multiple profiles. You'll find these and other services listed in Appendix A, "Resources."

Creating your own profiles

Creating your own printer profiles used to be a daunting, frustrating, and incredibly expensive undertaking. Today it's merely daunting and slightly expensive. You can get started for less than $500 with ColorVision's PrintFIX Pro (**Figure 7.12**), which is a device that reads color patches to create a printer profile, or for as much as $10,000 for automated systems that scan a great number of patches to create a printer profile and automatically average samples for the best possible results.

Figure 7.12 *ColorVision's PrintFIX PRO creates custom printer profiles using a spectrocolorimeter.*

Choices for the rest of us are the Gretag Macbeth EyeOne Photo (about $1,500, www.i1color.com), the X-Rite Pulse ColorElite (also about $1,500, www.xrite.com), and ColorVision's SpectroPRO (about $900, www.colorvision.com). These devices all work by moving the spectrophotometer across each color patch, which is measured and stored (**Figure 7.13**). When all patches are read, the profile is created. You'll need to do this for each paper you use, and for optimal results, for each lighting condition in which you plan to display your prints. When you consider the cost of entry for the hardware and the time involved in creating the profiles, it's not surprising that most photographers rely on services or manufacturers to provide their profiles.

Figure 7.13 *The higher-quality spectrophotometers all work by measuring the color values of a number of patches, which are then used to create the custom profile.*

Note

Programs are also available that use a regular scanner to read a color target and build profiles from that. I haven't covered those programs here because I don't feel that they offer an advantage over generic profiles and thus aren't worth the expense.

Chapter 4 covered all of the Print and Page Setup options, so I won't bore you with a repeat here. The critical detail to keep in mind is that when you select the option Let Photoshop Determine Colors in the Print with Preview dialog box (Print Preview dialog box in Photoshop Elements), be sure to turn *off* color management in the print driver. Failing to do this will give you two sets of color conversions—one by Photoshop and one by the printer. Certainly not what you'll want to see!

If you need to verify the proper setting in your print driver, click the Page Setup button and navigate to the printer settings for color management (refer to Chapter 4 for details on how to set color management options for most of the popular print drivers).

Once you've verified your printer settings and have the correct profile selected in the Print with Preview dialog box, it's payoff time. The only thing left to do is click the Print button to actually print your image.

Selecting and Using a RIP

When you need total control over every aspect of the print process, a *raster image processor (RIP)* is one way to go. RIPs are designed to improve the workflow and print quality, and are especially useful when you're doing large amounts of printing. The other primary use for a RIP, and the one that appeals to most individuals, is the increased control over how a photo is printed, particularly black-and-white images.

RIPs aren't for the faint of heart, though. Most are fairly expensive, with prices ranging from $500 to $5,000 depending on the number of features and the printer being used.

What a RIP does

A RIP completely bypasses the standard printer driver, talking directly to the printer to maintain complete control over how much ink is used, how the print heads are moved, and how colors are mapped from your working space to the RIP's profiles. All RIPs come with profiles that are tuned to work with their printing engine; most include a large variety of profiles for the majority of paper options. It's also common to have different profiles for color printing and black-and-white printing to maintain neutral color balance and better dynamic range.

Some RIPs work with PostScript, a page description language known for precise control over how ink is placed on a page. Another feature common to higher-end RIPs is hot folders, which allow you to save or place files in a special, RIP-monitored folder on your computer. When it detects a new file, the RIP starts up and automatically prints the file for you. You'll also usually find extensive layout options for placing multiple images on a single sheet of paper. When you're using expensive fine art papers, particularly in the wide-format rolls, the ability to place multiple images on a page can really save money by reducing wasted space.

Note

Epson sells the Stylus Pro 4800 with a RIP for an additional $200. This RIP is from ColorBurst, a company with a great reputation and an excellent product. On the surface it sounds like a great deal. Unfortunately, the RIP only works with the 4800 and the supplied profiles only. You can't add paper types, which greatly limits its usefulness.

ImagePrint

ColorByte Software's ImagePrint (www.colorbytesoftware.com) is one of the most full-featured RIPs available. Prices start at $495 for the "lite" version, which works with smaller printers like the Epson 2200/2400 and HP DesignJet 30, and go up to $3,295 for the Epson 9600 version with PostScript support. ImagePrint uses a fairly intuitive interface (**Figure 7.14**) that lets you put photos onto a page and then position, size, and rotate them.

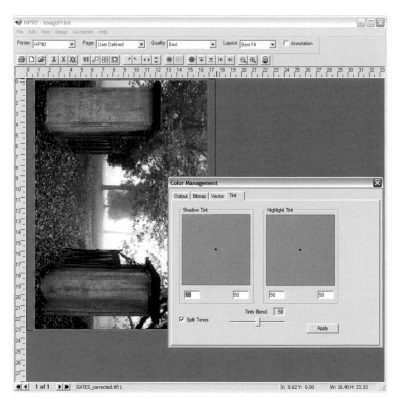

Figure 7.14 *ImagePrint offers excellent layout control for one or more images. One unique feature is the ability to apply split tones to a black-and-white image.*

When you have multiple images to print, you can use the ImagePrint File Browser (**Figure 7.15**) to drag and drop files onto the work area. ImagePrint will automatically position each image to optimize the amount of paper required for printing. And if you have black-and white along with color images on the same page, each image can have its own profile assigned to it—something that's impossible in a normal print driver or Photoshop.

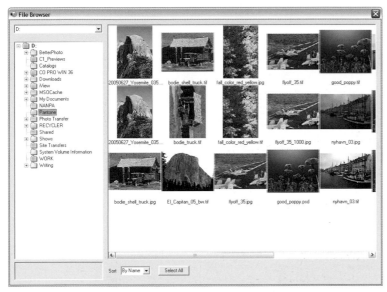

Figure 7.15 *The ImagePrint File Browser lets you select multiple images for placement on the page. ImagePrint automatically positions each image to take advantage of the selected page size.*

I also find ImagePrint's easy-to-use Color Controls (**Figure 7.16**) very useful. Tone, color, histogram adjustment, and ink control are all easily set for specific printing needs.

I prefer to use ImagePrint for all my black-and-white printing and for large print jobs of all types. The ability to schedule print jobs for a specific time, the options for setting profiles for individual images on a single page, and the extremely high quality of the supplied profiles all combine to make ImagePrint a key tool in my printing process.

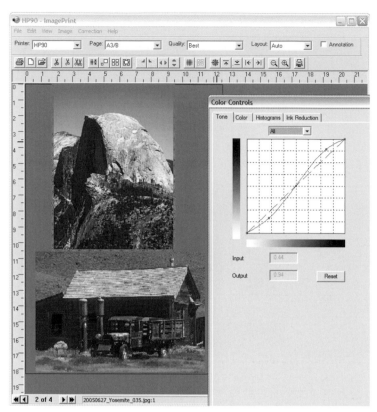

Figure 7.16 *The Color Controls options give you complete control over all adjustments, including tone and ink levels.*

QuadTone RIP

QuadToneRIP by Roy Harrington (www.quadtonerip.com) is a popular choice for many users for several reasons. First, it's inexpensive at $50. Second, it's fairly easy to create your own "curves," which are what QuadToneRIP uses for printer control, similar to a profile. All of the major features are found in a single window (**Figure 7.17**). QuadToneRIP is designed for use in black-and-white printing only using various monochrome ink sets, such as Media Street's QuadBlack and Piezography's Neutral inks.

Note

You can also use the standard Epson UltraChrome inks, but QuadToneRIP really shines with the monochrome inks.

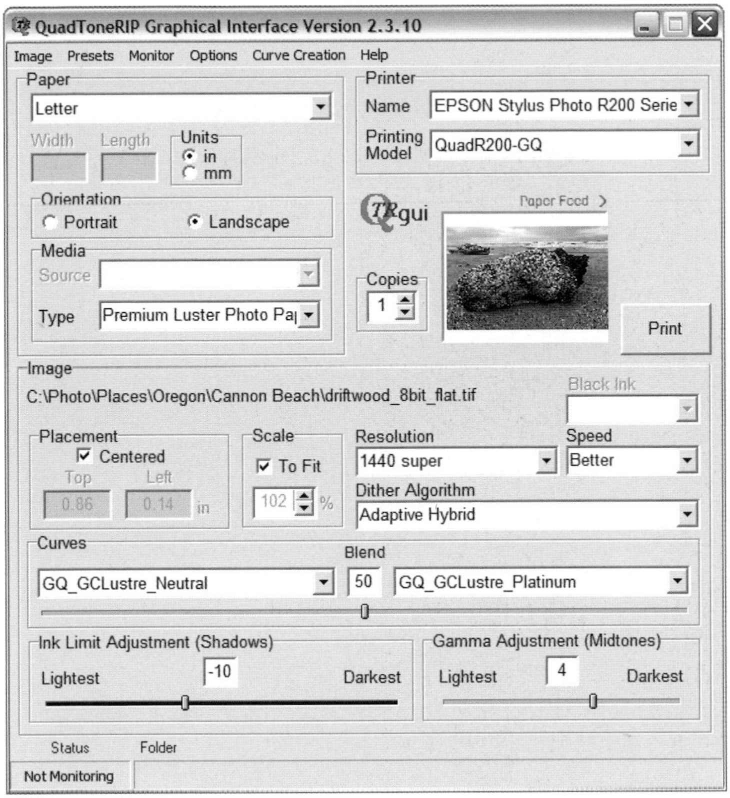

Figure 7.17 *QuadToneRIP is an inexpensive but very capable RIP designed for users of monochrome ink sets. You can easily create your own curves for specific inks and papers, and the RIP generates very high quality output.*

Qimage

Although it isn't technically a RIP, Digital Domain's Qimage (www. ddisoftware.com) is an excellent program that handles print jobs with ease. Available in Pro ($49.95) and Lite ($34.95) versions, the program has a large audience of dedicated users—and with good reason. You simply drag and drop selected images onto the page layout; Qimage automatically sizes and positions them for the best fit (**Figure 7.18**). Qimage also includes a number of preset templates for contact sheets and specific print sizes, along with an easy-to-use Custom feature that lets you create your own print packages.

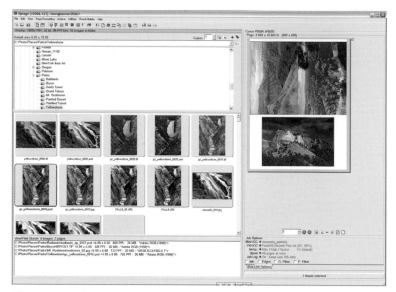

Figure 7.18 *Qimage is an amazing application that can handle almost any printing task. Just for good measure, Qimage throws in RAW image processing, color adjustment, border effects, and file management.*

Every time I launch Qimage I seem to find a new feature that surprises me. Along with some of the best print quality I've seen, the application does an amazing job of image scaling and correction. When it comes to printing, all the expected options are available, including rendering intents and profile selection (**Figure 7.19**) as well as soft proofing, cropping, and print-only sharpening.

When to use a RIP

Most users will never need to go to the expense of using a RIP. If you print a high volume of images, or you use multiple computers, then a RIP such as ImagePrint will save you time and money. Fans of black-and-white imagery will find that prints made from a RIP are higher quality, but this may not be enough to get you interested in shelling out a few hundred dollars.

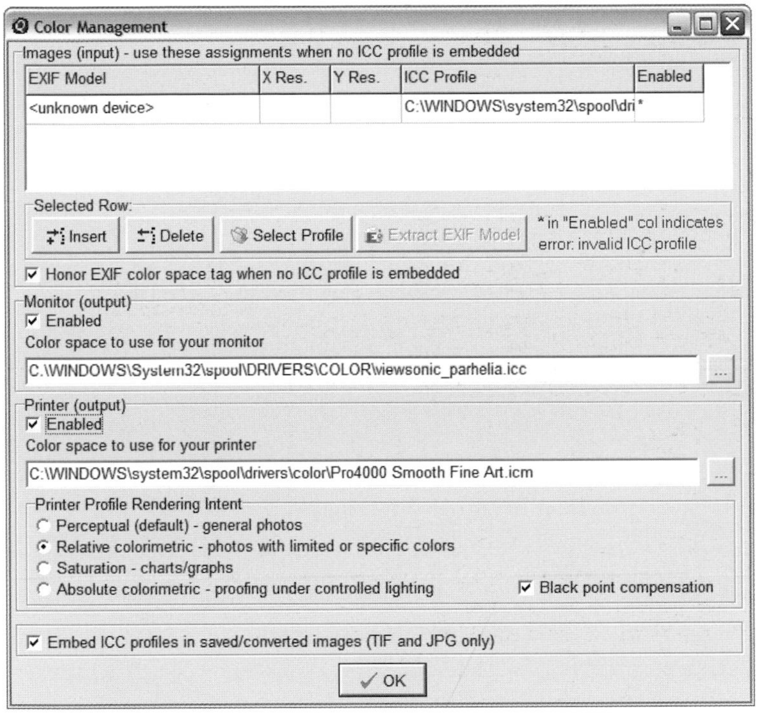

Figure 7.19 *Qimage gives you full control over how your photos are printed, with support for all printer profiles and rendering intents. The quality of Qimage's output is outstanding.*

If you're interested in trying a RIP, most of them offer trial versions to give you an idea of how they'll work for your needs. I do encourage you to try Qimage for high-quality output, especially if you don't use Photoshop. Having access to full printer profile support and rendering intents is a great way to improve your print quality.

A Final Printing Checklist

With so many options available, printing from Photoshop can seem overwhelming at times. The following checklist can help you ensure that you aren't missing something that might require printing a new version of your image.

1. Make any image corrections such as color balance, shadow and highlight adjustment, and image cleanup (Chapter 5).

2. Resize your image for the desired print size (Chapter 6).

3. Sharpen your image for output (Chapter 6).

4. Select Print with Preview (Print in Photoshop Elements) and set Color Handling to Let Photoshop Determine Colors, Printer Profile to the correct paper/printer combination, and Rendering Intent to either Relative Colorimetric or Perceptual.

5. Click Page Setup and verify that color management is turned off in the printer driver (Chapter 4).

6. Verify that the correct paper type, size, and orientation are set in the print driver (Chapter 4).

7. Click Print.

All that's left to do is to enjoy your image!

Moving On

Now that you know *how* to get a great print, you may find yourself printing more of your images than ever. There's just something about looking at your photo in print that becomes addictive. In the next chapter, I'll show you how to go beyond a regular print to create such special projects as books, calendars, and more.

8 | Creating Special Print Projects

Sometimes a simple print isn't quite what you envision for your image. If you've looked at coffee table fine art photography books and thought, "I could do that," you're right—you can! In fact, you can do books, calendars, and even wallpaper if you wish.

The digital revolution has opened a world of options beyond printing single images to square sheets of paper. From building montages to printing on fabric or canvas to designing scrapbook pages, this chapter will show you how. I'll even reveal a new twist on contact sheets and printing custom picture packages.

Printing Your Own Book

There is nothing quite like seeing your own images in print, especially a book. Of course, for the majority of us, that isn't a likely event. Heck, when I want to see my images in print I usually have to write a whole book around them (what you hold now being a prime example).

Luckily, self-publishing is now a very real option for just about anyone and in just about any quantity. You can print your book at home, or send your work out for printing. Whether you want one book or a limited run that is available on Amazon.com, you can find a service to print your book with all of the quality you expect.

Printing at home

Both Canon and Epson offer photo packages that enable you to print your own book, but the companies take entirely different approaches. Canon has two Photo Album Kits available, each including an album cover, clips, and 10 sheets of double-sided photo paper, all for about $30. Canon assumes that you'll be printing on one of its inkjet printers that includes the PhotoRecord software (**Figure 8.1**), which features a number of themes, clipart, and borders for your albums.

Figure 8.1 *Canon's Photo Album Kit uses the PhotoRecord software (included with Canon printers) to create a photo album.*

Epson on the other hand, has a complete package, the StoryTeller Photo Book Creator, which includes a book in either 5×7 or 8×10, glossy photo paper (single-sided), and a panoramic photo paper for creating a wraparound cover for your book. A kit with 10 pages runs about $20, and the 20-page kit is about $30. This is all bundled with the StoryTeller Publisher software (**Figure 8.2**), making it easy to lay out a custom book with templates, as well as a number of layout options. StoryTeller is a very nice package that works with any inkjet printer. The finished product (**Figure 8.3**) is something you'd be proud to share or give as a gift.

Figure 8.2 *Epson's StoryTeller Photo Book Creator is a great product that works with any inkjet printer, letting you create some sophisticated photobooks.*

Figure 8.3 *A finished StoryTeller book looks great and makes a wonderful gift.*

If you'd rather not deal with the printing at home and assembly of a book, some of the online print options may appeal to you. Personally, I had a blast using StoryTeller to create my own book to present to my son.

Online print services

Several very affordable options are available online for publishing one or more books with your images. This section covers a couple of the most popular options. You'll find more choices listed in Appendix A, "Resources."

iPhoto

One of the best-known online options for book printing is Apple's iPhoto (www.apple.com/ilife/iphoto). With several different book formats, including soft or hard cover, as well as size choices, iPhoto books (**Figure 8.4**) can include up to 100 double-sided pages. The only limitation is the requirement to use Apple's iPhoto software to create your book. Naturally, this means that you either need to own, or have access to, a Macintosh computer.

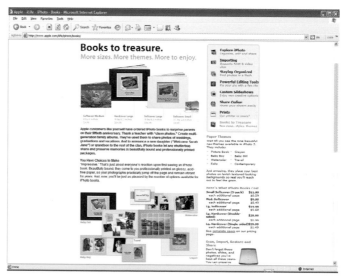

Figure 8.4 *Apple's iPhoto is a great way to get your images into a book format. A number of templates as well as book size options are available. It's only for Mac users, though.*

Creating a book with iPhoto couldn't be any easier. Launch iPhoto on your Mac, select your images in iPhoto, and click the Book icon in iPhoto's toolbar (**Figure 8.5**).

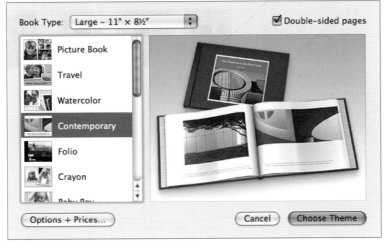

Figure 8.5 *Selecting the Book option in iPhoto starts with choosing the book type and theme.*

The next step is to select the book type and theme. Types include soft or hard cover along with various sizes. You can also choose whether you want single- or double-sided pages. Clicking on the various themes shows you examples of the cover and inside layouts for the book. When you've made your selections, click Choose Theme to proceed to the next step. Depending on the cover, size, and length of your book, you can plan on spending about $30, which is pretty amazing when you consider what you're getting in return.

Now the actual book building process begins. Starting with the cover (**Figure 8.6**), you drag the first image for your book onto the gray area and then click the text labels to name your book.

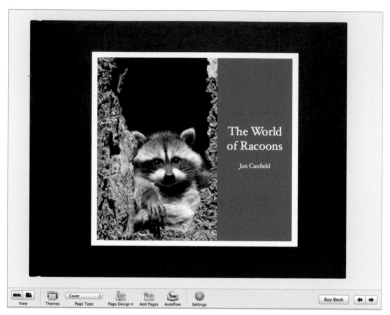

Figure 8.6 *Begin your book layout by placing the cover image and adding a title for your book.*

By holding down the Control key and clicking on your image, you can make adjustments to the image, such as Fit to Frame Size. If you'd rather, open iPhoto's editing tools for cropping and other adjustments.

To work on the inside pages, click the right arrow to move through your book's template pages. Drag and drop images onto the page template, and they'll be placed automatically for you. If your images in the filmstrip at the top of the iPhoto window are in the order you want them to appear in your book, you can use the Autoflow button to quickly build your book for you.

When you're done adding images and text to your book, just click the Buy Book button to go online for ordering. Here you can set cover color options and the number of copies you'd like to order (**Figure 8.7**). Click Buy Now, and you're instantly a published photographer!

Figure 8.7 *Ordering your iPhoto book is a simple process.*

Kodak Gallery

Formerly known as oFoto, the Kodak Gallery service isn't as elegant to use as Apple's iPhoto (but then again, I haven't found anything that is), but the finished product is very similar in quality and price, with a leather-bound book running about $40.

To get started with the Kodak Gallery Photo Books, you'll need to set up an account with their service at www.kodakgallery.com and upload the images you want to use in your book.

Select the Photo Books option from the home page (**Figure 8.8**), and then click Create Book to get started.

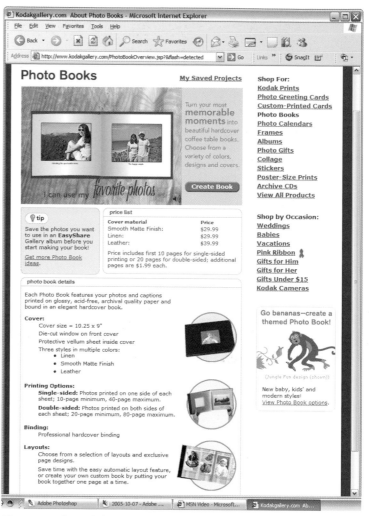

Figure 8.8 *The Kodak Gallery site (formerly oFoto) is a good online source for printing photobooks.*

Your first decision is what type and color to use for the cover of your book. Options include real or fake (aka faux) leather or linen (**Figure 8.9**). For fine art books, the leather choice adds a real feeling of quality to your book.

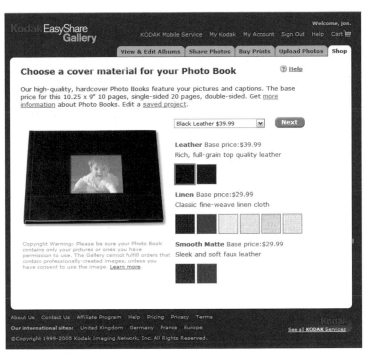

Figure 8.9 *Real or fake leather as well as linen covers are available for your book.*

Click the Next button to choose the interior layout design for your book (**Figure 8.10**). Several themes are available, from fun to fancy. Selecting one of the options updates the preview to show you how the printed page will look.

Clicking Next opens a new window with the option to create your book page by page or by using the Autofill feature. If you have anything other than book selections uploaded to your Kodak gallery, Autofill isn't the best option. And, because I'm a control freak anyway, I prefer to choose the Page by Page option for complete control over how my book is laid out.

Figure 8.10 *The Kodak site has several themes, or templates, you can choose from.*

Once you click Page by Page, you're taken to the Create Your Photo Book page (**Figure 8.11**), where the layout of your book takes place. A filmstrip of uploaded images appears below the page templates, and layout is a simple process of dragging images from the filmstrip onto the page. If you find that you're missing some of the images you'd like to use, you can upload from here as well.

To complete your book, click the Next Page button and continue to add text and images. When you've finished, click the Order button and you can browse through a preview of your completed book (**Figure 8.12**) before committing to the order.

Figure 8.11 *It's a simple process to drag your images onto the page, letting you quickly build your photobook.*

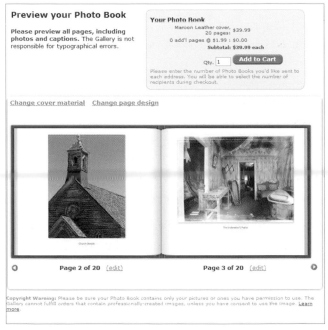

Figure 8.12 *You can preview your book online before committing to the order.*

Limited-run publishing

Other providers offer options for publishing a more traditional-style book, including distribution and resale. Some will print a limited number of books for you, whereas others will take care of everything, including obtaining an ISBN number and getting your book listed with Amazon.com.

Lulu

Despite the cutesy name, Lulu is one of the Web's best resources for self-publishing in a number of areas. Whether it's a photobook, calendar, or novel, Lulu can handle everything from editing to marketing.

Getting started with Lulu is simple enough—just visit www.lulu. com and set up a free account. Once there, select the Publish tab (**Figure 8.13**). This page features several helpful links and a tour of Lulu services that is worth viewing. When you're ready to start your own book, click Start a New Project. You'll see that Lulu can handle a number of publishing tasks, including creating books and calendars. For now, we'll take a look at the book publishing feature by clicking Book.

Figure 8.13 Lulu.com is an excellent online resource for printing, publishing, and selling your books and calendars.

Lulu can give you as much or as little support as you need for tasks such as editing, design, and layout, as long as you're willing to pay for the services. In general, you'll want to send your book contents as a PDF file with images saved at 300 dpi in the JPEG format. Lulu will send you a formatted version of your book for review and approval prior to submitting it for printing.

This might sound like an incredibly expensive and time-consuming process, but I was surprised at how inexpensive producing a book actually is. For example, an 8.5×11 full-color book with 50 pages is only a bit over $12. Of course, this assumes that you won't be needing any editing services.

For $34.95, Lulu's Basic Distribution Service will obtain an ISBN number for your book and have it listed in *Books in Print,* which is the database used by bookstores, libraries, and schools to find titles of interest. You'll also have your book listed with Amazon.com for one year.

> **Note**
>
> Having your book listed on Amazon.com and in *Books in Print* doesn't mean the book is in stock anywhere. Copies are still printed on demand as each order comes in.

Lulu also offers a Global Distribution Service for $149.95 that includes all of the features of the basic service in addition to including your title in Ingram's database (which is similar to *Books in Print* but is used by stores to actually order titles). Inclusion in Ingram's puts your title into the sales channels that other major publishers use, like Barnes and Noble, Amazon.com, and Borders. Your book will also be listed in the United Kingdom to help with sales outside the United States.

Infinity Publishing

If you'd rather just have a number of books printed for your personal distribution or to sell them on your Web site, Infinity Publishing (www.infinitypublishing.com) is a good option. The company offers several packages that include copies of your book, marketing materials, and books on how to market your own books. Prices start at $125.

> **Note**
>
> You'll find more self-publishing options in Appendix A.

Creating Photo Montages

Photo montages can be different things depending on who you ask. For some people, the term implies combining elements from multiple images to create a single image that would not have been possible otherwise.

For the purposes of this book, I define a *photo montage* as a single print with multiple images on the same page but not merged into a new creation, as shown in **Figure 8.14**.

Figure 8.14 *A montage is a document with multiple images on the same page.*

The easiest way to create a montage in Adobe Photoshop or Photoshop Elements is to start out with a new blank document in the size desired for the finished print. To do this, select File > New. Start off by naming your new file and setting the desired page size (**Figure 8.15**).

Figure 8.15 *Create a new document and specify the page size.*

Because you'll be printing this file, set Resolution to 300 pixels per inch and Color Mode to RGB Color. You can also specify a background color if you wish. I normally leave the background white, but if you want to create images with, for example a white border, a colored background will make your images stand out. Click OK to create the new document.

Next, open the images you want to place on the montage and do any resizing needed to get them down to the correct dimensions by selecting Image > Image Size (Photoshop) or Image > Resize > Image Size (Elements).

Now, select the image by choosing Select > Select All and copy it to the new document (**Figure 8.16**).

Note

Make sure the images are set to the same resolution as your montage document. Otherwise, the sizing will not be what you expect! Copying a 72 ppi image into your new 300 ppi montage will give you a very small photo.

Tip

Flatten your image if you have multiple layers to avoid accidentally dragging an adjustment layer instead of the image.

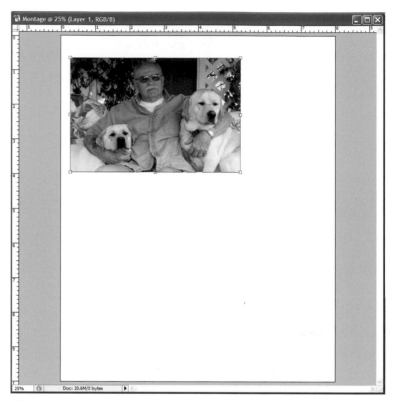

Figure 8.16 *Copy the image to the new montage document to get started.*

Select the Move tool and drag your image to the desired location, and do any resizing necessary.

At this point, I usually like to add a border to the image, giving it the appearance of a photograph placed on a regular scrapbook or photo album page.

Using the Marquee tool, drag out a selection around your image. Now, choose Edit > Stroke and add a border that fits the look you're going after. For this example (**Figure 8.17**), I've selected a 25-pixel stroke.

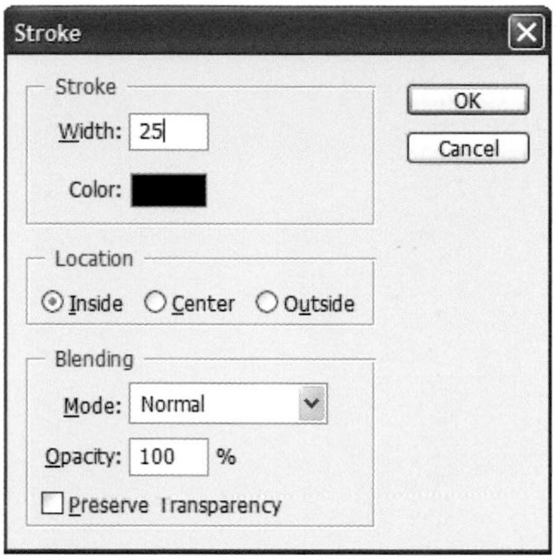

Figure 8.17 *Adding a stroke, or outline, to the image helps it stand out from the page.*

By default, the stroke color will be the same as your current foreground color, but you can select a new color by clicking on the color patch in the Stroke dialog box. This opens the Photoshop Color Picker, which lets you choose any color you like.

You'll also see three options for how the stroke is created: Inside, Outside, and Centered. These options control where the stroke is drawn in relation to the current selection. In the example, you selected the entire image so the correct option is Inside, which will draw the stroke to the inside of your selection. If you were to select Outside, the stroke wouldn't be visible because it would be created outside the image area. Choosing Center would show the stroke at only half the desired width.

Once the image is in the correct position, you can dress it up with borders or rotate it for a custom look. To rotate, click on the image with the Move tool and position the cursor just outside the image area. You'll see the cursor change to a bent arrow, indicating that you can drag the image to a new angle (**Figure 8.18**). Once you have the image at the desired angle, press the Enter key to confirm your choice.

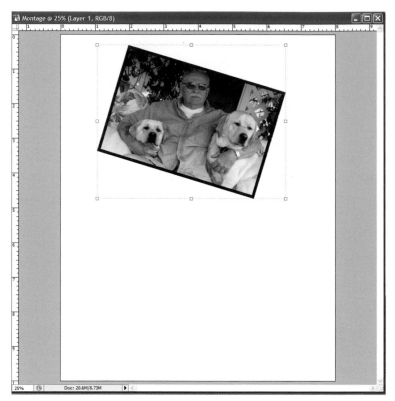

Figure 8.18 *Rotating images on the page makes the composition more dynamic and interesting.*

Repeat this process for each image that you want to use in your montage. Mix up the sizes and angles to give your creation a more exciting and unique look. Add a text layer if you like, and you have a custom print to share with family or friends.

Printing Contact Sheets

Photoshop and Photoshop Elements both include easy-to-use and very useful contact sheet printing options. Essentially a page full of thumbnails, contact sheets are a great way to quickly see the images you've saved to a CD or DVD. They also provide a way for customers to select images for enlargements.

Photoshop CS2 and Photoshop Elements (Mac)

To create a contact sheet in Photoshop, select File > Automate > Contact Sheet II. In the Macintosh version of Elements, select File > Contact Sheet II (Windows Elements users need to follow a different set of directions, which follow in the next section). The dialog box, shown in **Figure 8.19**, offers a number of options for creating your contact sheet. You can work with folders of images, images that are selected in Adobe Bridge, or images that are already open. If you select a folder as the source, you can also choose whether to include all subfolders.

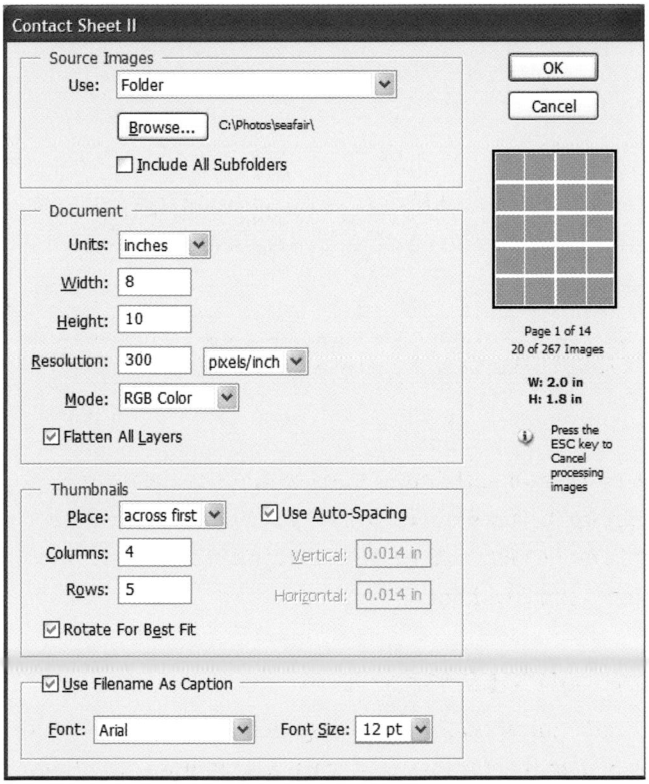

Figure 8.19 *The Contact Sheet II dialog box offers a number of options for creating contact sheets, which you can use for tracking images on CD or give to customers for ordering full-sized images.*

The Document settings have options for page size and image resolution. Because you'll be printing small versions of your images, I recommend using 300 ppi as the Resolution setting; for home printing, set RGB as the Mode option. Selecting Flatten All Layers reduces the size of your contact sheets but keep in mind that it prevents you from making easy edits once you create the sheet.

Select Thumbnails to specify how many images you want to place on each page and the order in which they appear—either across first or down first. I find that for examining details, using four columns and five rows is a good compromise between the number of images per page and the size of the image. Your selection here will be displayed in the preview on the right side of the dialog box, along with the number of pages required to print all selected images.

Finally, I suggest you enable the Use Filename as Caption option to make it easier to select images from the contact sheet for further editing or printing.

When you finish making your selections, click OK. Photoshop automatically opens each image, resizes it to the proper dimensions, and places it on a new document. When the process is completed, all the pages will be open and ready for printing (**Figure 8.20**).

You can also create contact sheets directly from Adobe Bridge. I find this method to be the quickest because I'm already in a file browser. Simply select your images in Bridge and choose Tools > Photoshop > Contact Sheet II. You'll see the same dialog box shown earlier. After you make your selections, Bridge launches Photoshop and begins creating your contact sheets.

Tip

Choosing 9 point as the type size keeps your captions from being truncated by the bordering image.

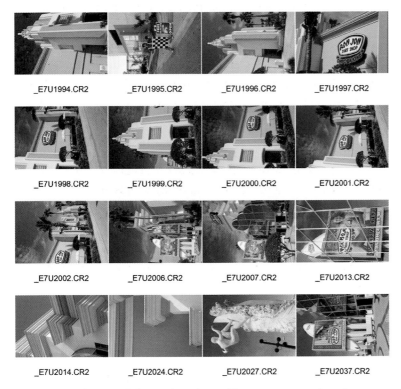

_E7U1994.CR2	_E7U1995.CR2	_E7U1996.CR2	_E7U1997.CR2
_E7U1998.CR2	_E7U1999.CR2	_E7U2000.CR2	_E7U2001.CR2
_E7U2002.CR2	_E7U2006.CR2	_E7U2007.CR2	_E7U2013.CR2
_E7U2014.CR2	_E7U2024.CR2	_E7U2027.CR2	_E7U2037.CR2

Figure 8.20 *After you click OK, Photoshop will create a contact sheet document that can be saved and printed.*

Photoshop Elements on Windows

Creating contact sheets in Photoshop Elements 3.0 and 4.0 on Windows is very similar doing so in Photoshop, but you'll have fewer options for customizing your contact sheet. The biggest difference is how you access the contact sheet feature—you need to use Adobe Organizer to create and print your images. To begin, select File > Print Multiple Photos and you'll see the dialog box shown in **Figure 8.21**.

Note

If you selected Print by mistake, you'll see a Print Multiple Images button in the Print dialog box that will take you to the dialog box shown in Figure 8.21.

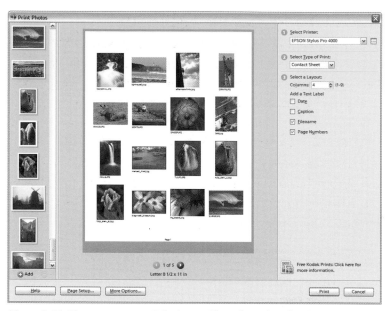

Figure 8.21 *Elements users on Windows will need to select the Contact Sheet option in the Print dialog box.*

Note

Users of Elements on Windows need to have these files in the Organizer or already opened in Elements before the files can be used.

Tip

I suggest including the filename to help find the images on your disc later.

By default, Elements shows only the selected or open image in the dialog box. This obviously isn't useful for a contact sheet, so you'll want to click the Add button to select all the images you want to include on your contact sheet.

If you have more than one printer, the first step is to select the printer you want to use from the Select Printer drop-down list. Next, select Contact Sheet from the Type of Print drop-down list. For layout, specify the number of columns you want to have and click the Text Label check boxes for Date, Caption, and Filename if you wish to include them on the contact sheet.

Once you've made your selections, click Print.

Customizing Picture Packages

Picture packages are a popular item with many event, school, and team photographers, and they can make a nice gift for family members as well. Photoshop and Photoshop Elements have a handy Picture Package feature that lets you build a variety of packages.

Photoshop CS2 and Photoshop Elements (Mac)

To get started, Select File > Automate > Picture Package, or on the Macintosh version of Elements, select File > Picture Package. You'll see the dialog box shown in **Figure 8.22**, which resembles the one for making contact sheets.

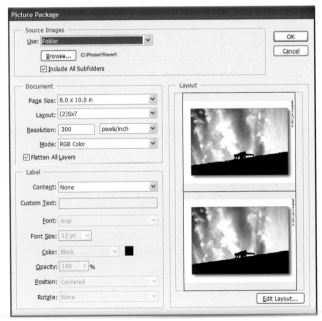

Figure 8.22 *Picture Package lets you quickly create standard or custom sets of images on a single page.*

After selecting the image source, whether it is the currently open image, a folder, or selected images in Bridge, choose the layout. A number of templates are included with Picture Package (**Figure 8.23**), but if you find that none of them have what you're looking for, you can create your own custom layouts.

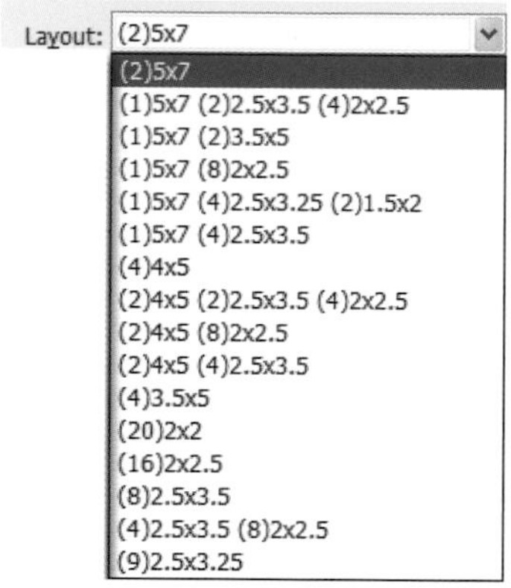

Figure 8.23 *The Layout list has a number of options for creating your own custom picture packages.*

To create a custom package, click Edit Layout. A new window opens with your current layout shown (**Figure 8.24**). The first thing you should do is rename the layout to avoid accidentally changing one of the existing templates.

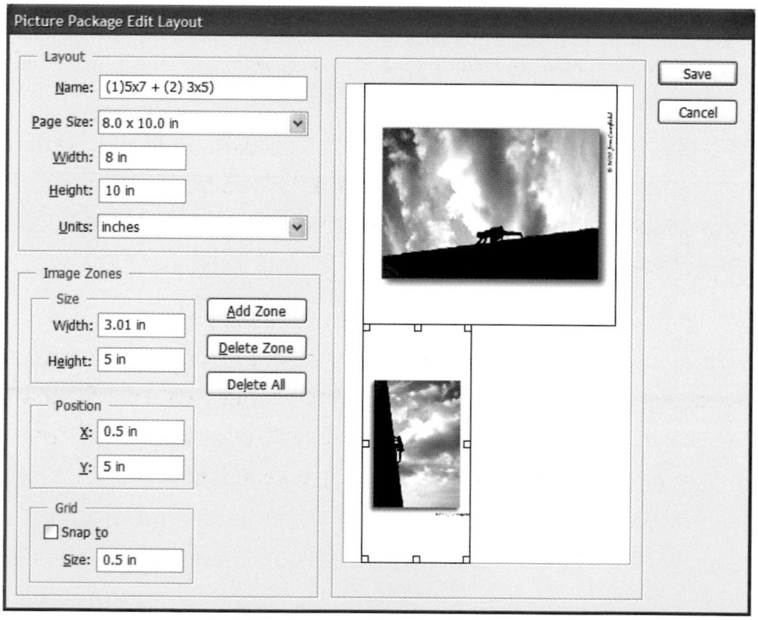

Figure 8.24 *Before making any changes, rename the layout to avoid overwriting the current one.*

Each image area is referred to as a "zone." To modify one of the existing zones, click to select it and either click Delete Zone to remove it or drag the size handles to resize the image. Your images will automatically rotate for best fit as you size the zone (**Figure 8.25**).

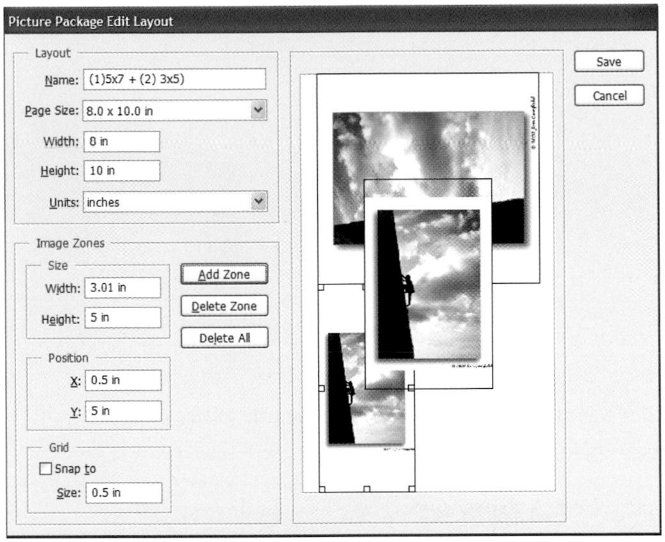

Figure 8.25 *You can drag, resize, or delete existing zones.*

To add a new zone, click Add Zone and Photoshop places a new copy of your image at the center of your layout. Drag the zone to the desired area on your page and resize to fit your needs (**Figure 8.26**).

You can also use more than one image for each page in your picture package, although it isn't obvious from the controls shown in the dialog box. Simply click on any of the zones to open a file dialog box; then select a new image, which will be opened and sized according to the dimensions on your package (**Figure 8.27**).

Tip

You can enter exact image dimensions in the Size fields if you don't want to drag the zone to a specific size.

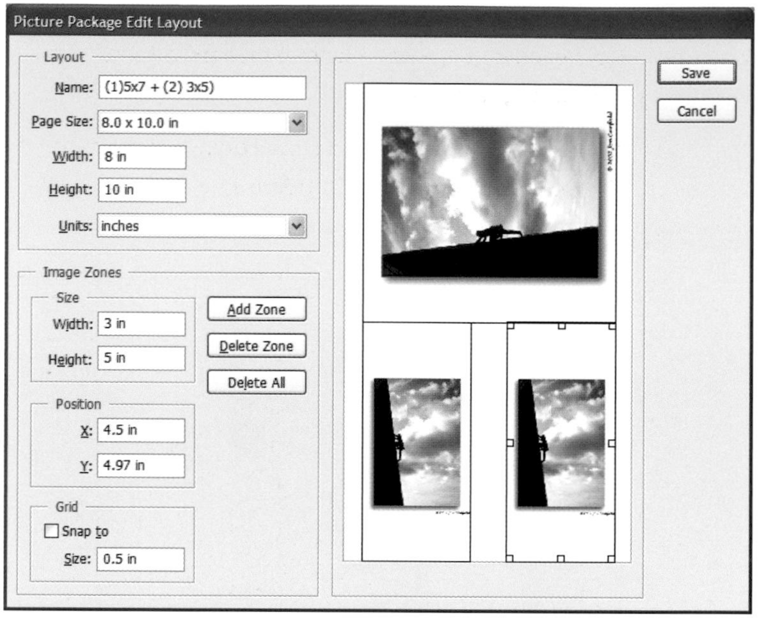

Figure 8.26 *Click Add Zone and drag the new zone into the desired position on the page.*

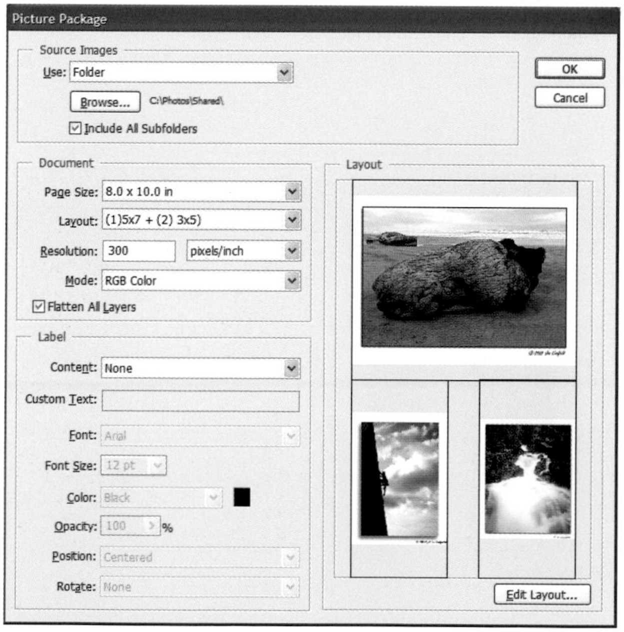

Figure 8.27 *Click on any image in the layout to replace it with a different image.*

Once you've made all your selections, click OK. Photoshop opens and sizes each selected image and places it on a new document ready for printing (**Figure 8.28**).

If you selected multiple images by choosing Folder or Selected Images in File Browser, Photoshop will create a new picture package page for every image selected.

© 2004 Jon Canfield

© 2002 Jon Canfield

© 2002 Jon Canfield

Figure 8.28 *After you click OK, Photoshop will create a new document with all images laid out and ready for printing. You can save the document for later use.*

Photoshop Elements on Windows

The Windows version of Elements accesses the Picture Package through the same dialog box as the contact sheet covered earlier. In brief, you'll select File > Print Multiple Photos (doing so launches Adobe Organizer if it isn't already running), and open the dialog box shown in **Figure 8.29**.

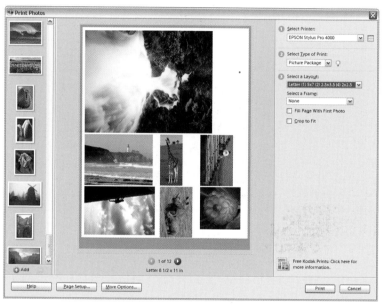

Figure 8.29 *Select the Picture Package option from the Print Multiple Photos dialog box.*

As before, you'll select your printer if you have more than one available and then choose Picture Package from the Type of Print drop-down list.

Elements includes a number of templates for your picture package, but you are unable to customize the layout as you can with Photoshop. If you have multiple images to be printed, by default the layout includes one of each selected image in the print package.

Clicking the One Photo Per Page option (Fill Page with First Photo in Elements 4.0) gives each selected image its own page, with multiple copies of the photo on each page (**Figure 8.30**).

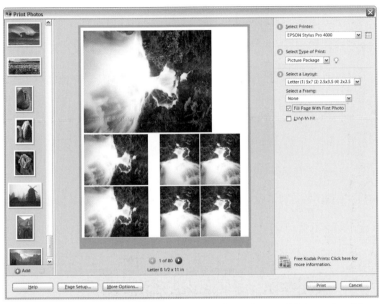

Figure 8.30 Using the One Photo Per Page option prints multiple copies of the same image, one page per image.

Crop to Fit resizes each image to fit within the template sizes. Because this changes the actual size of your prints, I recommend not using this option if you're trying to fit within a certain size, such as a wallet or ready-made frame.

One cool addition to the Windows version of Picture Package in Elements is the option to select a Frame for your images. There are several options in the drop-down list and choosing any of these will apply that frame to every image in the picture package (**Figure 8.31**).

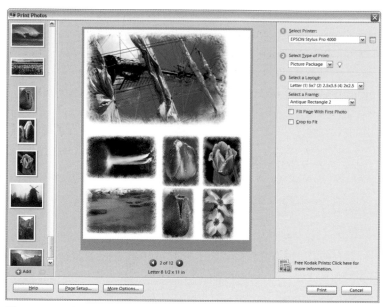

Figure 8.31 *The Windows version of Elements includes a feature to add frames to your images.*

Once you've made all your selections, click Print to generate your Picture Package.

Scrapbooking

Scrapbooks are arguably one of the most popular craft projects around. Digital photography has made scrapbooking even more popular because it gives you the ability to quickly make prints of just the images you want and in the exact size you need.

Most scrapbooks use 12×12-inch pages that are larger than what the average desktop printer can handle. If you have a wide-format printer, such as the Epson R1800, Canon i9900, or HP 8750, you can print complete pages in the correct size for your album, with all images, text, and graphic elements on the page.

HP even has a scrapbooking kit available for its printers (**Figure 8.32**). The HP Creative Scrapbook Assistant (about $30) is a software package that includes page templates, clipart, frames, mattes, and other doodads to embellish your scrapbook pages. Although other packages are available as well, this is one of the best for the digital imaging enthusiast.

Figure 8.32 *The HP Creative Scrapbook Assistant includes a number of templates and clipart that you can use to create a scrapbook page.*

If your printer can support the sizes, most inkjets are able to print directly onto the various types of scrapbooking papers available at craft stores. The exception to this, in my experience, has been the vellum papers. Ink tends to puddle up on the page and make a wonderful mess of everything it comes in contact with.

Printing on Fabric

Most of you are probably familiar with the iron-on transfers available for popular inkjet printers. Epson and HP both offer printable sheets that you can then iron onto a shirt or other fabric item (**Figure 8.33**). But, did you know that you can also print directly onto fabric?

Figure 8.33 *Printing on fabric is a unique way to customize clothing or quilts, such as this example.*

Printing your own fabric

By using regular freezer paper (which is similar to wax paper) and the fabric of your choice, you can print as large as your printer will handle.

To get started, cut a piece of freezer paper to the desired size (make sure it will feed through your printer). Now place your fabric onto the shiny side of the freezer paper.

Note

Make sure the fabric is no larger than the freezer paper and that no stray threads are hanging loose to catch in your printer.

Iron the fabric onto the freezer paper and you're ready to feed it through your printer (**Figure 8.34**).

Once the fabric has run through the printer, let the ink dry. To set the colors, place a piece of parchment paper over the fabric and use your iron on a high setting to set the colors. The finished fabric is now ready for whatever use you'd like.

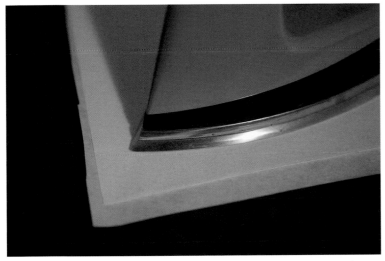

Figure 8.34 Iron the fabric onto freezer paper and feed it through your inkjet to create custom prints.

Custom fabric printing

The freezer paper method limits you to the size paper your printer can handle. If you want to print on large pieces of fabric, you'll need a service provider. For example, Silvia's Costumes (www.silviascostumes.com) prints from one yard to as much as you need in widths up to 60 inches on a variety of fabric types (**Figure 8.35**).

Figure 8.35 *Companies such as Silvia's Costumes can create custom-printed fabric in any size you need and on a variety of materials.*

Canvas

Many inkjet printers can use canvas material for printing. Very similar to traditional artist canvas, this media isn't suitable for every type of photograph, but it can give the right image an interesting look (**Figure 8.36**).

Especially when combined with a photo that has been edited to look like a painting (see Chapter 5, "Editing Your Photos"), prints on canvas have the appearance of a painted image rather than a traditional photograph.

Figure 8.36 *Some subjects lend themselves particularly well to printing on canvas.*

When printing on canvas, you should be aware of a couple of things. First, canvas prints tend to look a little flat compared to other paper types. I find that boosting the saturation by about 15, especially for landscape and flower images, restores the color that I want. In Photoshop, select Image > Adjustments> Hue/Saturation and raise the Saturation slider to 15 (**Figure 8.37**). Soft-proofing the results, as explained in Chapter 7, "Printing Your Files," will give you a good idea of the changes made prior to printing the image.

The second consideration when printing to canvas is that you should stretch the canvas onto a frame for best results. In order to do this, make sure you leave a border around your printed area of at least 1 and ½ inches to wrap around the stretcher frame (**Figure 8.38**).

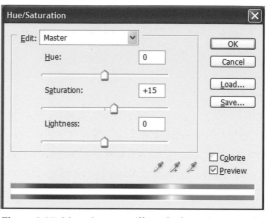

Figure 8.37 Many images will need a boost in saturation to look good when printed on canvas. This is especially true for landscape and nature-type images.

Figure 8.38 Leave a blank area on your print to compensate for the stretcher frame. This will be hidden by your frame.

The one exception to this is when you plan to display the print without a frame. In this case, you'll want the printed area of your image to wrap around the side of the stretcher frame.

Lenticular Prints

You might not be familiar with the term, but when you see a *lenticular* print you'll recognize it immediately. The lenticular process uses multiple images that are arranged in strips and viewed through a special lens (a lenticular lens to be exact). As you move the lens to different angles, different images are displayed. Although two images are the most common, you can add as many as six given a large enough lens.

There are several software packages available to assist with creating the print. These work by slicing your image into very thin strips and interlacing, or alternating, the strips. The resulting image is then saved and ready for printing.

One of the best programs for creating lenticular prints is Magic Interlacer. ProMagic (www.promagic.net) offers several variations of the program, ranging in price from $99 for a version that can make prints up to 8×10 to the $589 Pro package, which can do prints as large as you like. If you want to experiment with the process, ProMagic offers a free trial version of the software.

To get started, open Magic Interlacer Pro and start to examine the very crowded window (**Figure 8.39**). A pinnacle of user interface design it isn't, but it does a nice job with the finished product.

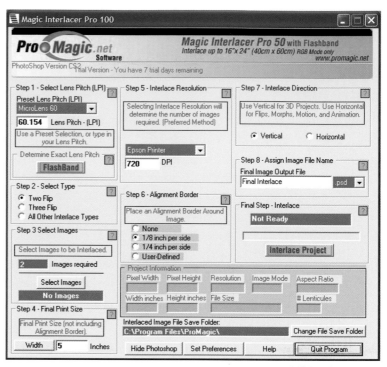

Figure 8.39 *The user interface may not be anything to write home about, but Magic Interlacer Pro does a great job of creating lenticular prints and is just plain fun to play with.*

Note

ProMagic also has software to create anaglyphs, which are those funky 3D images that require the glasses with red and blue lenses.

All versions of Magic Interlacer, with the exception of the Lite version, require Photoshop, which is launched with the program. Your first decision is how many images to use for your print. In this example, I'll use two images. Click Select Images and navigate to your image files (**Figure 8.40**). Once you've selected them, click the Add button to place them into your print. When you click OK, Magic Interlacer processes the files and returns you to the main screen.

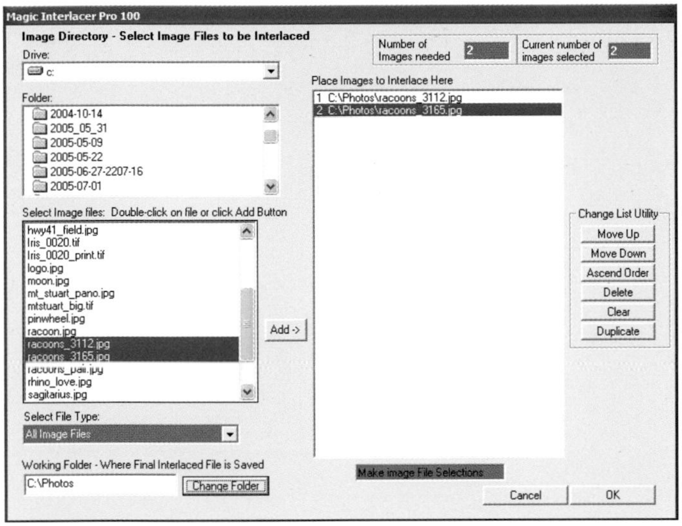

Figure 8.40 *Select the images you want to use for your print. You can set the order in which they appear, but this is only important if you're creating a sequence type of effect.*

Now, select the final print width for your lenticular print. In the next step, you'll select the type of printer you're using to get the optimal resolution for your print. Options include Epson, HP, Canon, and Lexmark.

If you want an alignment border—and you normally will to assist with lining up the print and the lens—select one of the options.

When you've made all your selections, click the Interlace Project button and let Magic Interlacer do its, well, magic. **Figures 8.41a, b,** and **c** show the two original images I used and the final interlaced image. To get the full effect, you'll need to print the image and place the lenticular lens over the print, but even here you can see how the effect works. Pretty cool!

Figure 8.41a

Figure 8.41b

Figure 8.41c

Figures 8.41a, b, and c *Using two different images, Magic Interlace Pro slices the photos into very thin strips and then interlaces them together to create a final lenticular print.*

Obviously this isn't something that you'll be doing often, but it's a fun effect. If you have kids or pets, it can be fun to create a lenticular print that uses photos at different stages of the subject's life, almost like watching a mini-movie of them growing up.

Murals and Wallpaper

Did you know that you can send your photos out to have them turned into murals or wallpaper to cover an entire wall or room in your house (**Figure 8.42**)?

Figure 8.42 *If you've ever wanted a wall-sized mural, shower curtain, or pillowcase made from your images, Gallery Street can take care of you.*

One of the online services for murals is Gallery Street (www.gallerystreet.com). This company can create murals in any size needed for a charge of $8.50 per square foot. Your mural will be ready in about four weeks. You can go wild and have custom shower curtains, tablecloths, and pillowcases made as well.

For wallpaper, Totally Custom Wallpaper (www.totallycustomwall-paper.com) can create any quantity of wallpaper you need using your own images. If you don't want to fill the wall with your photos, you can order borders to use as trim.

You'll find a number of other options for wallpapers and murals in Appendix A.

Moving On

As you can see from the variety of projects covered in this chapter, there are more ways to use your photographs than you might have imagined. If you've ever had the desire to do more than simply frame your images and hang them on the wall, you now know where to start.

To help you with preparing your images for output by one of the online services, the next chapter explains how to work with print services and prepare your images for output.

9 | Working with Service Providers

Unless you're made of money and have unlimited space available, there are going to be times when printing your own images just isn't practical. Whether you occasionally need to print at 16×20 or larger or to canvas or other special media, a service provider is usually the most cost-effective way to get the job done.

By knowing what to look for and what type of questions to ask before sending out your work, you can save time and money, along with a huge amount of frustration.

When to Use a Service Provider

It's hard to give up control over your photographs and prints. As a rule, we photographers tend to continually tweak our images to get them exactly right, often going through multiple rounds of image editing and printing until we have the perfect print. Sending your work out makes this process more difficult and forces you to trust someone with your "baby."

Although it might seem that always doing your own prints makes sense, there are times that sending your work out is more cost-effective than printing at home. For example, one year I decided to print calendars as gifts for everyone in my family. Many, many hours later I had a great set of calendars for everyone and was feeling pretty pleased with myself. Then I started adding up the cost in time and materials. Compared to sending the work out for printing, I spent about four times as much for each calendar as I would have if I'd gone through a service provider. Because they typically work at much larger volumes and buy their paper and ink in bulk, the costs are greatly reduced.

Obviously, if you need a print larger than what your printer can handle, it's time to look for someone else to print for you. It's hard

Note

As an example, the Epson R2400 uses ink cartridges that hold about 12ml of ink and cost about $15 each. The 7800 uses the same ink but in a larger 220ml cartridge that costs about $110 each. The same amount of ink for the R2400 would run almost $300!

to justify spending $5,000 on a large-format printer when you print only a few poster-size images a year.

Not only do you have more choices with regard to print sizes, most of the better service providers offer a number of output options (**Figure 9.1**). Rather than being limited to only inkjet prints, a LightJet or Pictography print might be a better option for your photo. You'll also have a broader selection of media options that are available only in large-format sizes. Any service provider worthy of the name can help you determine what media and printing process will be best for your needs.

Figure 9.1 *West Coast Imaging is an example of one of several good print services available. This provider's Web site offers detailed information on how to prepare your files, as well as the services you can request and results you can expect.*

Choose carefully

Not everyone who has a printer is a qualified service provider, just as not everyone who owns a car knows how to operate it safely. Printmaking is an art, just as photography is an art. You'll want to deal with someone who knows what they're doing and takes pride in their work.

Consider some of the advantages of using a service provider:

- A high-quality print service can offer advice on how to prepare your images for print by listening to your ideas and vision for the final product.

- Sending out your work for printing is often a great way to see what a good print can look like, particularly for an image that you've struggled with getting just right.

- Some media is only available in roll format for large printers. If you're looking for prints on vinyl or fabric in large sizes, a print service may be your only option.

- If you're printing in bulk, say 10 or more copies of something, as in my calendar example earlier, you can save a significant amount of money and time by sending out your work.

- Image correction is offered by many service providers.

Be prepared to pay for that final advantage, however. Although the cost is not trivial, it may be worthwhile to have someone with a wealth of experience perform corrections prior to printing. This puts the burden of quality completely on the service provider and has the added benefit of being a learning experience for you. If you have this type of work done, you should get a copy of the edited image, with all layers intact as part of the price. Going back and examining the adjustments made on your image is an excellent way to learn more about image editing and Photoshop.

Now for the flip side. The disadvantages of using a service provider are as follows:

- You're giving up control of your photo to someone else. Unless you have experience with the print service, or it has been recommended by someone you trust, the wait for that first print can be stressful.

- You lose the immediacy of printing yourself. Depending on where the print service is, it may be a week or more before you have your print back. If you go through a round of proofing before the final job (which I highly recommend, especially the first time you use a service), the turnaround times quickly add up.

- On average, the prints will cost you more. This seems to go counter to my earlier comments about the calendars, but it's not typical to send out a job that you can do yourself. In my example, the time saved would have paid for any per print differences. Most printers also offer significant discounts when printing multiple copies of a job. Don't forget to add in the shipping costs if the service provider isn't local.

The best advice when deciding to use a service provider is to be prepared. Think of it like a cab ride: if you know where you want to go, it's going to cost less than it would if you just say "drive."

What to ask

Remember that you're hiring someone to work for you, and it's completely reasonable to interview that provider. Knowing what to ask before sending out your work can save you money and frustration in the long run. So pick up the phone and get ready to ask the provider:

- **What printers do you use?** Because technology in everything digital advances so quickly, you'll want to be sure the printer is using recent models for the best output possible. Along with this, for inkjet prints you should ask what ink is used. If it's anything other than the manufacturer's ink, or a high-quality variation such as Pantone ColorVANTAGE or Lyson QuadTones, say thank you and hang up. Cheap replacement inks are not going to give you consistent results and may not last as long.

- **What type of media do you offer?** A number of different choices are available in fine art papers, RC photo papers, and so forth. It's nice to know exactly what you can choose, such as Hahnemühle Torchon or Somerset Velvet.

- **Do you provide custom profiles?** If you're going to pay to have your prints made, you obviously want the best possible results. A quality print service will create its own profiles for the best match with its printers and the media being used. Profiles should be available to you for soft proofing (more on proofing later in this chapter). If the provider can't answer your questions about profiles, run, don't walk away, and find someone who knows what they're doing.

- **Can you provide references?** Ask for a list of references, preferably from photographers whose work you respect. In particular, it's nice to know that the service provider has done work similar to what you need.

- **Are sample prints available?** Nothing says more about the quality of a print than a sample on the media and printer you're planning to use. At a minimum the service provider should be willing to supply you with a small print sample for evaluation. Better yet, ask the provider to do a small test print for you at a minimal charge.

- **What other services are provided?** In addition to printing, many quality providers offer scanning and image-correction services. Other services to look for include mounting, canvas stretching, and binding.

- **How long before my print is ready?** Most services are first-come, first-serve at the basic rates. You can expect at least a week on the turnaround time. If you're in a rush, faster service is usually available at a premium (sometimes a very high premium).

- **How much does it cost?** Ah, the all-important question. Expect to pay $12–$40 per square foot for the typical inkjet print, with the higher end common for fine art papers and canvas.

- **Can I upload images?** If the service provider has FTP upload available, you can reduce the time required to turn your job around as well as eliminate the need to burn a CD with your image and mail it.

Once you have the answers to these questions, you'll be ready to make an educated decision about how your image will be printed and begin to make the appropriate image adjustments.

Image Preparation

The more work you can do on your image prior to sending it out for printing, the more control you retain over the process and the lower your final costs will be. All color correction, image cleanup, resizing, and sharpening can and should be done by you before sending your files off to be printed. This type of preparation is commonly referred to as *preflighting*. Preflighting takes its name from the similar checklist done by pilots before a flight. Essentially, you're performing a safety check of every aspect of your image to be sure that it's exactly as you want it.

Most print services offer lower rates for preflighted files simply because you are taking on the responsibility for the image being correct. West Coast Imaging (www.westcoastimaging.com) is typical of the services with this option and includes detailed instructions on its Web site to properly preflight your images for each type of printer the service uses.

Preflighting consists of the following steps:

1. Size your image.

    Depending on the printing process, the service will specify the optimal pixels per inch for the image resolution and provide a list of standard print sizes.

2. Sharpen your image.

    This is where the option to have a proof print done comes in handy. If you're printing to a different type of printer, such as LightJet, you might not know what the best sharpening settings are. The service provider should be able to offer you guidelines, but don't be surprised if your first print isn't exactly like you thought it would be.

3. Add blank canvas area to your image. Select Image > Canvas Size (**Figure 9.2**) in Photoshop, or Image > Resize > Canvas Size in Photoshop Elements. Be sure the Relative check box is clear and enter your new dimensions for Width and Height. With the center Anchor box selected, the canvas will grow while the image remains centered in the new size (**Figure 9.3**).

This is done to make the final page size match the standard paper sizes available and adds a border to the printed image.

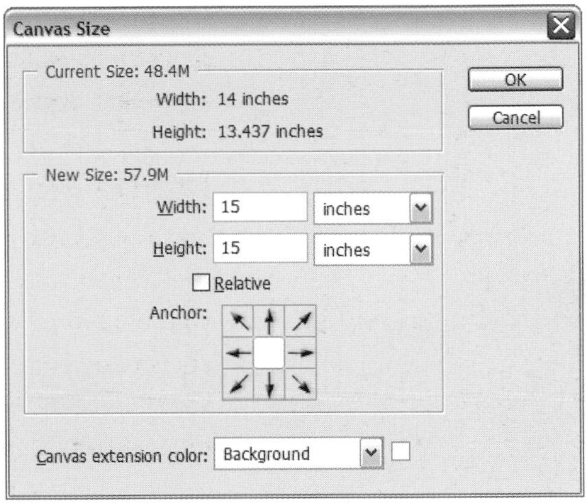

Figure 9.2 Add a border to your image with the Canvas Size command to make the dimensions fit one of the standard paper sizes.

Figure 9.3 After adding to the canvas size, your image will have a border surrounding it that matches the size of the printed page.

4. Add a stroke to your image. To create the stroke, choose Select > All and then Edit > Stroke (**Figure 9.4**). Add a 3-pixel stroke (or other number if specified by the print service), with the Location option set to Inside.

This creates a trim mark for the printer.

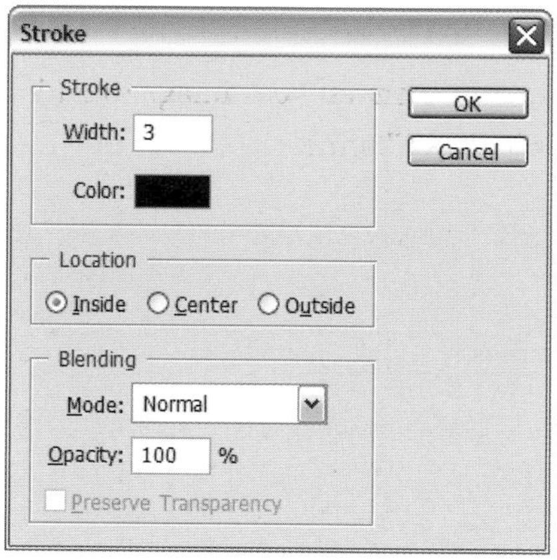

Figure 9.4 *Add a stroke to your image to provide the print service with a trim mark.*

5. Convert your image to the printer's color space. In Photoshop CS2, select Edit > Convert to Profile. For the Destination Space setting, select the supplied profile from the list. Unless directed to use a different Intent option, leave this setting at the default of Relative Colorimetric (**Figure 9.5**).

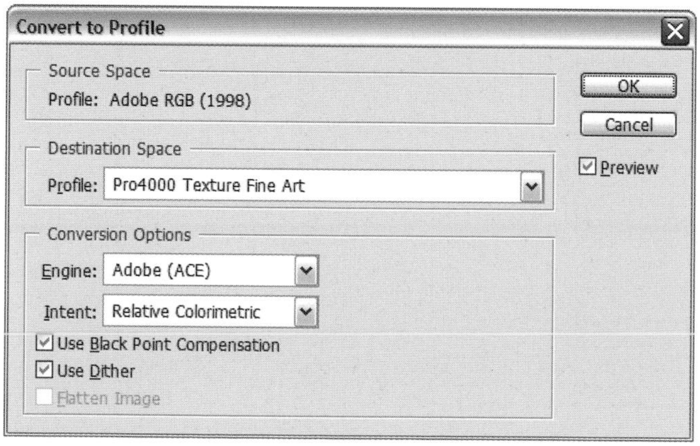

Figure 9.5 *Convert your image to the printer's color space using Convert to Profile.*

Photoshop Elements users don't have the same color management options as users of Photoshop CS2 do. On the Mac, choose Photoshop Elements > Color Settings and then choose Full Color Management. This lets the service provider know that your image is in the Adobe RGB color space (**Figure 9.6**). Windows users of Photoshop Elements will select Edit > Color Settings and choose Always Optimize for Printing (**Figure 9.7**).

6. If required by the service provider, convert your image to 8-bit by selecting Image > Mode > 8/Bits Channel.

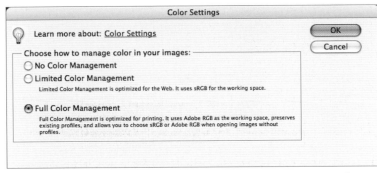

Figure 9.6 *Macintosh users of Photoshop Elements should select Full Color Management for best results when printing.*

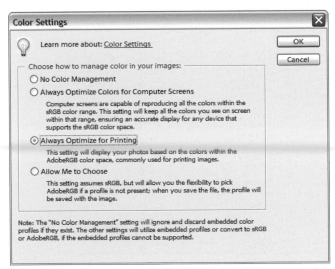

Figure 9.7 *Windows users of Photoshop Elements should select Always Optimize for Printing for best results.*

7. Flatten your image. Most print services don't want to deal with layered images. And the odds are that you aren't going to want to upload a file with all layers saved. Select Layer > Flatten Image.

These are just guidelines. Most print services will want you to use similar steps when preparing your images, but you should check with the provider before sending in your images.

Proofing

Proofing your image can add time to the print job, but for a very modest cost it gives you the opportunity to verify that all of your settings and adjustments are correct before committing to that large sheet of expensive paper.

Most print services offer proofing at a reduced rate, and if you're trying a new paper type and printer, you should take advantage of this option. If you'll be using a similar printing process as you normally do at home, then proofing is easily handled on your own. For instance, if you normally print on the Epson 2200 and you're having the image sent out for enlargement on an Epson 9600, they both use the same UltraChrome inks, which makes proofing at home a realistic option as long as you use the same type of paper the final print will be created on. Being able to fine-tune your image at home with a quick proof print before sending it out for the large print will save you time and money in the long run.

Moving On

By now you should have a good idea when using a print service is your best option. It's not always when you can't do the job yourself, but rather when it makes the most financial sense to let someone else handle your printing. Of course, there are times when you have no other options. When you reach that point, selecting the right service can make all the difference in the world. As a reminder, be sure to check Appendix A for a listing of excellent services.

Now that you have that beautiful print back from the service provider, or off your own printer if done at home, it's time to find out how to properly mount and display it. The next chapter will show you how.

10 | Presenting Your Work

After all the effort you've spent to take a great photo and make a beautiful print, you want it to have an immediate impact on the viewer. Regardless of whether it will hang in your home for only your family and friends to see, or whether you're planning to enter it into a competition or a gallery showing, matted and framed images are far more impressive and durable than bare prints. In this chapter I've asked a good friend, nationally known and respected photographer and exhibitor Ellen Anon, to show you how to correctly mount, mat, and frame your print.

Mounting Your Prints

Before you can frame or mat your print, you must mount it to something. Mounting protects your print and makes it more durable by giving it a stronger backing. As with everything else, you have choices as to what to use as a backing and how to go about attaching the print to the backing material.

How valuable is the piece?

Initially you must decide whether you want to use archival techniques. *Archival* means that the materials you use will be acid free and lignin free to prevent your print from fading or yellowing for at least 100 years. If your photo has significant value to you (whether for personal reasons or objective monetary value), such as a signed limited-edition print, it's likely you want to use archival materials. If you have chosen your printer, inks, and paper for their archival values, then you'll want to continue to choose archival materials. Certainly all prints that you sell or show in a gallery should be mounted archivally. The downside to using archival materials is that they are more expensive, but often it's money well spent.

On the other hand, if the print is just for fun and personal use, you may prefer to economize and use less expensive materials so you can frame and enjoy more pictures. Even nonarchival materials will help protect your prints and make them last longer than simply tacking them up on the wall. I'll explain the archival and nonarchival choices throughout each section. Appendix A, "Resources," has details on where to find archival and conservation mounting and framing supplies.

Choosing a mounting board

Theoretically there are a lot of objects that you could use as a backing for your prints. But most people prefer to mount their photo to something rather thin but firm and flat. Some commonly used choices are cardboard, various foam board products, two-ply mat board, mounting boards, and self-adhesive boards.

Cardboard backing is included with many preassembled frames and is generally the least expensive of all the backing materials. It has a high acid content, however, and is not an archival material. This means the acid is likely to discolor your print rather quickly. Further, cardboard is readily affected by changes in humidity, so it is not uncommon for cardboard to bow or warp, particularly with larger prints. If you care enough about your prints to be reading this book, you shouldn't use cardboard as your backing material!

Foam boards are the most commonly used backing material but vary tremendously in thickness and construction. Most foam boards have a center made of polystyrene foam and a paper or plastic outer covering. The most popular thicknesses for mounting photographs are $\frac{1}{8}$ inch and $\frac{3}{16}$ inch; they are available in both archival (acid-free, pH-neutral coverings and core) and nonarchival forms as well as black or white. In addition to being relatively inexpensive, foam boards are easy to cut.

Two-ply mat boards or mounting boards can also be used as a backing material. They are thinner (but denser) than foam boards, they may be lignin and acid free or nonarchival, and they are usually slightly more expensive. The best material for truly archival mount-

Tip

To make clean cuts in foam board, be certain to use a sharp blade and have another substance, such as a piece of cardboard, underneath the foam board. If you use a slightly dulled knife or razor blade, you might pull the center materials and end up with a messy edge.

ing is a cotton rag mat or mounting board. This is because the lignin in regular paper eventually breaks down and forms an acid that can yellow not only the backing but also your print.

Self-adhesive mounting boards have an adhesive already applied to them, thus enabling you to position your picture until you are satisfied. The adhesive becomes permanent after you apply firm pressure. The actual time it takes to make the bond permanent varies by paper type used for your print. Coated papers tend to become permanently affixed more quickly, making them less "repositionable." Self-adhesive boards are available in several thicknesses as well as in foam core. It's important to check that both the board itself and the adhesives are acid free and pH neutral if you have decided to mount archivally.

Mounting the print to the backing

The second decision you face is whether you are going to use conservation techniques or permanent mounting. Conservation techniques involve mounting your photo so that it can be removed from the backing at will without causing any damage, whereas permanent mounting is just as the name implies: permanent. Each approach has its advantages.

Conservation mounting preserves the value of your piece and is the way to go if you plan to sell your work. Although some buyers may love the way you matted and framed your picture, others may want to redo it to their own taste. It's even possible that your taste or room décor may change over time and you'll want to redo your print. Conservation mounting makes that possible.

Permanent mounting techniques are best for prints that don't have a high personal or monetary value. I wouldn't recommend them for signed, limited-edition prints because the mounting process can't be undone, is not archival (in most cases), and is likely to decrease the value of the piece.

Some people prefer to permanently attach their photo to the backing, believing that it is easier and produces less chance of warping. This is one of those controversial areas. Although technically

Note

Mounting boards differ from mat boards in that the surface of a mounting board is smooth and acid free but generally doesn't look as nice as a mat board. A mat board has a colored surface paper that may be smooth or textured. While the core and backing of the mat board are often acid free, the surface may or may not be.

conservation mounting techniques are supposed to reduce the chances of any rippling or warping occurring within a mat or frame, when done by amateurs sometimes warping does occur.

The best way to decide which is right for your prints is to look more closely at what's involved with each approach.

Conservation mounting

Conservation mounting requires not only that all the mounting materials be acid free, lignin free, and pH neutral, but also that your print be completely removable with minimal, if any, exposure to adhesives. In addition to the advantages of being able to change the mounting for aesthetic reasons, not having the print permanently attached means that the print can move slightly as it expands or contracts with changes in the environment. Traditionally it was believed that this reduced the chances of the print buckling or warping within the mat.

There are two main approaches to conservation mounting. One uses mounting corners, and the other uses hinges. Using *mounting corners* is much easier in my experience, but you have to choose your corners carefully. Photo corners can be made from a variety of materials, some of which are not archival because of both their adhesives and corner material. For example, paper corners, unless made from acid-free, buffered materials, could break down over time and damage your photo.

I prefer MaxiView Corners (**Figure 10.1**). Unlike traditional triangular corners that can cover a substantial amount of your photo, these corners are cut to cover only a small portion of your picture—just enough to hold it securely in place. While using them, I've had no trouble with my prints warping. They are available in two sizes: 1¼ inch, which works well on prints up to 11×14 inches, and a 3 inch for larger prints. Both sizes are made from acid-free polypropylene, and they use a permanent acrylic adhesive that is 100% water based. Note that your photos never come into contact with the adhesive. You can buy MaxiView Corners at a variety of online retailers, including www.lightimpressionsdirect.com.

Figure 10.1 *MaxiView Corners securely mount your print while covering a minimum of its surface. They are one of the easiest ways to do conservation mounting and are available in sizes appropriate for both large and small prints.*

Another popular method used in conservation mounting is to create *hinges* that attach the print to the backing (**Figure 10.2**). This is a carryover from mounting artwork such as watercolor paintings. Advocates of this approach recommend making the hinges using Japanese papers because they're strong and don't discolor or weaken over time. Japanese papers are available under a variety of names, but to be certain the paper is conservation quality, check that it's made from 100% kozo fibers. Unfortunately, some of the Japanese papers marketed for hinging contain wood pulp and are therefore not archival and not suitable for conservation mounting.

Figure 10.2 *Japanese paper hinges use a paste made from wheat or rice to attach the print to the hinge and the hinge to the mount.*

The basic approach with hinging is to attach the hinge to the print using a starch paste adhesive, and then attach the other side of the hinge to the backing board using more starch paste. Detailed instructions for making the hinges as well as rice or wheat starch paste are available on the Internet. Search for "Japanese paper hinge" or "how to do conservation mounting."

Permanent mounting

Permanent mounting means attaching your print directly to the backing with an adhesive. Although it seems straightforward, there are again several options. *Dry mounting* uses an adhesive that is a tissue, acetate, or acetate rubber cement, whereas *wet mounting* uses a paste, spray, or liquid adhesive. I prefer the dry methods because the wet adhesives are often messy and it's very easy to create a disaster with them.

Both wet and dry adhesives can require the use of just pressure to create the bond between the photo and the mounting board (in which case the process is referred to as *cold mounting*), or they can require the addition of heat as well (in which case it's called *hot mounting*). The mounting boards that contain an adhesive that I mentioned earlier are an example of cold mounting.

3M (www.3m.com) makes PMA (Position Mounting Adhesive), which can be used with the nonadhesive backing boards. It's available in rolls from 11 to 24 inches wide and can be pressure set using a roller system or a squeegee (**Figure 10.3**). This is a dry adhesive.

Figure 10.3 *Position Mounting Adhesive (PMA) by 3M is an easy-to-use and repositionable way to dry-mount your print.*

The cold mounting process is basically the same whether you use PMA or the peel-and-stick boards. To cold-mount your print:

1. Cut the mounting board to the desired size and mark where you want to position your photograph.

2. Wipe the back of your photo and the mounting board to remove any dirt or stray hairs. Anything that gets trapped between your print and the backing will show through as a bump when you press the photo into place.

3. If you're using the PMA, remove the protective backing from one side and lightly place the print onto the adhesive. Once it's in the proper position, use a squeegee or roller to create the bond. Next trim the excess PMA.

4. Peel the protective backing off the other side of the PMA, or off the mounting board if you're using a peel-and-stick board.

5. Lightly place your print onto the backing board and reposition it as needed.

6. When it's where you want it, apply firm pressure to it with the squeegee or roller to create the bond to the board. Be sure to remove all air bubbles because even a small air bubble will cause light to be reflected differently and detract from the appearance of your print.

> **Tip**
>
> If you're using PMA, cut a piece just slightly larger than the size of your print. Making it slightly larger makes it easier to use.

If you prefer to use a wet method, you may want to try the 3M Photo Mount spray adhesive, which is pH neutral. To use Photo Mount:

1. Cut your mounting board as desired and mark where you want to position your photograph.

2. Wipe the back of your print and the board to remove all dirt, because even a small hair will appear as a crease or bump when you're done.

3. In a well-ventilated area, spray an even coat of Photo Mount on the back of your print.

4. Lightly place the photograph onto the mounting board and reposition it until you're happy with the placement.

5. As described in the PMA method, apply even pressure to activate the bond.

Most hot-mounting techniques use a tissue-type adhesive or acetate along with a heat press. The basic technique is to place the adhesive between the print and the mount, which is prepared the same as for the cold mounts. You then place the photograph and the board into a heat press that activates the adhesive while simultaneously applying pressure. A protective sheet prevents the inks from sticking to the press.

The primary advantage of hot mounting over cold mounting is that once you own a heat press, it's more economical. Many framing stores use this technique. However, dry-mount presses themselves are expensive. An entry-level Seal 160M currently sells for just under $1,400, but it seems to work quite well with inkjet prints, particularly the Epson UltraChrome inks. Although you could use an iron instead of a press, the results can be erratic because the procedure depends on even pressure and even heat.

Laminating

Another option that is often overlooked is lamination. Often used to protect photos at trade shows, *laminating* is a permanent process that is not archival but may protect, waterproof, and improve fade resistance by offering some UV protection. The technique is a useful alternative when traditional behind-glass framing isn't possible. For example, you could laminate tiny photos to use as luggage tags or huge prints that might be quite costly to frame.

Laminate is available in pouches or roll style in a variety of styles and thicknesses. The pouch style works better for smaller prints and thinner mounting boards. As you run the pouch through the laminator, the photograph is sealed between two layers of film.

Roll laminators (**Figure 10.4**) are more common for photographic purposes because they can handle larger sizes and thicker mounting boards. You place your mounted photo between two sheets of laminating film that have either a heat-activated or cold-press adhesive on them and then run them through rollers that activate the bond. The film is available in gloss, luster, and matte finishes.

Figure 10.4 *Place your mounted photo between two sheets of film and run it through the laminator to protect prints that are not going to be framed behind glass.*

Cold-roll laminators are available for under $700, whereas the heat-seal models usually are over $1,000. Pouch laminators are considerably more affordable. You can find 4½-inch laminators for under $50, while 9-inch models may run closer to $150. If you foresee the need to do large numbers of prints, or laminate large sizes, heavy-duty models are available at a cost of around $300. The film itself tends to be inexpensive; for example, a box of 100 12×18-inch pouches 3 mil thick is under $25.

If you have only an occasional print you'd like to laminate, many printing shops offer laminating services.

Protective sprays

Protective sprays are another approach to protecting your print from scratches, moisture, UV fading, and environmental damage. The sprays create a surface barrier that makes the print more durable. Unfortunately, many of them create a coating that changes the texture and appearance of your print. Your best bet is PremierArt Print Shield by Premier Imaging Products (premierimagingproducts.com) (**Figure 10.5**), which provides protection from light, water, moisture, airborne contaminants, and even fingerprints while maintaining the surface texture of your print. It works well on glossy paper as well as matte papers. Testing by Wilhelm Imaging Research (www.wilhelm-research.com) verifies using this spray increases print permanence.

If you are not going to place your print under glass or acrylic, using PremierArt Print Shield is a good idea, especially if you've gone to the effort of mounting and matting it.

Tip

Before using any protective print spray, it's a good idea to "cure" the paper to remove the excess glycol to avoid outgassing. To do this, place a piece of plain paper over the print for 24 hours. While this is less of a problem with pigment UltraChrome inks, it's still a good habit.

Figure 10.5 *PremierArt Print Shield protective spray offers protection from environmental contaminants without changing the surface texture of your print.*

Matting Your Prints

When done well, matting can tremendously increase the impact of your photo. The mat adds importance to your print and encourages the viewer to gaze at it longer.

Matting serves several additional purposes as well:

- It separates your photo from the environment around it to make it a focal point of interest.

- If the print is also framed, the mat separates the picture from the frame to create a space that encourages the viewer to focus on the image. This gives the piece a stronger presence.

- Practically speaking, it physically separates the print from the glass if it is framed. This is important because inkjet prints that are pressed against glass tend to deteriorate more quickly, and spots or fogging may occur on the glass.

- Matted prints are simply more marketable, because they're ready to be hung or framed and look more impressive.

So, now that you know why you should use a mat board, take a look at the matting options that are available.

Choosing the mat board

You have a number of choices to make about your mat. There are archival mats and nonarchival, as well as varying thicknesses of mats. Of course, a huge variety of colors is available as well. In addition, you can use a single mat or something more dramatic, such as a double mat.

Archival mat boards are constructed from cotton, and the core as well as the surface and backing papers are completely acid free and lignin free. These are called *rag* mats.

Regular, nonarchival mat boards are made from wood pulp that is buffered during the manufacturing process to make them pH neutral. The core and back of the boards are acid free, but not the surface paper. Even so, some of these papers are rated as lasting 100 years.

Mat boards are available in varying thicknesses: two-ply, four-ply, six-ply (rare), and eight-ply. The four-ply mats are the most common. Two-ply mat board is quite thin and lacks some of the impact of the heavier mat boards, although it can be used when

Note

The term "rag" dates back to the fifteenth century when cotton rags were the principal raw materials used for papermaking. The term is used today to refer to papers and boards made of 100% cotton fiber pulp.

Tip

If you plan to show your work, check with the gallery for any requirements they may have on mat weights.

double-matting a picture. Even most double mats use four-ply boards, however. Eight-ply mat board is quite a bit more expensive and can be more difficult to cut, but it gives your picture a very elegant appearance. If you are showing your work in a gallery or selling it, you can often command a higher price for your piece if you use eight-ply board because the finished product looks more impressive and expensive. The extra thickness of the mat allows the 45-degree bevel edge to become more prominent, which is a nice finishing touch.

Choose your mat colors carefully, because it's quite easy to overwhelm your photo with strong colors. Many people prefer to use black or some shade of white (**Figure 10.6**). You'll be amazed at how many shades of white mat board are available and how some look wonderful with your piece (and others quite drab). If you prefer to use a color, there are two approaches that are often successful. One is to choose a color that appears in your photo that you wish to accentuate.

Figure 10.6 *Simple white mats can be an effective choice for many images. (Image copyright Ellen Anon, www.sunbearphoto.com)*

Often it's a good idea to go just a bit lighter than the actual color in the photo because there is a lot of surface area in the mat and the greater area can make the color appear overwhelming if you're not careful. An alternate approach is to select a color that is the opposite of the main color in your image. This works because opposite colors are complementary, but if you're not good with colors, you may want to consult someone for help if you go this route.

You can also order a set of corner samples so you can see how each color works with your print. One Web site that offers these samples is www.framingsupplies.com.

Another approach is to use Photoshop to help you simulate different color mats. Many Web sites that sell mat boards, including Dick Blick Art Materials (www.dickblick.com), have online color samples that you can view. To simulate the appearance of matting your print with one of these colors you can apply the colors as borders (**Figure 10.7a**, **b**, and **c**).

To preview what your print will look like with different color mats, follow these steps:

1. Take a screenshot of the color samples and save it.

2. In Photoshop, open the files of the image you'll be mounting as well as the screenshot of the color samples.

3. With the image you wish to mat active, choose Image > Canvas Size.

4. Assuming you already sized your print to the print size, check the Relative box and add 2 or 2½ inches to each dimension. Leave the anchor point set to the center.

   By default the new canvas will use your existing background color.

5. Click on the added canvas with the Magic Wand tool to make a selection. Make sure the Contiguous option is selected and

use a low tolerance so you don't accidentally select some pixels within your photo.

6. Use the Eyedropper tool and click on the desired color from the screenshot of the color samples to set that color as your new foreground color.

7. Select the Paint Bucket tool and click within the border on your print. The border will be replaced by the color you selected and will simulate matting your print. Repeat this as many times as you want to find the best color mat to use.

Figures 10.7a

Figures 10.7b

Figures 10.7c

Figures 10.7a, b, and c Different color mats can create a very different feel to your photograph. Some aspects of a picture may be drawn forward while others recede. Be sure to select a mat color that complements your print. In 10.7a, the mat color draws your eye to the fawn and helps the surrounding colors recede. 10.7b gives more prominence to the flowers and grasses, and lets the fawn blend into the surroundings. The black mat used in 10.7c gives more weight to the whites in both the flowers and the fawn. Which is best is a subjective choice; any of the three work well. (Images copyright Ellen Anon, www.sunbearphoto.com)

A compromise between a plain white or black mat and a colored mat is to double-mat your picture, using white or black as the outer mat, with an accent of another color for the inner mat (**Figure 10.8**). Of course, you could also use black or white for the inner mat as well. This often makes for a dramatic presentation of your print.

Figure 10.8 *Double-matting is often an extremely effective way of finishing your print. It shows that you've taken the time to attend to details to create a finished product with considerable impact. (Image copyright Ellen Anon, www.sunbearphoto.com)*

Mat boards can also have cores that are a different color than the surface. Commonly the core is either white or black, although some specialty mats have various colored cores as well. Using a contrasting core, such as a white mat with a black core, or vice versa, provides a pleasing accent bevel around your piece that makes for a very polished presentation and is more economical than using a double mat (**Figure 10.9**).

Figure 10.9 *Contrasting black or white or color core mats add an eye-pleasing detail flattering to many images without creating any additional work while cutting the mat. (Image copyright Ellen Anon, www.sunbearphoto.com)*

Because the purpose of the mat is to draw attention to your picture rather than to the mat, usually a simple mat works best. Colors, accent lines, and cuts should complement your photograph and not compete for attention.

Cutting the mat

Cutting the mat demands precision and for most people, it takes a while to become proficient. Most people ruin quite a few mats when they first begin cutting them. Being just an $1/8$ of an inch off on one cut will ruin the entire mat. Tools are available that make the process considerably easier and more reliable, but the better ones are expensive. If you need only an occasional mat, you might consider using a precut mat rather than dealing with the frustration of doing it yourself.

Precut mats are available in an amazing array of sizes, styles, and colors, in both archival and nonarchival materials. The standard sizes are 8×10, 11×14, 16×20, and 20×30 inches. The openings are cut to standard sizes as well, but they may or may not correspond to the size of your print. Different cameras shoot to different proportions, however, so sometimes "standard" isn't what you need.

Many precut mats use two-ply mat board but some are four-ply, so look carefully at what you're selecting. Some have fancy designs on the mat that may look nice on the mat by itself—but that may compete with your photo rather than complement it.

If commercially available mats don't meet your needs, consider having a mat custom cut for you. You specify the dimensions and the mat, and then the expert cuts the mats for you. An additional advantage of this approach is that your prints don't have to be a standard size—you can make them whatever size best suits the image and your needs. Of course, you can specify the dimensions so that the overall size fits a standard frame if you wish. Your local framing store may offer this service at prices that may or may not be competitive with such online resources as www.framingsupplies. com, www.matcutter.com, and www.lightimpressionsdirect.com.

How large a mat do you need?

If you are using a precut, standardized mat, your choice for overall mat size is pretty straightforward: You select the mat that has an opening that fits your print. Someone else decided how wide to make the borders. If you are cutting the mat yourself or ordering a custom-cut mat, however, you have to make the decision.

There are no hard-and-fast rules for border width; personal prefer- ence plays a big part. Generally, the larger the print, the larger you make the border. For example, if your print is 8×12 inches, a 2-inch border around most sides will look nice. You may want to weight the bottom edge and make it slightly wider, perhaps 2½ inches (**Figures 10.10a** and **b**). The same photo printed at 12×18 will look better with borders of 2½ to 3 inches. In most cases, a width of 2 or 3 inches is a good starting place, and you won't want to go beyond 5 inches unless you are seeking to create a special, dramatic look. Ironically, a very small photo, such as a 4×6 print, will gain new importance and prominence when placed in an oversized mat, perhaps one with 5-inch borders. Just be careful not to make the mat too large, or you may overpower the picture without gaining a dramatic effect.

Figures 10.10a and b Border widths are a matter of personal preference, but
a reasonable starting place is 2 to 3 inches for a print about 10x15 inches (a).
Weighted bottoms can add impact (b). When matting pictures for a gallery
show, larger mats may give the picture more impact. (Images copyright Ellen
Anon, www.sunbearphoto.com)

On the opposite end of the spectrum, you can mat a horizontal panorama with small borders on the left and right edges and add wide borders on the top and bottom to help even out the proportions (**Figure 10.11**).

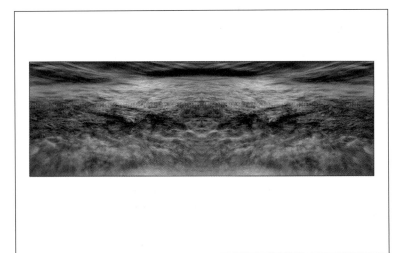

Figure 10.11 Using narrower side borders on a panorama or a picture that has unusual dimensions can help give a sense of balance to the print by changing the aspect ratio of the finished piece. (Image copyright Ellen Anon, www. sunbearphoto.com)

For a double mat, make the outer mat slightly narrower than the inner one by about ¼ inch on each edge. This results in a pleasing layered look to the final print.

Calculating the exact dimensions

One of the most critical steps in cutting your own mats, as well as when ordering a custom-cut mat, is to take *precise* measurements. This isn't the time to hurry because the smallest miscalculation will render the mat useless.

To calculate the dimensions of your mat:

1. Accurately measure the size of your print—not the paper but the print itself.

Note

If you are planning to display your work in a gallery, they may have set guidelines for the final dimensions regardless of the size of the print itself. In such cases, make sure you request full guidelines for mounting, matting, and framing your pieces.

2. Subtract ¼ inch from step 1's length and width measurements to determine the size of the opening you will need.

    This ensures that the mat just covers the edges of your print and that no plain paper peeks through unexpectedly on a side. For example, if your print measured 8×12 in step 1, you'll need an opening that measures 7¾×11¾ inches.

3. Decide on your border width. For this example, I'll use 2½ inches all around.

4. Add the width of the border for each side to the size of the opening.

    In this case, add 2½ to 7¾ inches (the size of the opening), then add another 2½ inches (the border on the other side of the print) to get a measurement of 12¾ inches in one direction. The other dimension is 2½ plus 11¾ inches (the size of the opening in the other direction) plus another 2½, for a total of 16¾ inches. So the 8×12 print with 2-inch borders all around needs a mat that is 12¾×16 ¾ inches with a window opening of 7¾×11¾ inches.

If you wish to weight the mat (to have one border slightly wider than the others), then simply add that measurement in to the appropriate side to determine the size of your mat.

Cutting the window

Once you have a piece of mat board cut to your exact external dimensions, you still need to cut the window. You can do this with tools as basic as a straight edge and a razor blade or with the aid of a mat cutter. Mat cutter prices range from under $150 for a basic setup to over $50,000 for computer-driven systems. More sophisticated cutters do make life a lot easier, but most of us don't need outrageously expensive computer-driven models.

A basic mat cutting setup, such as the Altos 4501 (www.altosezmat.com), uses simple adjustments and allows for straight or beveled edges. It can handle any length mat because it is open ended and adjusts in ⅛-inch increments up to 6 inches wide for the borders.

Altos also has circle, oval, and freehand cutters available. If you decide that you want to get fancy with your cuts, Altos also offers books and videos with advanced cutting examples.

If you're going to cut a lot of mats, you may want to consider investing in a more sophisticated mat cutter, such as the Logan Framer's Edge mat cutter Model 650 for around $650 or the Fletcher 2200 for near $1,400 (**Figure 10.12**). The more expensive units have features that prevent bowed cuts, simplify repeat cutting of mat borders, and have stop systems to prevent you from making overcuts (or undercuts) that can ruin your mat. You can also find models that handle board lengths up to 40 and even 60 inches.

> **Note**
>
> Aside from measurement errors, overcuts and undercuts are one of the most common errors and result in a lot of wasted mat board. A system that provides stops is well worth it if you cut mats frequently.

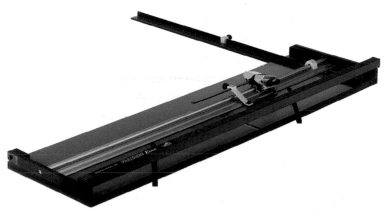

Figure 10.12 If you're planning to cut a quantity of mats, it's worth investing in a quality mat cutter. Features such as stops to prevent over- and undercuts help prevent you from ruining numerous mats.

You can program the computer-driven systems to make not only the basic straight and beveled cuts, but V grooves and other designs as well. The advantage of these systems is that once they are programmed accurately, the boards are cut with no mistakes. Their downside, of course, is cost.

Regardless of which tools you use to cut your mat, the basic steps are quite similar:

1. On the *backside* of your mat board, mark off the borders (**Figure 10.13**). Use a sharp pencil and make as precise a line as pos-

sible. It's actually the corners that are the most important areas to mark.

If you are using a high-end mat cutter with stops, you can just set the measurements on the stops and border width on the cutter itself. Making the pencil lines, however, is a good way to double-check your accuracy.

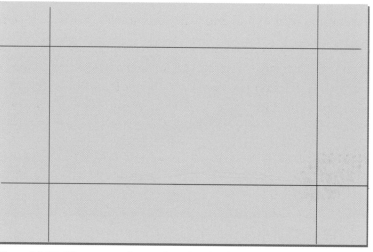

Figure 10.13 *After you cut the mat board to the desired size, precisely mark off the borders on the back of the mat board using a very sharp pencil.*

> **Tip**
>
> If you're cutting using a straight edge and a razor blade, place weights on the ends of the straight edge to help prevent it from moving as you cut against it.

2. Place your mat board on the cutter and adjust the settings for the proper size.

3. Make sure to use a sharp blade and cut along the guides, turning the board for each cut. If your border widths are all the same, you can cut all four sides without having to reset any of the measurements. But if you've weighted one side, be sure to reset the measurements accordingly.

When cutting mats, it's very easy to make a seemingly small mistake that ruins the entire mat. I've learned the hard way to avoid distractions while I'm in the process of cutting a mat. Take your time, think through what you're doing, and you'll be able to save a lot of money by cutting your own mats.

> **Tip**
>
> When cutting mats, I prefer to hinge the mat to the mounting board before I attach the print to the mounting board. I lay the print in place and adjust it slightly to make sure the mat lies exactly where I want it. I then place a covered weight on the print to prevent it from moving while I add the MaxiView Corners. I finish by using 3M ATG tape to fasten the other three sides of the mat to the mounting board.

Framing Your Prints

In most cases, if the print is worth the work of matting, it's worth framing. Aesthetically, a framed piece is considerably more impressive. In addition, the extra protection offered by the frame and the glass will add to the durability and longevity of your print. Inkjet prints are subject to fading and color shifts not only from UV light exposure but also common pollutants in the air. Framing under glass significantly reduces the damage from these environmental hazards.

Whether you opt to purchase ready-made frames, order custom-cut frames and assemble them yourself, or have a frame shop do the work, you will encounter a variety of options in materials, colors, sizes, style, and prices. Most museums and galleries, for example, prefer simple black metal or polished wood frames (**Figure 10.14**).

Note

Sometimes framing isn't the right option. For example, perhaps the print is simply destined for your portfolio as a sample of your work. In this case you may prefer to laminate the print and mat it, or just mat it but not frame it.

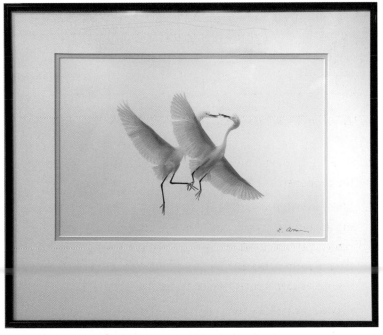

Figure 10.14 *Simple black frames are preferable for displaying in museums, and galleries favor simple black frames as well. They give a uniform and elegant appearance to the prints and complement most styles of photography. (Image copyright Ellen Anon, www.sunbearphoto.com)*

But gallery style framing is also popular for home displays because of its clean, classy, and elegant look. In addition, it's a style that tends to work well with almost all subject matter. When choosing more ornate frames, try to choose one that complements your image rather than competing with it.

As for mats, you can go to your local craft store, home décor store, photo store, framing store, or even discount superstore and find a selection of preassembled frames. If your matted print is a standard size, a preassembled frame may be more economical if you can find a style you like. Some people even browse yard sales to buy framed pieces extremely cheap so that they can reuse the frame!

If your print is not a standard size, another option is to order custom-cut moldings and assemble the frames yourself. These frame pieces are available online in a variety of materials and styles. Those from Nielsen (www.nielsen-bainbridge.com) are generally good quality, as are some of the others. Most are metal frames, but you'll find a considerable variety of colors, finishes, and styles (**Figure 10.15**).

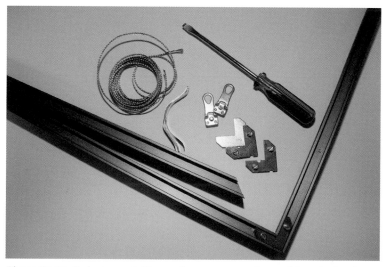

Figure 10.15 *Ordering metal frames by segments and assembling the hardware is quite easy and only requires a simple screwdriver.*

You order these frames in segments, and normally the price listed is for two pieces at each length. You tell the supplier the size of your matted piece, and it calculates how large to make the frame. The frames are easy to assemble with just a screwdriver, but be sure to inquire whether the hardware is included or if you have to order it separately. You will almost surely have to order hangers and picture wire separately, along with rubber bumpers or spacers to hold the picture slightly away from the wall on the bottom. Online sources such as www.framingsupplies.com and www.lightimpressionsdirect.com offer a wide variety of choices.

One thing you must take into consideration when selecting a frame style is the thickness of your matted piece—that is, the combined width of the backing board, the print, the mat, and the glazing material (whether glass or acrylic). Some frame styles are deeper than others (**Figure 10.16**). Generally it's not a problem to select a deeper frame, although they tend to be slightly more expensive, because you must use spring clips to hold your matted piece securely into the frame. It is a problem, however, to select a frame that isn't deep enough to hold your matted print and the glazing material!

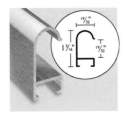

Figure 10.16 *The "rabbet," or thickness, of the frame is an important dimension to check to make sure that the frame is thick enough to hold the glass or acrylic, the mat, your print, the mounting board, and a spring hinge. In this diagram, the rabbet is* ¹⁹⁄₃₂ *of an inch.*

Note

The term "rabbet" is used to describe the depth or thickness of the frame.

Of course you can also opt to have your print professionally custom-framed at a frame shop, but this is often a very expensive proposition. If you have a special print, however, it may be worth the price.

PictureFrames.com (www.pictureframes.com) offers custom framing and matting as well as ready-made frames online. They offer a unique Personal Frame Shop, which you can use to preview your matting and framing choices on your print (**Figure 10.17**). You can try various combinations until you find just the right one. You upload a JPEG file of your image, and then as you make your mat and frame choices, the image preview (as well as the pricing) updates.

Figure 10.17 *The Personal Frame Shop (www.personalframeshop.com) allows you to preview your matting and framing choices online to determine the ideal combination.*

Glass or acrylic?

Glass or an acrylic is used as a protective barrier in most frames to prevent environmental contaminants from reaching, and slowly destroying, your artwork. Glass was the default choice for glazing in frames for many years and is still commonly used. It's available in clear as well as antireflective styles and in a variety of thicknesses and grades. Normally you want the thinnest glass commercially available because glass is quite heavy, but you may want to consider museum grade or nonglare glass. Some glasses, particularly those with an antireflective coating on them, have a slight color cast that can be problematic.

Glass is generally readily available and can be purchased precut from regular glass shops as well as craft stores or museum shops. For a recent gallery show of mine, I was directed by the gallery owner to a regular commercial glass store for my glass because the cost was less than half of what it was from venders selling glass specifically for framing. You can order sheets of glass and cut it yourself, but unless you're framing huge quantities, it's unlikely to be worth the trouble. Glass breaks easily, and the edges are sharp. For me, it's well worth the small extra premium I pay to have the glass cut by someone who does it regularly. Even so, when I'm putting together a number of prints for a gallery show, I always end up with numerous glass cuts on my hands and arms as I assemble the framed prints.

Acrylic or Plexiglas is becoming a popular alternative to glass for several reasons. It is much lighter than glass, and particularly in large prints—those over 16×20—this can be a good thing. Not only would a 24×36-inch print framed using glass be quite heavy to move, it would also be quite difficult to hang and require special hardware on the wall. For pictures that need to be shipped to other locations, acrylic makes the process safer by reducing the chances of glass breakage, as well as more economical due to its weight. Similarly, if the print is to be hung in an area where it might fall or children are around, acrylic may be a better choice even for smaller prints due to the reduced chance of shattering.

Acrylic is available in clear as well as antireflective styles that block up to 97% of the ultraviolet light. However, the antireflective styles may have a dull appearance, and you may want to see a sample before deciding to use them. If you do decide to use antireflective acrylic, it will arrive with protective sheets on both sides. Once you remove these sheets, it will be quite difficult to determine which side is supposed to face outwards, so some advance planning is called for. Further, when you remove the protective sheets a static charge seems to develop, turning the acrylic into a dust magnet. This can make it challenging to assemble your frame without trapping dust inside.

Acrylics scratch quite easily, and this can detract from the appearance of your print. Small scratches can be removed using a product called Novus #2, which available online from a number of sources, including www.delviesplastics.com.

To clean acrylic, use a soft, nonabrasive cloth dampened with lukewarm water with a small amount of mild dishwashing detergent (⅛ teaspoon detergent to 6 ounces of water) or use Brillianize, a product specifically designed for cleaning acrylic. Wipe clean until dry. Don't use a paper towel because it's too abrasive and may scratch the acrylic. Chemical cleaners such as most window cleaners or all-purpose cleaners can also harm acrylic surfaces.

Alternative presentations

Sometimes you just want to do something different. Ultimately you are limited only by your imagination to creatively use available materials to present your images. This could mean constructing a frame yourself out of an unusual material. For example, Jon once framed a picture of an old barn with pieces of wood that had fallen off the barn.

Another approach would be a "floating" presentation where the edges of the print are not covered by the mat, thereby creating the impression that the print is floating. Often the edges of the print are torn or deckled rather than being the smooth crisp edges of the paper. Simply trying to tear the edges of an inkjet print by hand can be a hit-or-miss operation resulting in a high number of ruined prints. Using a straight edge to guide the tearing will give slightly better results, but the edges themselves will probably be too uniform and lack the torn appearance you're seeking. One solution is offered by Inkjet Arts (www.inkjetart.com), who sells several styles of rippers that essentially are stainless steel or Lucite pieces that have deckled edges that you use to guide your tearing (**Figure 10.18**).

Figure 10.18 This "ripper," available from www.inkjetarts.com, enables you to create deckled edges on your prints.

Deckle the edges of your paper after you have printed it because the torn edges may make it difficult for some printer rollers to carry the paper through without jamming. You have to plan ahead for your paper size when using this technique. If you want to leave a one-inch border with a deckled edge around your print, you'll need to have at least two inches of border around the image when you first print it so that you have something to hold onto as you tear the edges.

One effective way of presenting a print with a deckled edge is to mount it to a piece of four-ply mat board that is about ¼ inch smaller than the deckled print. Then mount the combination to a

Tip

Avoid the deckle edge rippers made for scrapbooking. They aren't stiff enough to work well with heavy photo papers.

mounting board. This will raise your print and create a small drop shadow that adds to the illusion that it is floating (**Figure 10.19**). You may then add a double mat or an eight-ply mat, and allow the window to reveal some space around the edges of your print. You'll need to use at least a double- or eight-ply mat to have the depth that you'll need. Complete the look by adding a frame and glass or acrylic as desired.

Figure 10.19 *Properly mounting and matting a deckled print gives it a limited-edition fine art feel.*

PhotoGlow (www.photoglow.com) offers a unique and striking presentation option using backlit frames. Unlike the commercially available backlit frames you may have seen at airports or other commercial locations, PhotoGlow's frames are evenly illuminated and quite thin. In fact it's difficult to tell that it's a back-lit frame by just looking at the frame itself. However, one look at the image tells you something is quite different! The backlighting adds vibrancy, depth, and drama to your image (**Figure 10.20**). PhotoGlow frames are available in numerous sizes from 5×7 to 24×36 inches, as well as custom-created sizes, all in different finishes. To use these frames you'll need to print your picture on backlit film. The downside of these frames is that they are not archival. But if you'd like to make your photograph become a conversation piece, this could be a good choice.

© 2003 Jon Canfield

Figure 10.20 *The PhotoGlow frame gives your image incredible depth for a very striking presentation. It's easy to see how much more depth the image has when the PhotoGlow frame is turned on (left side) compared to the normal style frame on the right.*

Moving On

The bottom line is that the final presentation of your print should reflect your personal taste while enhancing the image. Properly mounting, matting, and framing your photograph will add years to its life and increase its impact on those who view it. Ultimately people will perceive you as a better photographer because your work is presented so professionally.

A | **Resources**

Throughout the book I referenced a number of sources for the various products featured. You'll find all of those sources and a number of others listed in this appendix for easy reference. As new and updated information becomes available, I'll post it on the Web site at www.printlikeapro.com.

Color Management

If you're serious about your image editing and printing, you already know that color management will have a big impact on the quality and predictability of your output. A number of choices are available when it comes to color management solutions. You can't go wrong with any of them, but these are all considered top-quality options.

ColorVision

A leader in the color management field with a number of products ranging from entry-level to pro, ColorVision tends to have the best prices for the features offered and are excellent to work with. The product line (from least to most expensive) includes:

* ColorPlus
* Spyder2PRO Studio
* PrintFIX PRO Suite
* SpectroPRO Suite
* Datacolor ColorFacts Professional

    ColorVision, Inc,
    5 Princess Road
    Lawrenceville, NJ 08648
    (609) 895-7430, (800) 554-8688
    customerservice@colorvision.com
    www.colorvision.com

Fuji

Fuji has a full set of profiling tools available. Each is available separately or as a complete set. These are all software solutions that require you to purchase a spectrocolorimeter separately:

- Monitor Profiler

- Camera Profiler

- Scanner Profiler

- RGB Output Profiler

- CMYK Output Profiler

- ColourKit Profiler Suite

   FujiFilm Electronic Imaging Ltd.
   www.colorprofiling.com

Gretag Macbeth

Gretag Macbeth has a reputation among color professionals of being high quality and very accurate. The Eye-One products are available in several configurations. Eye-One Photo is of special interest to photographers; it allows you to create monitor and printer profiles. Many companies also use the ProfileMaker software to create profiles for their papers and printers. The product line includes:

- Eye-One Display 2

- Eye-One Photo

- Eye-One Proof

- ProfileMaker

   Gretag Macbeth LLC
   617 Little Britain Road
   New Windsor, NY 12553
   (845) 565-7660
   www.i1color.com

Monaco/X-Rite

Monaco is familiar to most Epson printer owners because a special offer for EZ Color is included with many photo printers. The Optix series and Pulse ColorElite are professional-quality tools at very reasonable prices. The product line includes:

- Monaco EZ Color
- Monaco Optix XR
- X-Rite Pulse ColorElite

  X-Rite Photo Marketing
  8 Westchester Plaza
  Elmsford, NY, 10523
  (914) 347-3300
  info@xritephoto.com
  www.xritephoto.com

Editing Software

Adobe might be the standard by which everyone else is judged, but other image editing options are available that might be more your style. Although I covered Adobe Photoshop and Photoshop Elements almost exclusively throughout the book, the other programs listed here are also worth checking out.

Adobe

The standard in image editing, Photoshop and Photoshop Elements are without a doubt the most popular programs among digital photographers.

  Adobe Systems, Inc
  345 Park Avenue
  San Jose, CA 95110
  (408) 536-6000
  www.adobe.com

Corel

Corel offers Paint Shop Pro which is a very good alternative to Photoshop at a much lower price. Painter and Painter Essentials are also available from Corel.

Corel Corporation
1600 Carling Avenue
Ottawa, Ontario
Canada K1Z 8R7
(800) 772-6735
www.corel.com

Microsoft Corporation

Digital Image Suite is Microsoft's offering in the image editing area. A great product that will appeal to casual or new digital imaging enthusiasts, it also works with most Photoshop plug-ins.

Microsoft Corporation
One Microsoft Place
Redmond, WA 98052
(800) 642-7676
www.microsoft.com

iView Multimedia

My favorite image management program, iView MediaPro is the only way I'm able to find my images. If you shoot lots of digital images, you need to be organized. iView MediaPro is the best tool for organizing. Enough said!

iView Multimedia Ltd
30-40 Elcho Street
Battersea Park
London
SW11 4AU
www.iview-multimedia.com

ACD Systems

This company offers excellent image-management tools along with image-editing software (Canvas) and printing utilities (FotoSlate Photo Print Studio).

ACD Systems of America
1150 NW 72 Avenue
Suite 180
Miami, FL 33126
(305) 596-5644
www.acdsystems.com

Extensis

Portfolio is a very useful image-management solution. Also available is the Extensis Photo Imaging Suite, which includes Portfolio, pxl SmartScale, Mask Pro, PhotoFrame, and Intellihance Pro.

Extensis, Inc
1800 SW First Avenue
Suite 500
Portland, OR 97201
(503) 274-2020
(800) 796-9798
www.extensis.com

ProMagic

Offers image-processing software for creating lenticular prints and anaglyphs.

ProMagic Software
109 Willow Drive
Zephyr Cove, NV 89448
(775) 588-2603
support@promagic.net
www.promagic.net

Apple Computer

Along with building the Macintosh, long a favorite with photographers, Apple has software and services that are designed to help you get the most from your digital imaging. iPhoto is a very good cataloging and editing program, and the online printing service is great. iPhoto books are among the best out there.

Apple Computer
1 Infinite Loop
Cupertino, CA 95014
(408) 996-1010
www.apple.com

Plug-ins

Sometimes all you need is one more feature to customize a program to your needs. These plug-ins all add their own specialty to Photoshop, and some can be used as standalone programs as well, handy for those of you that don't use Photoshop-compatible programs.

These are only a few of the thousands of plug-ins available. If you can imagine an effect, someone has probably written a plug-in to create it. These are some of interest to digital photographers.

onOne Software

From image resizing to masking to borders and beyond, onOne Software offers a range of software, including:

- Genuine Fractals
- Mask Pro
- Intellihance Pro
- PhotoFrame

- pxl SmartScale
- Genuine Fractals Print Pro

  onOne Software
  15350 SW Sequoia Parkway
  Suite 190
  Portland, OR 97224
  (503) 968-1468
  (888) 968-1468
  sales@ononesoftware.com
  www.ononesoftware.com

Fred Miranda

Offers excellent plug-ins and actions for Photoshop. Fred is a great photographer and really understands what photographers need. Highly recommended, especially SI Pro 2, BW Workflow Pro and Resize Pro. He also hosts one of the most popular photography forums on the Web.

  www.fredmiranda.com

PictoColor

iCorrect Portrait and iCorrect EditLab Pro are excellent plug-ins to correct color cast problems easily and accurately. Correct Photo is a standalone program with image correction and editing features and includes PictoColor's outstanding color correction software.

  PictoColor Corp
  151 West Burnsville Parkway
  Suite 200
  Burnsville, MN 55337
  (952) 894-8890
  service@pictocolor.com
  www.pictocolor.com

AutoFX

Offers an amazing collection of plug-ins and filters. Photo/Graphic Edges is my favorite tool for edge and border effects. Mystical Tint Tone and Color also with Mystical Lighting can add unique effects to your images with a simple-to-use interface. The programs run as plug-ins or standalone.

> AutoFX Software
> 151 Narrows Parkway
> Suite E
> Birmingham, AL 35242
> (205) 980-0056
> www.autofx.com

nik Multimedia

You just can't beat Color Efex 2.0 or Sharpener 2.0 for features or quality. Color Efex has most of the image enhancement filters that you'll ever need, and Sharpener 2.0 is simply the best method of sharpening images for output that you can find.

> nik Multimedia, Inc.
> 7588 Metropolitan Drive
> San Diego, CA 92108
> (619) 725-3150
> infous@nikmultimedia.com
> www.nikmultimedia.com

Pixel Genius

Started by some of the biggest names in the Photoshop world, Pixel Genius has a set of plug-ins that will have special appeal to photographers. Photokit Sharpener and Photokit not only do a great job but also teach you how to do these effects on your own as you go along. Highly recommended.

> Pixel Genius
> www.pixelgenius.com

RIPs

When you're ready to go beyond what the printer driver is capable of doing, or your workload needs the extra help from a dedicated printing tool, RIPs (Raster Image Processors) can take you to the next level.

ColorBurst

ColorBurst is available in several different versions starting at the low end for the Epson 4000 up to models for wide-format printers (up to 60 inches) from Encad, HP, and Roland.

> ColorBurst Systems
> 101 E. Holly Avenue
> Sterling, VA 20164
> (703) 404-1795
> cse@colorburstrip.com
> www.colorburstrip.com

ColorByte Software

ColorByte Software is the maker of my personal favorite RIP, ImagePrint. Available in several different levels from a Lite version, which is available for Epson 2200, 2400, HP DesignJet 30 and 90 printers, up to a the PostScript version that supports large-format printers from Epson, HP, and Roland.

> ColorByte Software
> 10004 N. Dale Mabry Hwy
> Suite 101
> Tampa, FL 33618
> (813) 963-0241
> sales@colorbytesoftware.com
> www.colorbytesoftware.com

Wasatch

Wasatch SoftRIP is available for a number of printers including Epson, Canon, Encad, HP, Mimaki, and Roland.

Wasatch Computer Technology
333 South 300 East
Salt Lake City, UT 84111
(800) 894-1544
wct@wasatchinc.com
www.wasatchinc.com

Onyx Graphics

The Onyx RIP is a favorite of many service providers with full Pantone color matching and excellent workflow features for busy printers. Onyx RIP supports a wide variety of printers (one of the widest selections of any RIP).

Onyx Graphics
6915 South High Tech Drive
Salt Lake City, UT 84047
(801) 568-9900
(800) 828-0723
www.onyxgfx.com

QuadTone RIP

An inexpensive RIP designed to produce excellent black-and-white prints, the program is easy to use and supports a wide variety of printers.

Roy Harrington
P.O. Box 3962
Los Altos, CA 94024
www.quadtonerip.com

StudioPrint

Offering high-quality output for a variety of printers, StudioPrint is geared more toward the print service with large-format printers.

ErgoSoft US
34 Technology Way
Nashua, NH 03060
(603) 882-0248
sales@ergosoft.com
www.ergosoftus.com

Qimage

Qimage isn't technically a RIP but it does do a fantastic job with printing. If you're not sure a RIP is for you but you'd like more control over page layouts, give Qimage a try.

Digital Domain, Inc
P.O. Box 1189
Sykesville, MD 21784
www.ddisoftware.com

Papers and Inks

There are more paper and ink sources than I could ever hope to list here, so I'll stick to ones that I know are high quality and that have given me good results.

Crane

Makes Museo papers in a variety of sizes and weights. All are excellent quality, especially on pigment ink printers.

Crane & Co, Inc
30 South Street
Dalton, MA 01226
(800) 268-2281
customerservice@crane.com
www.crane.com

Hahnemühle

Offers a wide variety of quality fine art papers including Photo Rag and Torchon. They're not cheap, but you'll love the results!

Hahnemühle USA
722 Calhoun Street
Woodstock, IL 60098
(815) 502-5880
www.hahnemuhle.com

Hawk Mountain

Provides a wide variety of fine art and traditional-style papers. It is also a good source for PremierArt Print Shield and edge decklers.

Hawk Mountain Papers
314 Ziegler Road
Leesport, PA 19533
(610) 916-8938
(800) 807-2248
paper@hawkmtnartpapers.com
www.hawkmtnartpapers.com

Red River Paper

Offers papers, greeting cards, and inks. Sample kits are available to try different paper surfaces.

Red River Paper
8400 Directors Row
Dallas, TX 75247
(214) 637-0029
(888) 248-8774
www.redriver.com

LexJet

LexJet has it all—from the company's own papers to Epson-branded media. It also sells ink, printers, software, graphics tablets, and color management solutions.

LexJet
1680 Fruitville Road, 3rd Floor
Sarasota, FL 34236
(941) 330-1210
(800) 453-9538
info@lexjet.com
www.lexjet.com

Moab

Offers outstanding fine art and traditional photo papers. Entrada is my hands-down favorite fine art paper. And, they're great people to work with!

Moab Paper Company
59 South Main Street
Suite 3 PMB 220
Moab, UT 84532
(435) 259-3161
(877) 259-3161
www.moabpaper.com

Photographer's Edge

Provides a number of different styles of cards that can be customized with messages and your own photos.

Photographer's Edge
855-C Garden of the Gods Road
Colorado Springs, CO 80907
www.photographersedge.com
(719) 528-3988
(800) 550-9254
www.photographersedge.com

Pantone

Set the standard used by everyone for color reproduction. It makes sense that this company would do ink right too. If your printer is supported, the ColorVANTAGE inks are the best you can get.

Pantone, Inc
590 Commerce Boulevard
Carlstadt, NJ 07072
(201) 935-5500
www.pantone.com
www.colorvantageinks.com

Lyson

Has a reputation for quality inks, especially their black-and-white inksets. The Daylight Darkroom software and ink solution is one of the best black-and-white printing solutions available.

Lyson, Inc
801 Landmeier Road
Elk Grove Village
Chicago, IL 60007
(847) 690-1060
sales@lysonusa.com
www.lysonusa.com

Media Street

Offers a number of replacement inks for many popular inkjets in both refillable cartridges and continuous flow systems. The company also has the new QuadBlack black-and-white printing system that offers top quality at a price that's hard to beat. Check out its digital picture frame too.

Media Street
44 West Jefryn Blvd Unit Y
Deer Park, NY 11729
(631) 242-5505
(888) 633-4295
www.mediastreet.com

Inkjet Mall

Offers the complete line of Cone Edition inksets. Cone Editions was the first black-and-white inkjet printing system and is still widely recognized as one of the best available. Inkjet Mall also offers its own Piezography and PiezoTone inks.

Inkjet Mall
17 Powder Spring Rd.
East Topsham, VT 05076
(802) 439-3127
(888) 426-6323
www.inkjetmall.com

Printers

You'll find a range of printers that can do just about any printing task you could imagine. Whether its inkjet, dye sublimation, or laser imaging, it's out there!

Canon

For photographers, the Pixma lineup and the wide-carriage i9900 printers have great color and good display life. The imagePROGRAF line of large-format printers offer outstanding color and speed in sizes up to 44 inches wide.

Canon USA
One Canon Plaza
Lake Success, NY 11042
(516) 328-5000
www.canonusa.com

Epson

Epson has the widest selection of printers for photographers. From the R200 to the high-end Stylus Pro 9800, you'll find something that will fit your needs. The newest UltraChrome II printers have the best black-and-white printing of any inkjet printer available.

Epson USA
3840 Kilroy Airport Way
Long Beach, CA 90806
(562) 981-3840
www.epson.com

Kodak

Kodak has a number of products available for a range of users—from the EasyShare printers for snapshots to its very nice dye-sublimation printers and large-format Encad printers. Kodak also has a complete line of inkjet papers that work with most inkjets.

Eastman Kodak Company
343 State Street
Rochester, NY 14650
www.kodak.com

Lexmark

Offers a number of low-cost printers for those on a tight budget.

Lexmark International, Inc
740 New Circle Road NW
Lexington, KY 40550
www.lexmark.com

Mitsubishi

They're not just cars! Mitsubishi has some excellent printers that use dye sublimation for high-quality prints. The CP-9500DW is one of the best printers available for event photographers.

Mitsubishi Imaging Products
9351 Jeronimo Road
Irvine, CA 92618
(888) 307-0388
ipdinfo@mdea.com
www.mitsubishi-imaging.com

Olympus

Olympus has a range of dye-sublimation printers for 4¥6 prints. The quality is superb, and the printers are easy to use.

Olympus America, Inc
2 Corporate Center Drive
Melville, NY 11747
(800) 798-2777
www.olympusamerica.com

Durst

If you can afford one of these, you've hit the big time. Durst offers large-format Rho inkjets and the Lambda Laser.

Durst Image Technology
50 Methodist Hill Drive
Suite 100
Rochester, NY 14623
(585) 486-0340
www.durst-online.com

Océ

Designed for busy print services, the Océ VarioPrint and LightJet printers aren't going to be sitting in your home office.

Océ-USA Holding Inc
5450 North Cumberland Ave
Chicago, IL 60656
(773) 714-8500
www.oceusa.com

Fuji

The Fuji Frontier systems are at the heart of many minilabs using traditional chemicals to produce digital prints on conventional papers. The Pictography system uses laser exposure for high quality output on matte and glossy photo papers.

Fuji Photo Film USA
1100 King George Post Road
Edison, NY 08837
www.fujifilm.com

Xerox

The Tektronix Phaser uses solid ink for highly saturated prints, but for photography it's not the best choice.

Xerox Corporation
P.O. Box 1000
MS 7060-583
Wilsonville, OR 97070
(877) 362-6567
www.office.xerox.com

Print Services

When the print you need is beyond the ability of your equipment and you want the best quality possible, these services can handle the job for you.

Calypso

One of the highest-quality print services for photographers, Calypso provides top-notch output and great service. The company also offers framing, scanning, and other services.

Calypso Imaging, Inc.
2002 Martin Avenue
Santa Clara, CA 95050
(408) 727-2318
(800) 794-2755
www.calypsoinc.com

Nash Editions

Graham Nash was one of the pioneers in digital printing and now runs Nash Editions, widely regarded as one of the top print services in the world.

Nash Editions
2317 North Sepulveda Blvd.
Manhattan Beach, CA 90266
(310) 545-4352
www.nasheditions.com (If you visit the Web site, click on the camera lens to access the site. Not the most intuitive interface.)

West Coast Imaging

Outstanding service and quality is West Coast Imaging's specialty. The provider also offers workshops, scanning, and more.

West Coast Imaging
49774 Road 426
Suite B
Oakhurst, CA 93644
(559) 641-7338
(800) 799-4576
info@westcoastimaging.com
www.westcoastimaging.com

Color Folio

Color Folio has done prints for some of the biggest names in photography but even if you don't have a big name, you'll still get the same high quality service

> Color Folio
> 2550 Lewis Drive
> Sebastopol, CA 95472
> (888) 212-7060
> info@colorfolio.com
> www.colorfolio.com

Online Printing

For specialty projects, whether it's a coffee mug, poster, or mouse pad, or you just want 4×6 prints of some of your images, the online services listed here can provide what you need and normally at very reasonable costs. Many of these services will give you free prints when you sign up, which is a great way to evaluate the service.

Mpix

Mpix has the highest quality of any of the online services; it uses real photo paper and offers print sizes up to 20×30 inches. Special products include magazine cover mockups and calendars.

> www.mpix.com

Kodak Gallery

Formerly Ofoto, Kodak Gallery can print snapshots, books, calendars, greeting cards, and more, and also features online storage and image sharing.

> www.kodakgallery.com

Shutterfly

Shutterfly offers very good quality and a number of specialty products, including books, calendars, cards, coffee cups, and more.

> www.shutterfly.com

dotPhoto

dotPhoto can be counted on for prints, greeting cards, calendars, and more as well as sharing images. You can even send your photos to a cell phone.

www.dotphoto.com

Snapfish

Now part of HP, Snapfish has the lowest print prices I've seen anywhere. (You can't print at home this cheap!) Print quality is excellent, and a wide range of specialty products is available—ever want to see yourself on a deck of cards?

www.snapfish.com

Lulu

Lulu is the premier online book printing and publishing service. Whether you want to print one book for yourself or market your book to stores, Lulu can handle it.

www.lulu.com

Mat and Frame Supplies

When your print is done, you want to show it off in the best possible light. The right frame and mat can make all the difference in the world. The suppliers listed here can provide everything you need to showcase your work.

Dick Blick

Provides excellent service and some of the best prices on name-brand supplies.

Blick Art Materials
P.O. Box 1267
Galesburg, IL 61402
(800) 723-2787
info@dickblick.com
www.dickblick.com

Light Impressions

One of the largest mail order suppliers of quality framing and matting supplies as well as archival storage solutions

Light Impressions
P.O. Box 787
Brea, CA 92822
(800) 828-6216
www.lightimpressionsdirect.com

PictureFrames.com

An outstanding resource for framing and matting supplies. PictureFrames.com will even print and frame your work for you.

Graphik Dimensions, Ltd
2103 Brentwood Street
High Point, NC 27263
(800) 332-8884
www.pictureframes.com

PhotoGlow

Offers backlit frames in a variety of styles and sizes.

PhotoGlow
152 Whittier Drive
Dennis, MA 02638
(508) 737-9199
ed@photoglow.com
www.photoglow.com

Index